WALSALL MATCH OF MY LIFE

WALSALL MATCH OF MY LIFE

SIMON TURNER

pitch

First published by Pitch Publishing, 2026
2

Pitch Publishing
9 Donnington Park, 85 Birdham Road
Chichester, West Sussex, PO20 7AJ
www.pitchpublishing.co.uk
info@pitchpublishing.co.uk

Set in Adobe Caslon and ScalaSans

Typeset by Pitch Publishing

Cover design by Olner Design

Printed and bound in India by Thomson Press India Private Limited

The authorised representative in the EEA is Easy Access System Europe OÜ, Mustamäe tee 50, 10621 Tallinn, Estonia gpsr.requests@easproject.com

A CIP catalogue record for this book is available from the British Library

ISBN 978 1 83680 485 7

Papers used by Pitch Publishing are from well-managed forests and other responsible sources

MIX
Paper | Supporting responsible forestry
FSC® C010615

Contents

This book is dedicated to

Roger Turner

father, friend and fellow fan

'The great pleasure in life
is doing what people say
you cannot do'

Walter Bagehot

Acknowledgements

Many endeavours rely on the kindness of strangers, and in putting this book together I have certainly been the recipient of much goodwill. Thanks, firstly, must go to Dan Briggs, whose assistance was vital to getting this project off the ground. I am also grateful to Steve Davies and Dave Evans for the help they provided. The *Express and Star* kindly offered me access to their photograph archive, and the time given to me by Alison Smith while I was there was greatly appreciated. Jane at Pitch Publishing has been as supportive as ever, and I shall remain forever thankful to her for agreeing to add a book on Walsall to their *Match of My Life* series. Duncan Olner, meanwhile, has produced yet another vibrant cover design. I also mustn't forget to mention my wife, who has shown incredible patience through the long days and nights I have devoted to writing this book. Val, you are truly the match of my life. There is, of course, one group of people to whom I owe more thanks than any other: the players. They were, without exception, generous with their time and their memories. Without them, there would have been no book, and more importantly, no great matches for Saddlers fans to remember.

Foreword

Fellows Park, the Hillary Street end. That's where it all started for me. I was only five years old when my father took me to my first Walsall match, back in 1962. I have some wonderful memories of games played at that famous old stadium, such as the FA Cup victory over Manchester United. Now, that was a night!

I've been privileged to see some thrilling Saddlers matches over the last 50 years or so, several of which are featured in the pages that follow. I had forgotten much about these games, but this book reminds me of every detail and brings them back to life so vividly, even more so because we see them through the eyes of those that played in them. Learning more about the footballers and why these matches mattered so much to them is particularly enlightening.

We can, of course, still find highlights of some of these games on YouTube, but there is something special about reading the accounts of them given here. They stimulate the mind and trigger your own recollections of the matches as you saw them. To me, that means so much more.

This is an affectionate book, written by a Walsall supporter with a real eye for detail. It is a great read for any Saddlers fan, especially if, like me, you have been around a few years and can remember some, if not all, of the matches brought to life here. So, sit back and read and let your memories of those great games come flooding back.

Leigh Pomlett, 2020

Introduction

Whenever I tell people that I support Walsall, invariably their first question is: why? Given the club's rather conspicuous lack of success over recent years, I must admit that it is a fair challenge. The answer I usually give is that Walsall is where I am from. That is part of the reason, but not the whole truth. My reply explains why I started following the club in the first place, but not why I have kept faith with them over the years. So why have I stuck with the Saddlers? Like many other Walsall supporters, the club has somehow become part of me. I could no more switch my team now than I could change my DNA. For better or worse, being a Saddlers fan is simply part of who I am. And, for what it's worth, I wouldn't change that for the world.

It's fair to say that putting this book together has been a bit of an adventure. Tracking down the players, inviting them to be interviewed and then spending time with them has been a great thrill. When I was much younger, on the rare occasions that I managed to persuade a girl to go out with me, I would arrange to meet her by the 'Hippo' on The Bridge. I would get there early and wait nervously, wondering if she would turn up or not, fearing all the time that she would have come to her senses and stayed at home.

Meeting players for this book was a very similar experience. To their credit, not one of them let me down.

Some say that you should never meet your heroes, but I thoroughly enjoyed spending time with mine. Interviewing Alan Buckley, the man who scored the first goal I ever saw, was a special moment, whilst being in the company of other childhood idols such as David Kelly and Craig Shakespeare was not an experience I shall easily forget. As for wandering around a garden centre with Dean Keates as we tried to find a coffee shop that we could see but just couldn't reach, well, that's a story for another day …

In creating this book, I have tried to cover as wide a span of Walsall history as possible. The matches that are recalled are spread across half a century and the players interviewed range from septuagenarians to those who have only recently hung up their boots. I hope, therefore, that my efforts will appeal to several generations of Saddlers fans. Within the pages that follow you will read of giant-killings, magnificent cup runs, heroic promotions and even a 12-goal thriller. If you enjoy reading this book only half as much as I have enjoyed writing it, then you're in for a treat. As the saying goes, it's been emotional.

Simon Turner, 2020

ALLAN CLARKE

Allan Clarke
Striker, 1963–66

Ashington may have produced the Charlton brothers and Bury may have given us the Nevilles, but those towns have got nothing on Short Heath. The Clarke family produced no less than five footballing brothers, four of whom played for the mighty Saddlers. Allan, the second eldest of the five, had easily the most successful career in the game. Nicknamed 'Sniffer' due to his ability to scent even the slimmest of chances, he was a born goalscorer.

Clarke joined Walsall at the tender age of 15 and soon made his way into the first team. Within a couple of years, his goals almost single-handedly saved the club from relegation. That may have proved a heavy burden for some, but Clarke's young shoulders were more than capable of bearing the strain. The goals continued to flow and even the most optimistic of Saddlers fans knew it was too good to last. Early in 1966, Clarke left for the bright lights of Fulham, aged still only 19.

Before the decade was out, Clarke was twice the subject of British record transfer fees, with Leicester City splashing the cash to acquire him in 1968 and Leeds United doing likewise in 1969. It was with the West Yorkshire club that Clarke reached the pinnacle of his career. In the space of six seasons he won a league title, an FA Cup and a Fairs Cup (the spiritual predecessor of the UEFA Cup and Europa League). During that spell Leeds also finished second in the league on three occasions, twice lost the FA Cup Final and were runners-up in the European Cup.

Unsurprisingly, international honours also came Clarke's way. He made his debut in the 1970 World Cup finals, coolly converting a penalty to give England a victory over Czechoslovakia. He went on to score a total of ten goals in 19 appearances for his country, a better ratio than Wayne Rooney, Bobby Charlton or Michael Owen ever managed. Allan Clarke was, indeed, the Harry Kane of his day. Over half a century has elapsed since Walsall produced a striker of his calibre, and goodness knows how many more decades will have to pass before Saddlers fans get to glimpse a young talent like his again.

Stoke City 0 – 2 Walsall

FA Cup Third Round
Saturday, 22 January 1966
Victoria Ground, Stoke-on-Trent
Attendance: 32,676

Stoke City	**Walsall**
Bobby Irvine	Terry Carling
Calvin Palmer	Frank Gregg
Tony Allen	John Harris
Eric Skeels	Graham Sissons
Maurice Setters	Stan Bennett
Alan Bloor	Nick Atthey
Dennis Viollet	Howard Riley
Peter Dobing	Allan Clarke
John Ritchie	George Kirby
Roy Vernon	Jimmy McMorran
Harry Burrows	Colin Taylor

Managers

Tony Waddington	Ray Shaw

Scorers

	Howard Riley (16)
	Allan Clarke (45)

Referee
F. Cowen

I ONLY had one aim in life when I was young, and that was to be a footballer. Nothing else mattered. When I was 12 and 13 years old, I used to play for the South East Staffordshire District team on a Saturday morning and my father would give me a rub down the night before the game. I remember him saying to me once while he did this, 'Do you want to be a footballer when you grow up?' 'Of course, I do,' I replied. 'Well, you don't want a girlfriend then?' he asked. 'I'm not interested in girls,' I said. 'I just want to be a footballer.' And that's how it was. I never had a single girlfriend at school, not one.

I wasn't much interested in school, either. Each year I would come home with a report from my headteacher and it always said the same thing: 'If Allan concentrated in his lessons like he does on the football field, he'd be top of the class.' That never changed throughout my education, from when I started at New Invention Infant School as a five-year-old until I left Short Heath Secondary Modern at the age of 15. Thankfully, my dream of becoming a footballer came true, but if it hadn't, I would probably have ended up working in a factory. I didn't get the qualifications to do anything different. The one thing I regret in life is not studying when I had the chance to. When I talk to kids who want to become footballers, I always tell them not to neglect their education because football is a short career. When I finished playing at the age of 34, I hadn't earned enough money to pay my mortgage off. No one in my era did. We all had to find other ways of earning a living.

I used to train with Aston Villa's first team during school holidays, and the plan was that I would join them once I turned 15. They used to give me two free tickets for every home match and so I regularly went to watch them with my dad. Villa were in the top division at the time and had some great players, including Gerry Hitchens who went on to play for Inter Milan and England. Joe Mercer was the Villa manager back then, and his number two was Ray Shaw. That was the first time I came across Ray, who was to become an important figure during the early part of my career. A few years later, he took over as manager at Walsall, gave me my first long run in the team and was in charge when we played against Stoke City in the FA Cup.

About three to four weeks before I was due to leave school, I told my mom and dad that I didn't want to join Villa. I knew a lot of lads who were going to go there, and they were all England schoolboy internationals. I'd never even had a trial for my country, so I wasn't sure about how I'd get on in that company. Saying that, I think I should have been given a chance as I was banging in goals all the time for the South East Staffordshire District and Birmingham County Boys teams. Unfortunately, there was a lot of politics involved in schoolboy football in those days. Maybe if I'd been born down south it would have been different. A few years later, the baby of our family, Wayne, followed in my footsteps. Like me, he played for the District and County teams but, unlike me, he got a trial and was picked to play for England Schoolboys. I'd made a name for myself in the game by that time, and I'm sure being Allan Clarke's younger brother didn't do Wayne's chances any harm at all. Anyway, my dad was very supportive about me not going to the Villa. He told me I could go to whichever club I wanted to, and so I joined Walsall.

I started at Walsall in 1962 as an apprentice, or as a ground staff boy as we were all called back then. There were eight of us, six of whom worked with the groundsman, maintaining Fellows Park. I looked after the professionals with Stan Bennett, who had started at the club a year before me. We cleaned boots, got the training kit out, took it to the laundry when it needed washing and put the baths on. The only time we saw a ball was on Tuesday and Thursday nights, when we trained with the amateurs. That all changed during my time in the game. I later spent 12 years in management and my apprentices worked with the professionals every single day. Looking back, the start that me, Stan and the other ground staff boys had in football gave us a lot of discipline, which was no bad thing.

You won't believe this, but when I left school and joined Walsall, I was only 4ft 5in tall. Whenever I played for South East Staffordshire District and Birmingham County Boys, I was referred to in the local papers as 'Tiny Clarke' because of my height, or lack of it. I did a lot of growing during my spell with the Saddlers and was a six-footer by the time I was 19. All that growing absolutely drained me of energy, and I was often in bed by eight o'clock in the evening as a result.

I made my debut just over a year after joining Walsall. It came in a home game against Reading and their centre-half kicked absolute chunks out of me. Bill Moore gave me my first start, but he left the club about a month later and I only played four more games that season. The new manager knew I wanted to play more often, and I was able to establish myself in the team at the start of the following campaign. The Walsall fans gave me a lot of encouragement as I made my way in the game. I couldn't afford a car at the time, so if we had a home match, I would have to catch two buses: one from Short Heath into Walsall town centre, and another out to Fellows Park. I would be with Saddlers fans on the bus, and before the game they would ask, 'Are you going to score today, Allan?', and I'd reply, 'Of course, I am!' The supporters paid my wages and I never forgot that. It was marvellous to be able to mingle with the fans before and after matches, but it wouldn't happen nowadays. Money has taken over football and supporters can't get anywhere near the players they go to watch. It's sad really, but there you are.

One of the most exciting players in that team was the left-winger, Colin Taylor. He was at the club when I started out as a ground staff boy but left a year later to join Newcastle United. He only stayed with them for one season before being re-signed by Walsall. By the time he came back I had made my way into the first team and so we played together in the forward line until I left the club. A few years later I moved to Leeds United and Peter Lorimer was one of my team-mates. He was called 'Hotshot Lorimer' because of the power of his shooting and was once proven to have the hardest shot in football. Colin Taylor may not have been as well known a footballer as Peter, but he could hit the ball just as hard, I can tell you. The only difference between them was that Peter was right-footed, while Colin would naturally strike the ball with his left.

One memory I have of Colin was when we played a midweek league match away at Port Vale. He had the ball about 40 yards from goal and I was yelling at him to pass it to me. I shouted to him twice, but he obviously didn't hear me. Not many footballers can shoot at goal from that distance, but because of his shooting power, that was well within Colin's range. Anyway, he decided to give it a go, and the Port Vale full-back made the mistake of getting in the way. He was about ten yards in front of Colin and the ball hit him right on his forehead. The poor fellow went down as if he'd been shot. He was knocked out cold! That happened right in front of me, and you just don't forget things like that.

Walsall reached the third round of the 1965/66 FA Cup by beating Swansea by six goals to three at Fellows Park and then knocking out Aldershot by two goals to nil away from home. Getting a tie against Stoke City was a big deal for Walsall. Not only was it a local Staffordshire derby but Stoke were a top-ten Division One team at the time. They had some cracking players in their side, such as the striker Dennis Viollet who had previously been at Manchester United and had survived the Munich air disaster. Over the years I played with some great footballers including Alan Ball, Gordon Banks, Bobby Charlton, Bobby Moore and Martin Peters. However, the best footballer I ever played with, and against, was the Leeds United and Scotland midfielder, Billy Bremner.

Me and Billy were very similar in that we didn't have a nerve in our bodies. The bigger the crowd, the more we wanted it. No manager ever had to inspire Billy Bremner or Allan Clarke. We motivated ourselves. That was something I had from a very young age as I always believed in my own ability. Throughout my career I never worried about centre-halves; I let them worry about me. I'm not being brash in saying that. I am just one of those fortunate people who isn't easily perturbed by things. So, I wasn't at all apprehensive before Walsall took on Stoke. Some players can get nervous before a big game like that, but not me. My only emotion was excitement. We were a Third Division side taking on one of the best teams in the country, and I couldn't wait for the kick-off.

The tie was held at the Victoria Ground, which was where Stoke used to play before they moved to their new stadium. There were over 30,000 spectators in the crowd, and that was just perfect for me. At that time Walsall's kit was red shorts and white shirts with 'WFC' emblazoned in red across the front of them. There were no strip sponsors back then. Like now, Stoke City played in red and white stripes, which meant there was a clash of colours. Walsall therefore borrowed some claret and blue shirts from Aston Villa, and we played in those instead.

In the summer before we drew Stoke in the FA Cup, Walsall signed George Kirby to play up front with me. He was coming towards the end of his career but had played for some top clubs, such as Everton, Sheffield Wednesday and Southampton. George was a hard lad and I learnt a lot from him about how to look after myself on a football field. Maurice Setters was one of the Stoke centre-halves that afternoon. He'd previously been at West Bromwich Albion and Manchester United and had clearly crossed paths with George before. After the captains had tossed the coin to see who would be kicking which way, the two teams changed ends and George and Maurice walked past each other. As they did so, Maurice called out: 'Are we going to have a quiet afternoon, George?' 'That's up to you, Maurice!' came the quick reply.

A few weeks before the cup tie against Stoke, we played a league match away at Millwall, which was always a tough place to go. George was up against their centre-half and he fouled him near the halfway line, about 20 yards away from me. The referee blew up, stopped play and awarded a free kick to the opposition. The Millwall trainer came on to the pitch to treat the injured player, when suddenly one of the home spectators ran past me with a weapon in his hand. He was headed straight for George, so I shouted out to warn him. George turned around in the nick of time, grabbed hold of this fan and then completely flattened him. I remember thinking 'Well done, George!' The Old Den had quite a reputation in those days, but for all the wrong reasons.

Stoke came at us from the start of the game, but we managed to weather the storm. Then, after about quarter of an hour, Jimmy McMorran was on the receiving end of a hard tackle. He tried to carry on for a bit, but soon limped off and spent much of the rest of the game in the dressing room. There were no substitutes allowed in the FA Cup back then, so we had to carry on without him. Taking on a top tier side with 11 men was hard enough, but now we had to do it with ten. We were awarded a free kick for the foul on Jimmy and the ball was launched into their penalty area. It rebounded off George before Howard Riley got hold of it and smashed it into the net to give us the lead.

Not too much longer afterwards, Stoke thought they had equalised when a shot from Dennis Viollet ended up in the back of our net. The trouble was that it had come through a hole in the side netting! The Stoke players appealed for a goal, but thankfully the referee decided to consult with the linesman who was able to confirm what had really happened. The net was repaired and so we carried on, taking the game to Stoke. Just before half-time, I went through on goal and their keeper brought me down. The referee immediately pointed to the spot, and so I picked the ball up, placed it down and sent the goalkeeper the wrong way. The Stoke manager, Tony Waddington, was so unhappy about what their keeper had done that he never played him in the first team again.

I was the regular penalty taker for Walsall, and it was a job I took seriously. Before the start of a match, when the captains were tossing up to see who would kick off, the players used to take shots at the goalkeeper to allow him to get a feel of the ball. I would use that time to take a good look at the opposition keeper, seeing whether he was naturally left- or right-handed. Most goalkeepers favoured their right, but there was the odd one who was different. Once I'd found out which was their weaker hand, I knew exactly which side of the goal my penalty would go to if we got one. I watch Premier League players take spot-kicks these days and I don't think they're doing their job like I did. You have to do your preparation; you have to be ready.

Later that season I moved to Fulham, but I wasn't first in line to take penalties there. That duty fell to Bobby Robson, who was coming towards the end of his playing career before going on to become one of the country's finest-ever managers. I remember playing in a match at Craven Cottage once and we were awarded a penalty. As Bobby put the ball down on the spot, I leant in and said, 'Take your time, son.' There I was, a 19-year-old, advising an ex-England player! Bobby was probably thinking, 'Who the hell is this lad, telling me what to do?' But that's how I was at the time, a young man full of confidence and self-belief.

We started the second half two goals in front and Stoke put us under a lot of pressure. It didn't help that they had an extra man because of the injury to Jimmy McMorran. George Kirby went back to help the defence, and we managed to hold out for a famous victory. We lost away to Norwich City in the next round, but I don't remember anything about that match at all. The win over Stoke sticks in the memory because it was an act of giant-killing in a local derby; it was what the FA Cup is all about. Games like the one against Norwich just fade away.

The fact that Walsall had beaten a First Division side was just unbelievable, and that was where I wanted to play: right at the top. The publicity from our win over Stoke didn't do my chances any harm at all, particularly because I had scored a goal. I remember on a Sunday morning my mom and dad would get a newspaper and there would often be snippets in there about which big clubs were looking at me. That happened for a while, but no one came in for me, so I stayed in the shop window, banging goals in for Walsall. I would have loved it if a local club like Aston Villa, Birmingham City, West Bromwich Albion or Wolverhampton Wanderers had come after me, because I could have stayed at home with my mom and dad. But they didn't.

In the end, the only club that made a firm offer to Walsall was Fulham. Their manager was Vic Buckingham, who had previously been in charge at the Albion, Sheffield Wednesday and Ajax. I went into training one day, about six weeks after we'd beaten Stoke, and Ray Shaw told me that the manager from a First Division club had come up from London. Ray wanted to know whether I wanted to speak to him. 'Of course, I do!' I replied. So, I met Vic Buckingham, we managed to agree terms and the club accepted Fulham's offer for me. They paid a transfer fee of £37,500, which was a huge amount of money for Walsall in those days. It paid a lot of wages for a long time. It also turned out to be a decent piece of business for Fulham, because 18 months later they sold me to Leicester City for £150,000. That wasn't a bad profit at all.

I was still only 19 and had realised my ambition of joining a First Division club. Fulham had some great players at that time. In addition to Bobby Robson there was Johnny Haynes, who had captained England and was the first '£100 a week footballer' when the maximum wage was abolished. They also had George Cohen who was the right-back in the England side that won the World Cup that summer. I moved down to London on my own and went into digs until the end of the season. I had planned to get married in the summer, but Fulham had already arranged a tour of the Far East and the dates clashed. I discussed it with Vic Buckingham, and we agreed that I would play in the first four of the six games before flying home on my own. So, I went out there, played in places like Hong Kong, Penang and Singapore, and then came home to get married to Margaret. We've been together ever since.

I only managed to get as far as the fourth round of the FA Cup with Walsall, but I had more success in the competition later in my career. I joined Leicester City in 1968, having turned down an opportunity to sign for Manchester United. They had players like George Best, Bobby Charlton and Denis Law in their side, but I could see they were on the decline. In the one season I spent at Leicester City, we reached the final of the FA Cup, losing 1-0 to Manchester City. I was in the final again a year later, that time as a Leeds United player. We lost in a replay to Chelsea, but two seasons later I finally tasted victory, scoring the only goal when Leeds beat Arsenal to win the FA Cup for the first and, so far, only time in their history.

Leeds United were the best team in England for a decade, so if anyone was going to win anything, they had to get past us first. Sadly, these days it's almost as if my era never existed. The television pundits talk about how many appearances a player has made in the Premier League, or how many goals he has scored or assists he has made. You'd think football didn't begin until 1992. It drives me crackers. England actually won a World Cup during my time as a player. They're not winning it now. You need great players to win a World Cup, and my era had them in abundance. There were no weak international sides when I played for my country, but there are plenty now. I reckon if we had played against them in my day, I would have scored three or four goals myself, let alone what my team-mates would have got. Yet England struggle to beat some of these sides. It's an absolute joke.

There's so much more money in football now than there was when I played. When I started out as a ground staff boy at Walsall, I was on £5 a week like all the others. It went up by £1 a week until you got to 18, when the club either had to give you a professional contract or else let you go. I was the club's top striker by the age of 17, so they signed me on professional terms a year earlier than they normally would have done. Even then, I was only on £25 a week. When I was in the First Division with Leicester City, I was on £100 a week and they told me I was their highest-paid player. When Leeds United came in for me in 1969, I asked for another £10 a week, but the gaffer, Don Revie, had done his homework and found out what Leicester were paying me. He told me he couldn't give me that as all his players were on the same wage. Who was I to disbelieve the gaffer? So, I signed for Leeds United without getting a pay rise. I did it because I wanted to play for Leeds, but what modern player would do that? In my opinion, money has spoilt the game. It has absolutely ruined it.

Looking back, I can see now that I got a break when Vic Buckingham took a chance on me as a teenager. I came through the ranks at Walsall with Nick Atthey and we're still friends now, nearly 60 years after we first met. Nick was good enough to play in the First Division, but he never got a break like I did and so spent his whole career at Walsall. It really is a thin line. After Nick had spent ten years at the club he was entitled to a testimonial game and so he asked me whether Don Revie would bring Leeds United down to Fellows Park. I had a word with the gaffer, who was always there to help people, and he agreed. That game took place just a couple of weeks before Leeds played Bayern Munich in the 1975 European Cup Final and was the only time I turned out against Walsall during my playing career. It ended in a 3-3 draw and I got one of the goals, which was good.

When I was at Leeds United, reporters often used to ask me what I planned to do when my playing career was over. My answer was that I wanted to have a go at management. All the great managers at the time had started out at the bottom. Bill Shankly had managed Carlisle United; Brian Clough had been at Hartlepool United while Don Revie had taken over at Leeds United when they were in the Second Division. I wanted to do the same thing: begin at a club in the Third or Fourth Division and learn the ropes there. I also told reporters that, ideally, the club I'd like to start in management with was Walsall. That's what I would have loved to have done. I heard once that somebody mentioned me in the boardroom at Walsall, but it never came to anything.

Instead, I ended up at Barnsley and took them to promotion in my first season in charge. A few years later, I took them to play against Walsall in a league match at Fellows Park. That was a very proud day for me, putting out a team to take on the club where I had started out as a 15-year-old boy. I remember Colin Taylor coming into the visiting dressing room after we had won that match, and it was great to see him again. Ever since I left the Saddlers to join Fulham, I have always looked out for the Walsall score on a Saturday afternoon, and I always will.

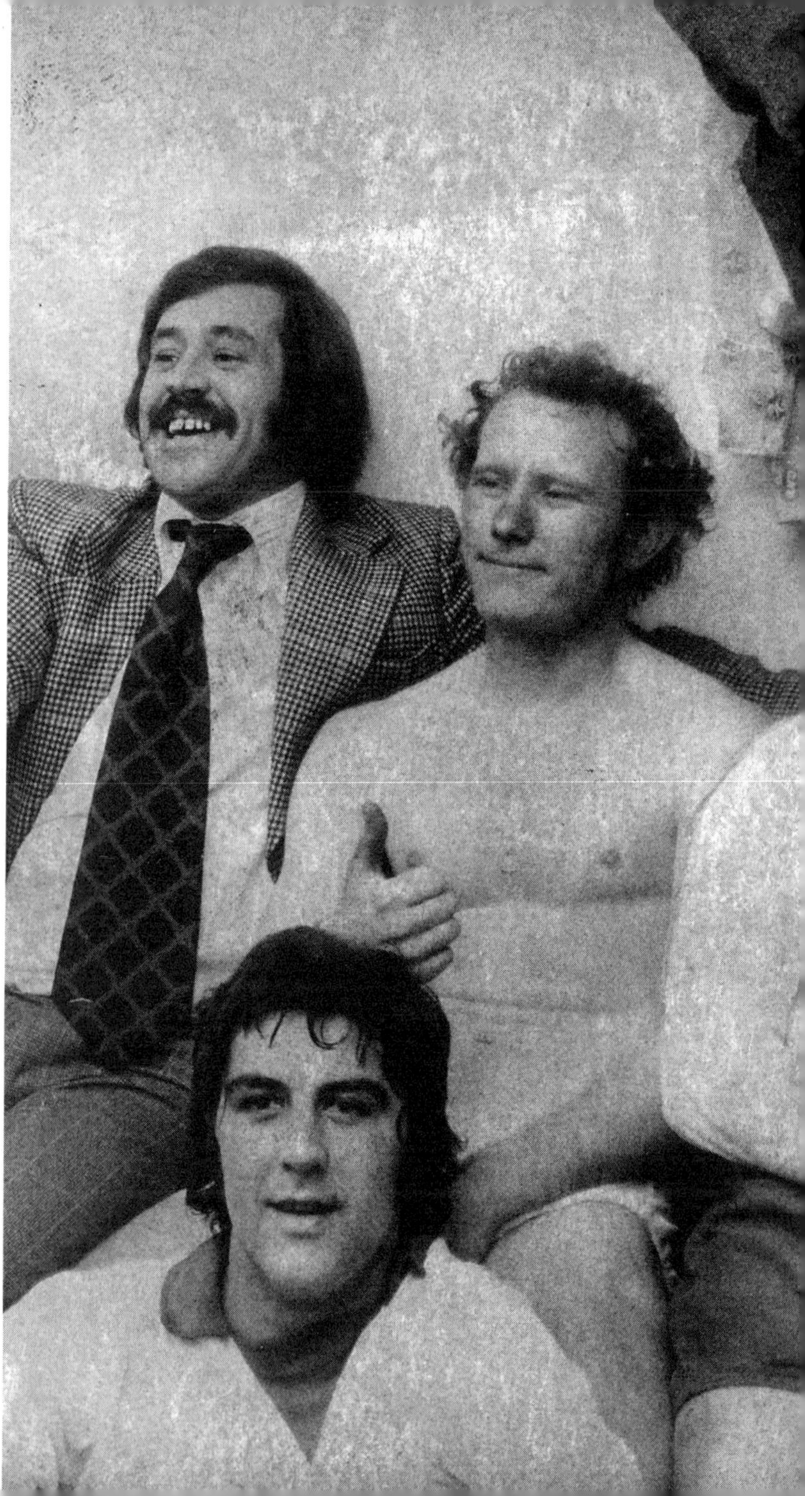

Alan Buckley
Striker, 1973–84

As home debuts go, Alan Buckley's was rather impressive. He scored a hat-trick in a 6-1 victory over Shrewsbury Town, immediately winning over Saddlers fans with a dramatic statement of intent. This was no flash in the pan, merely a portent of what was to come. Within a couple of seasons, he was averaging a goal a game in league matches at Fellows Park. Back in those days it wasn't a question of whether he would score at home, merely when. Alan Buckley scored the first goal I ever saw, but such was his prowess in front of goal I'm sure many other Walsall fans could say the same. No other player has scored more goals for the club, and no one probably ever will.

Like so many other players who arrive at Walsall, Alan Buckley came because a bigger club deemed him surplus to requirements. Nottingham Forest's loss wasn't simply Walsall's gain; it was more like a lottery win. And if you doubt that, just consider where the club would have been without him. Between 1973 and 1986, Alan Buckley was at the forefront of everything Walsall did, and for the most part it was a great time to be a Saddlers fan.

Alan Buckley's importance to Walsall became painfully apparent when he briefly moved to Birmingham City in October 1978. He left behind a team that was 11th in the table, but without his goals they ended the season in the bottom four. The club was in the league basement for the first time in two decades, and they needed a hero. Alan Buckley was duly brought back as player-manager, and he led them to promotion at the first time of asking, scoring 18 goals in the process. The 'Buck' was back.

Over the following seasons he slowly morphed from one of the club's greatest-ever players to one of its finest-ever managers. There have been many wonderful teams that never won anything but will be remembered forever because of the football they played. Think of Brazil's 1982 World Cup team, or Kevin Keegan's Newcastle United. Alan Buckley's Walsall were one of those sides. They consistently pushed for a promotion that remained frustratingly out of reach, but they shall not be forgotten any time soon. Sometimes the most precious of memories are worth any amount of shiny silver cups.

Walsall 3 – 2 Manchester United

FA Cup Third Round Replay
Tuesday, 7 January 1975
Fellows Park, Walsall
Attendance: 18,105

Walsall	**Manchester United**
Mick Kearns	Alex Stepney
John Saunders	Tony Young
Colin Harrison	Stewart Houston
Dave Robinson	Brian Greenhoff
Stan Bennett	Arnie Sidebottom
Nick Atthey	Martin Buchan
Brian Taylor	Jim McCalliog
George Andrews	Sammy McIlroy
Bernie Wright	Stuart Pearson
Alan Buckley	Lou Macari
Alan Birch	Gerry Daly (Ron Davies)

Managers

Doug Fraser	Tommy Docherty

Scorers

Bernie Wright (21)	Gerry Daly (39)
Alan Buckley (109, 111)	Sammy McIlroy (114)

Referee
Peter Willis

I MAY be Walsall's record goalscorer, but I didn't even get to play up front in my first game for the club. My career started at Nottingham Forest, and though I scored lots of goals for the reserves, I wasn't given much of a chance to establish myself in the first team. An opportunity arose for me to go on a month's loan to Walsall and I went because I wanted to play football. The Saddlers manager, Ronnie Allen, really wanted a midfielder, but I managed to agree that I would only go if I could play as a forward. Anyway, I played as a striker in a practice match shortly after arriving and scored a hat-trick. I thought I'd laid down a marker with that, but then Ronnie decided to play me out on the left wing for the opening game of the season. I just couldn't believe it. We lost 2-0 and thankfully he saw sense and put me in the forward line for the next game. It was a League Cup tie at home to Shrewsbury and I scored three goals in a 6-1 win.

Despite getting that hat-trick, Ronnie persisted in playing me in midfield from time to time. I signed for the club permanently, but our form was indifferent, and Ronnie got the sack just before Christmas. I wasn't the only player to join Walsall from Nottingham Forest that year as the club had also taken on Doug Fraser. He was a full-back who was coming to the end of a fine career, having won the FA Cup with West Bromwich Albion as well as being capped for Scotland. Because we both still lived in Nottingham, we used to travel in the car together to Walsall. One day, I went down with him as a fellow player and when we came back, he was the acting manager! That was the bright idea of the chairman, Ken Wheldon. Even though he had plenty of money, he was a skinflint. Appointing Doug as player-manager meant he got two employees for the price of one.

Doug was great for me. His opening game in charge was away at Blackburn Rovers, which was always a tough place to go. The first thing he said to me was, 'Buck, you're playing up front on Saturday.' We beat them 2-0 and I scored both goals. From then on, I always played as a striker. Doug's main quality as a manager was that he put his trust in you and let you get on with it. I don't recall him ever telling me what to do, or how to play. I had my attributes and the other players in the team had theirs and he never tried to change us. Doug kept us fit, but he was never really into coaching. We went on a good run after beating Blackburn, and I think Doug's approach was simply 'if it ain't broke, don't fix it'.

Doug was not one for tactics either. He set us up to play 4-4-2 and never tinkered with it after that. If you listen to all the so-called pundits these days, you'd think football is a different game now to how it was when I played. But it's not. It's still about whether you can create something when you have the ball, and how hard you are to play against when you haven't. Apparently, some modern managers study graphs after matches to check whether their players have run 10.9 kms. If they have then it's assumed that they've had a good game. Well, if that's the case then I never played well in my life because I never ran that far. To my mind, it's about how effective you are as a player that matters, not how far you've run.

Doug did well after taking over from Ronnie and got given the job on a permanent basis, though he didn't play much more after that. He kept us up without too much trouble and put a fine team together. In goal we had Mick Kearns who was a good shot-stopper, though his greatest quality was that he understood the game. He was quite thoughtful about football and we used to have some good chats about it, although we didn't always agree. Despite that, we got on very well together and I liked his wry sense of humour. Mick's a one-off.

People rave about how the Manchester City goalkeeper, Ederson, can pick out a player with a pass, but Mick used to do that for me. When he had the ball in his hands I would drift out to the left and Mick would kick it straight out to me every time. Mick also was good at organising the defence in front of him, which I'd never seen a goalkeeper do before. When I was at Nottingham Forest it was always the manager who would tell players who to pick up, which area of the pitch he wanted them in and who to mark at set pieces. Mick took on that job at Walsall, which I think Doug welcomed. The only weakness in Mick's game was that he didn't command the box as I thought he should, especially given his size. Ron Green played a lot of games in goal for me when I became Walsall manager and he would come off his line and try to catch absolutely everything. I liked that.

The two centre-halves in front of Mick were Stan Bennett and Dave 'Sugar' Robinson. Stan wasn't the best footballer in the world, nor was he the quickest, but he would always do what was needed, even if that was clearing the ball into the terraces or kicking someone. Mick would often come up to me after a match and have a chuckle about something Stan had done, such as kicking the ball over the stand when it came to him on the edge of the area. Mick would much sooner have a Dave Mackay-type player in central defence who could bring the ball down and stroke it around. But that wasn't Stan's game. Personally, I was never bothered about where the ball ended up, as long as Stan had got rid of it. Sugar couldn't run either, but he was a very intelligent player and a real 'steady-eddie' next to Stan.

Colin Harrison was the left-back in that team, but he could have played anywhere. In fact, he was a central midfielder when I made my home debut against Shrewsbury Town and went on to become a right-back after Doug left. It's fashionable these days to have right-footed players on the left wing, but we did that years ago. Colin was used that way as he only ever kicked with his right foot. He was a reliable full-back who never got beaten, never gave the ball away and would always play quality balls forward. Colin was a fantastic player really. On the other side of the defence was John Saunders, who joined us from Leeds United. He was a tall, dark-haired, swarthy chap who looked more like a centre-half than a right-back. John was a lovely lad, but not the hardest of players. You could never see him going out and kicking anybody.

Brian Taylor played in front of John on the right flank. He was another one who could have taken up any position on the pitch, though my dad was never sure about him. My dad used to come and watch me play at Fellows Park and stood just to the left of the goal at the Hillary Street end. He told me there had been times when Brian hadn't passed the ball to me, even though he'd seen that I was in a good position to score. I raised it with Brian once, because I thought I should be scoring all the time. He was fine about it, but there were still times when he didn't play me in when he could have done. Brian was a bit of a mystery to me. On the opposite side of the pitch we had Alan Birch. 'Acker' was an intelligent player who worked his socks off running up and down the left wing.

He was a local lad and only 18 years old when we played Manchester United.

The central midfielders in that team were Nick Atthey and George Andrews. Nick was a little dynamo; a Nobby Stiles type of footballer. He didn't score many goals, but that was because he was the sort of player who would sooner set up a chance for someone else than shoot himself. George was equally unselfish. I often used to get the impression that he would rather head the ball down to me than try to get a goal. He would play just behind me and Bernie Wright, bombing into the box late from midfield. I used to tell him that he must have a radar in his head, because every time he headed the ball down it seemed to end up right on my foot. I scored a lot of goals from George's knockdowns. Like Colin and Nick, he was a very good footballer. I think those three never really tested themselves by playing at the highest level that they could have done. But that was how it was back then. Players often ended up staying at one or two clubs for their whole careers.

My striking partner, Bernie Wright, was a real character. I'll never forget the moment when he arrived, while I was warming up for my first practice match at the club. He had the build of a rhinoceros, wild hair, long sideburns and stubble before stubble even existed. I remember on one occasion he and Miah Dennehy were playing football on the car park at the ground when they squared up to each other over something. Dave Serella got hold of Miah, but it took about half a dozen of us to hold Bernie back. He had the strength of an ox. Bernie was a nice lad though, and we hit it off right away in a footballing sense. He would do the long runs through the channels, and if he couldn't go for goal himself, he would always head the ball down to me or play me in. Bernie was very quick for a big guy and his touch was good. He was also a real team player. Whenever we defended set pieces, Mick would tell him who to come back and mark and Bernie would never question him.

The 1974/75 season was Doug's first full campaign as a manager, and that was when we went on probably the greatest FA Cup run in Walsall's history. We were drawn away against Ashford Town in the first round and played them on a midweek afternoon for some reason. I don't remember why. Anyway, we beat them 3-1 and then defeated Newport County by the same scoreline in the second round. The day of the third-round draw started like any normal day at Walsall. The apprentices came in with all the training kit and chucked it down on to the treatment table in the middle of the dressing room. It was first come, best dressed at Walsall in those days. Then we heard the cup draw and just couldn't believe it. *Us lot* were going to play at Old Trafford. We were off to the 'Theatre of Dreams', and it was a dream for us.

That Manchester United side was managed by Tommy Docherty and nearly all of them were internationals. They had Alex Stepney in goal, who was a European Cup winner, as well as players like Martin Buchan, Lou Macari and Stuart Pearson. Manchester United went on to win the FA Cup two years later with pretty much the same team that we played in 1975. It's not like now when the big teams put out their reserves for cup matches. We played Manchester United's first 11. We took on the best they had got.

If somebody had said to me before we went to Old Trafford that we would get a 0-0 draw, I would have replied that there was more chance of putting us lot on the moon. But that's what we did. Mick, Colin and Stan organised us at the back and we were well worth the draw. It wasn't as if we were hanging on at all. Mind you, it certainly helped that Mick took half an hour to take a goal kick. Like I said, he understood the game. Towards the end of the match we won a throw-in, down towards the corner flag, and the ball came to me. Normally I'd do a trick and would then be off and away, trying to score a goal. But for once in my life, I did the right thing. I just stayed where I was and juggled the ball from foot to foot, passing the time away. Eventually Brian Greenhoff got it off me and put it out for another throw-in, but I'd wasted precious seconds.

There were a lot of Walsall fans at that game, and there was sheer disbelief amongst them that we'd got a draw. It was the same with the players, and I remember how excited we were on the coach on the way home. It was beyond our wildest dreams to be taking Manchester United back to Fellows Park.

We didn't have to wait long for the replay. Nowadays there's often a gap of a week or more between matches, but we played at Old Trafford on the Saturday and the replay was on the following Tuesday. We had Sunday off and then did some training on Monday, but all we wanted to do was get out there and play. We fancied ourselves a bit, you see. We'd had a little test up at Old Trafford and knew what we were about. We were also playing at Fellows Park, and we didn't lose many at home. I'm not saying we were favourites, but we knew we had a chance to do something special.

My brother, Steve, had recently joined Luton Town from Burton Albion and he came up to watch the match with Andy King and John Seasman, who also played for the Hatters. We lived in Heath Hayes at the time and they came up to our house for something to eat prior to the game. They stood on the terraces to watch the match, and John met a Walsall girl that night who he later went on to marry. You really couldn't make this stuff up.

There was an incredible atmosphere at Fellows Park for the replay. Like the players, I reckon the fans sensed that something extraordinary could happen and so the noise was deafening, even before kick-off. The fact that it was an evening fixture also added to the occasion; there's always something special about a night game. The recorded attendance for that game was about 18,000 or so, but I think there were a lot more there than that. I remember carrying the ball down the right wing towards the Hillary Street end and having to dodge spectators' feet. There were that many in the stands that they'd come over the wall and were sitting on the ash track around the pitch. That's how full it was. I found out later that Ken Wheldon had a turnstile at the ground which would click as people paid and went through it, but it didn't register them as being part of the crowd. I reckon he probably had two or three turnstiles fixed like that for that match against Manchester United.

We hadn't been playing all that long when Brian Taylor crossed the ball into the box, and I ran towards it. It fell for Bernie instead and he struck it first time with the outside of his left foot, thumping it into the net like it was a training game. It was an amazing shot. Manchester United came back at us and were awarded a penalty, shortly before half-time. The ball bounced up and hit Stan Bennett on the arm and the referee pointed to the spot. It was cruel, really. It was one of those decisions that big clubs often get given and smaller clubs don't. Anyway, Gerry Daly put the penalty away and it was level at the break.

There weren't any goals in the second half and so it went to extra time. For us, just taking Manchester United that far was an achievement in itself. It was nip and tuck after that, but we always looked like we could score, and in the second period of extra time we did. John Saunders put a cross into the box for George Andrews and Alex Stepney came out to get it. I didn't care whether he was a European Cup winner or not, I knew George was going to win that header. George had a natural spring and was always favourite to win balls like that. He got there ahead of Stepney and nodded it down to me, just like he always did. The ball bounced awkwardly, and I couldn't believe that I had so much space around me. I was sure that Martin Buchan was going to suddenly appear from nowhere, but he didn't. If I'd snatched at the chance, I'm not sure I would have scored. Instead, I took my time and it was as if everything went into slow motion. I controlled the ball with my thigh, nudged it down to my foot and put it to the side of the defender standing on the line.

Not long afterwards, George was brought down in the box and the referee awarded us a penalty. Taking those was my job. I used to have a habit of bending down and tying my bootlace before walking back to hit the ball. It allowed me to take stock of what was going on and gave me time to clear my head. I remember putting the ball on the penalty spot, down at the Hillary Street end, and the crowd roaring so loudly that I thought the stand was about to collapse. I walked back, turned around, stopped, and suddenly you could have heard a pin drop. It was as if all the fans had left the ground. Everybody knew what was at stake, because a goal now would probably settle the game.

I always used to take penalties the same way, side-footing it with power to the right of the goalkeeper. As I stood there, I thought to myself that Manchester United would have done their homework and would be expecting that. So, I decided to put it the other side of the net instead and give it a bit more height than usual. I hit the ball cleanly, but Alex Stepney still managed to get his fingertips to it. Thankfully, the power of the strike carried it into the net and the place absolutely erupted. We were two goals up, and for the first time in the match I reckon all the lads in the team thought, 'we'll beat these'. And we did. Manchester United did get a goal back, which made the last few minutes a bit heart-stopping, but we held on.

I shook hands with Martin Buchan after the final whistle and there was no animosity from the Manchester United players because they'd lost to us. When we got back to the dressing room there were six bottles of lemonade laid out for us, which was supposed to be a treat. We'd just beaten one of the biggest clubs in the world and all we got to drink was fizzy pop, but that was Ken Wheldon for you. Normally, there'd be the odd person in the players' lounge after a match but it was packed solid that night. Everybody was in there. I fought my way through the crowd and bumped into my dad, who had a little smile on his face because I'd scored a couple of goals.

I was involved in a lot of unforgettable matches for Walsall. There were games where I notched hat-tricks, one against Rotherham United when I got four, and others in which I scored spectacular goals. But that victory over Manchester United is my most memorable match. That's because of what the result meant to everybody: to us as a group of players, to the club and to the fans. To have got a draw at Old Trafford, and then to have taken Manchester United back to our place and beaten them shows that it was no fluke. Over three and a half hours of football, we were the better team. Later, when I became manager of Walsall, we got some great results in the League Cup, beating Arsenal at Highbury and then drawing with Liverpool at Anfield. Those were good nights, but not as wondrous for me as beating Manchester United in front of a packed Fellows Park. That will always be my favourite Walsall moment.

We beat Newcastle United at home in the next round with a George Andrews header, but then the adventure ended in a 2-1 defeat away to Birmingham City. That FA Cup run put the club on a firmer financial footing, which at least made Ken Wheldon happy. He was proud of us when we got a draw at Old Trafford, but what really excited him was getting a replay. I remember seeing the '£' signs in his eyes in the coach on the way home. It was the same again after we beat them at Fellows Park. He was pleased with the result, but what he really wanted was for us to draw another big club. To be fair, he focused on the club's finances because somebody had to. I know Ken Wheldon was never well liked by Walsall supporters, but I could never understand why because he kept the club going for years.

In fact, I think Ken Wheldon had a lot more warmth and feeling for Walsall Football Club than people ever believed he had. Only he would have paid £175,000 to bring me back from Birmingham City to be Walsall's player-manager. I know that the club had received the same sum when they'd sold me to the Blues a few months earlier, but what you have to understand is that some of that fee had to go to Nottingham Forest because of a sell-on clause in my contract. I reckon it cost the club £60,000 to get me back, which was a lot of money for them in those days. I suppose what it also showed was how much Ken Wheldon thought of me. In many ways I was his blue-eyed boy, but then you're going to be if you score 30 goals a season, year after year.

Walsall won promotion in my first season as player-manager, but we just couldn't get going once we got back into Division Three. I had a bad knee, Don Penn was scuppered, and things weren't looking good. We had a supporters' evening, which I didn't think was a good idea because it's just asking for trouble if the team is struggling. Ken Wheldon wasn't bothered. He just sat there and let me take all the flak. Anyway, after a while he got up and started talking about moving the club to a new stadium, which completely took the attention off me. No one wanted to complain about how badly I was managing the team after that. A lot of people thought his plan to leave Fellows Park was treasonous, but the club had to leave because it was a dump. When we played Liverpool in the semi-final of the League Cup in 1984, a wall collapsed under the pressure of the away fans and people got injured. Moving to a new stadium was Ken Wheldon's way of taking the club forward, and it finally happened a few years after he sold up and left.

I liked Ken Wheldon, though the two of us used to have some incredible rows when I was the manager, some real humdingers. I've always been one for saying what I thought, and he always stood his ground. But I'd go in the next morning and it was all forgotten. He'd simply say, 'All right, ma lad,' like it had never happened. I liked that. I bumped into him from time to time after we had both left Walsall, but a while later I got a call from Jack Harris, who had also been a director at the club. He told me that Ken Wheldon was ill and that I should go and see him if

I could. I didn't, and he died not long afterwards. I regret not going now.

I was the Walsall manager until Terry Ramsden took over the club in 1986 and I got the sack. Ken Wheldon rang me that night and told me he didn't have a clue that was going to happen. He couldn't believe what they'd done, given all I'd achieved at the club over the years, but that's how football is. Chairmen and directors like to bring in their own people, and they didn't know me at all. Nevertheless, I felt that I should have been given until Christmas to prove myself. We'd finished sixth the season before, having scored more goals than any other team in the Football League. I felt cheated and it was hard to watch Tommy Coakley win promotion a couple of years later with so many of my players.

If there's one thing that's certain in football management, it's that you'll get the sack one day. I remember when it happened to Doug, about three years or so after he'd taken over. Ken Wheldon came into the dressing room and told the players that the club couldn't afford to get relegated, so they were going to have to let Doug go because things weren't going well on the pitch. After he left, the lads all started talking amongst themselves, but the first thing I did was go and knock on Doug's door. We had travelled to Walsall together in the car from Nottingham for years and had a good relationship.

I told Doug I couldn't agree with what they'd done and that I was really sorry he was leaving. He said that I'd been golden for him; I'd played my socks off, not given him one minute's trouble and had stuck by him when I could have gone off and played for bigger clubs, which was nice to hear. That night, me, Miah Dennehy and Dave Serella went to watch Nottingham Forest play at the City Ground, and we met up with Doug after the game in a pub opposite the stadium. We had a drink and I never saw Doug again after that because he left football completely. The last I heard he was working for the Prison Service at Nottingham jail, though I suppose he must have retired by now.

It's been gratifying that some of the players I managed at Walsall have stayed in the game and had success. Richard O'Kelly was my first-ever signing for the Saddlers when he joined from Alvechurch in 1979. He was also one of the first players I recruited when I took over at Grimsby Town nine years later. He suffered a double leg fracture at the end of his first season with the club and sadly never played football again. I told him to stay at the club with me and I'd look after him. Unfortunately, the club didn't have two halfpennies to rub together, so after he recovered, he had to go everywhere, doing everything in the game in order to earn a living for his family. A year or two later things improved at Grimsby and they told me that they could afford a youth coach if I wanted one. I told them I had got just the man for the job: Richard O'Kelly.

He was at Grimsby with me for a few years, and then I took him with me to West Bromwich Albion as youth coach when I was poached for the manager's job there. That suited him down to the ground, given that he's an Albion fan. Anyway, after I got the sack there, he stayed on for a few years before going all over the place again, doing all sorts of jobs once more. It's great to see him working with Dean Smith in the Premier League. In my opinion, there's no one that deserves that more than Rich. He's always lived for the game and tried as hard as he could to be the best that he can be. You can put your life on him.

I knew that Rich would become a top coach because I saw what he could do when he worked with me. Craig Shakespeare, however, exceeded all my expectations. I never envisaged that he would achieve what he did as a coach, but then I never saw that side in him. Unlike Rich, Shaky was only ever a player for me at Walsall and Grimsby. I can remember when he came into the office with his mom to sign for the Saddlers at the age of 16. He spent all his formative years with me at Walsall and I like to think that I gave him a good grounding in the game which has served him well over the years.

One of the other people that worked with me for several years was Arthur Mann. He was a player for me at Kettering, a youth coach at Grimsby and then my assistant manager at the Albion. I'd have trusted Arthur with my life. When I got the sack from the Albion in 1997, Arthur left the club shortly afterwards as he didn't want to be there without me. In the months that followed we used to play tennis together, as well as watching Walsall from time to time. Arthur never said as much to me, but I think his dearest wish was for me to go back and manage the Saddlers again. He knew what a big part of my life the club had been. I was living in Four Oaks at the time, so I was only down the road. The offer never came, but if it had done, I'd have come back to Walsall. Of course I would.

MICK KEARNS

Mick Kearns
Goalkeeper, 1973–79, 1982–85

For almost 50 years, Mick Kearns has been a near-constant presence at Walsall Football Club. He has ridden the waves with the rest of us, revelling in the good times and anguishing over the bad. A lot has changed over that half a century. When Mick Kearns joined the Saddlers, goalkeepers were able to pick up back passes, rarely wore gloves and weren't awarded a foul every time an opposing striker breathed on them. It's still football, but not quite the game Mick played as a young man.

Mick Kearns started his career at Oxford United, making his debut at the age of 19 and playing almost 70 league games for the club. The next stop was Walsall, and it was to prove life-changing. He went straight into the Saddlers first team and missed only five games over the following five and a half seasons, being an ever-present between August 1974 and October 1977.

There weren't any promotions during Mick Kearns's time as a player at Walsall, but there were some incredible cup runs. He was part of the Saddlers sides that beat Manchester United, Newcastle United and Leicester City in the FA Cup in the 1970s, and then famously came out of retirement to keep Arsenal at bay when Alan Buckley's team knocked them out of the League Cup at Highbury in 1983. He also kept goal for the Republic of Ireland on 18 occasions and still holds the record for being Walsall's most capped player.

Mick Kearns finally hung up his boots in 1985, but he just couldn't keep away. He was soon back at the club as its community relations manager and later became the goalkeeping coach, with Jimmy Walker benefitting greatly from his expertise. Mick was also a regular co-commentator on Saddlers matches for BBC Radio WM. It was never good to hear that Walsall had conceded a goal, but there was always the consolation of waiting to find out whether he would say 'Jimmy will have been disappointed with that ...'. Not quite a catchphrase, but it wasn't far off being one. Mick Kearns took a well-deserved retirement in 2013 but can still be regularly seen at the Banks's Stadium in his role as a club ambassador.

Chesterfield 0 – 1 Walsall

FA Cup Second Round Second Replay
Tuesday, 21 December 1976
Baseball Ground, Derby
Attendance: 5,990

Chesterfield	**Walsall**
Steve Hardwick	Mick Kearns
Len Badger	Brian Taylor
Ken Burton	Brian Caswell
Bill McEwan	Roger Hynd
Les Hunter	Dave Serella
Sean O'Neill	Nick Atthey
Alan Jones	Miah Dennehy
Malcolm Darling	Mick Bates
Rod Fern (Wilf Smith)	Bernie Wright
Andrew Kowalski	Alan Buckley
Dave Bentley	Alun Evans

Managers

Arthur Cox	Doug Fraser

Scorers

	Bernie Wright

Referee

P.J. Richardson

LOOKING BACK, I've made two big decisions in my life. One was to sign for Walsall Football Club, and the other was to make my home in Aldridge. I've never regretted either of them. I started my career at Oxford United but lost my place in the team and ended up on the transfer list. The Saddlers showed an interest, so I came up to Walsall and Ken Wheldon, who was the chairman at the time, sold the club to me. I signed up and eventually relocated to Aldridge, where I have made many great friends over the years. There's a lot of luck in life, and I feel very fortunate to have got those two decisions right.

Ronnie Allen was appointed as Walsall manager in 1973, during the same summer that I joined the club. He brought some good footballers in, including Alan Buckley and Doug Fraser. Ronnie recruited players who could get on the ball and play, but for whatever reason, it just didn't work out for him. We had some bad results, went ten games without a win and Ronnie left the club only six months after joining. Doug Fraser was asked to take over as player-manager, though he didn't turn out for the team much after that. He had a similar philosophy to the game as Ronnie and we suddenly took off, steering clear of the relegation zone and finishing the season in 15th place. Then, in Doug's first full season in charge, we had that great FA Cup run during which we beat Manchester United and Newcastle United. We finished eighth in Division Three that season, then seventh the following year and were playing entertaining football, which the fans loved.

Doug's approach was simply to let us go out and play. He had been a full-back so he would talk a little about how he wanted the team to defend, but that was pretty much it. The players took much more responsibility for organising themselves on the field in those days than they do nowadays. If we saw that things needed changing, we didn't wait for a signal to come from the dugout, we just did it. I don't believe that a team needs a manager when it's playing well. Managers are only useful when things are going wrong, such as when you're a goal down at half-time, or if you're drawing at home against a team that you're expected to beat. A good manager can be priceless at times like that.

The 1976/77 season was Doug's fourth as manager, but we struggled to perform as well as we had done previously. We didn't win any of our first six league matches and were bottom of the table in mid-September. A few weeks later we played away at Brighton and Hove Albion, and that was a complete and utter disaster from start to finish. The match was due to be played on a Tuesday night and our next fixture was away to Portsmouth on the following Saturday. The chairman had the bright idea that, rather than hire a coach, the players would drive down on the day of the Brighton match and then stay over for the Portsmouth game. I drove and three or four of the other players took their cars as well. It was crazy. It's nearly 200 miles to Brighton and many of the motorways that you'd use today hadn't even been built back then. It took us hours and hours to get there.

We were under pressure for much of the first half against Brighton, but we'd been kicking against the wind, so we were pleased to go in 0-0 at half-time. We thought we'd get some relief in the second half as the wind would be behind us, but they absolutely murdered us. In a 28-minute spell, Brighton scored seven goals. Peter Ward got four and Ian Mellor notched a hat-trick. Ian went on to work with the Professional Footballers' Association and our paths often crossed when I was community director at Walsall FC. He never let me forget that game. The cause of all our woes was that long journey down. We were exhausted but we managed to cope until we went a goal behind. After that we collapsed, with our tiredness becoming a convenient excuse for not making runs or failing to close opponents down. We all got drunk that night, but things got a little better at the weekend and we managed to get a 1-1 draw against Portsmouth.

Our form continued to be poor, however. We were in and around the relegation zone for much of the first half of the season, which meant that the FA Cup was a good distraction for us. Our first-round opponents were Bradford City and we drew 0-0 with them at Fellows Park before winning 2-0 away in the replay. We travelled to Chesterfield in the next round and got a 1-1 draw. That meant that Walsall were in the hat for the third-round draw, which was held at 11.00am on the following Monday. It wasn't on television like it is now, so we all had to huddle around a radio to hear who we would be playing if we managed to beat Chesterfield.

The only radio we had at the club was an old crystal set that had been there for years and years. It had an aerial that went up into the roof and would crackle so badly if anybody walked past it that you couldn't hear a word that was being said. As the draw was underway the players compared notes on which of the big teams were still in the bag, and then we heard Manchester United's name being read out. There was silence as we waited for the next ball to come out, and when we heard that either Walsall or Chesterfield would be going to Old Trafford there was pure elation. Everyone was ecstatic.

But we still had to beat Chesterfield if we were going to play Manchester United. The replay was held at Fellows Park and that ended in a 0-0 draw after extra time. In those days FA Cup ties weren't decided on penalties and further games had to be played until there was a winner. Second replays were also held at neutral grounds, with it being deemed that Derby County's Baseball Ground was a mutually convenient venue for a tie between Chesterfield and Walsall. They had the same rules for the League Cup at that time as well. Not long after I joined the club, we played Manchester City in the second round of the competition and drew 0-0 with them at Fellows Park and then again at Maine Road. A second replay was needed, and ironically that was held at Old Trafford.

The reason why that FA Cup replay against Chesterfield is my most memorable game is because I think it was my finest performance for Walsall. In addition, it was also an important match for the club as a trip to Manchester United hung on the outcome. There was only one team in that game, but unfortunately it wasn't the Saddlers. We only got into their half of the pitch on two occasions: once when we kicked off and once when we scored. The remainder of the match was played in our half and shots rained in constantly on our goal. In fact, it was just like when we played forwards versus defence in training. Every time I kicked the ball away, it just boomeranged back again. However, it turned out to be one of those games when I just couldn't put a foot wrong, no matter what I did. If I had turned around, the ball would just have hit me on the back. I remember making one save when the ball was crossed into the box and all I could do was spread myself to try and stop the shot from going in. The ball struck my hand and it looked as if I had made an incredible save, but really it was just a bit of luck.

Whenever a team is under the cosh like that but still come through, it is always the goalkeeper and the centre-halves that get the credit. And rightly so. The two defenders in front of me that night were Roger Hynd and Dave Serella. Roger was a very experienced player who came to Walsall from Birmingham City at the end of his career. He had played for Glasgow Rangers in a European Cup Winners' Cup Final and was a very enthusiastic character. He was also the player-coach at the time and would rally everyone on the pitch. Dave Serella wasn't as accomplished on the ball as Roger was, but he was a very brave centre-half, a real out-and-out defender. Despite not being the tallest, Dave was good in the air and he complemented Roger very well.

Two Brians made up the remainder of that resolute defence: Caswell and Taylor. Brian Caswell was the most versatile footballer I ever played with at Walsall. He played left-back that night, but could play anywhere in the back four, or anywhere in midfield for that matter. Brian Taylor was a very pacey, skilful right-back who was better going forward than he was defending. Playing in front of the back four, helping to protect them, was Nick Atthey. Nick was one of the most consistent players that I played with at Walsall. He always gave 100 per cent and was a tremendous servant to the club, making over 500 appearances for Walsall over a period of 15 years, though that season was to be his last. Nick had a superb spring for a small player and was forever heading the ball away from danger. He read the game very well and was adept at breaking up play. In my opinion, Nick Atthey was as good a defensive midfielder as we've ever had at the club.

When Nick won the ball off the opposition, he would often pass it to Mick Bates who was a much more creative player. Mick had spent most of his career at Leeds United, being part of that great squad of players that Don Revie put together that won countless trophies in the 1960s and 1970s. Teams were only allowed one substitute player back then and Mick Bates was often Leeds's number 12, with Billy Bremner and Johnny Giles usually being first pick in midfield. He signed for Walsall out of the blue and it was quite a coup for the club to get a player of his ability. Another player we had in that team who had played at the top level was Alun Evans. He started his career with Wolves, spent a few seasons at Liverpool and then joined us from Aston Villa. Alun came to us at the end of his career and had a bad knee, though his experience got him through games. He scored one or two vital goals for the team and was a big help to the younger players at the club.

One of our strikers against Chesterfield was Alan Buckley, who was a truly incredible goalscorer. He didn't have much pace and couldn't go past a man with the ball at his feet, but he still managed to score 20 or more goals for five seasons on the trot. The reason for that was his football brain. Alan's quickness of mind was Premier League standard and that enabled him to read situations better than most defenders he came up against. He would anticipate where the ball would land more swiftly than they could, getting in front of them before they had even realised danger was present. Alan spent some time playing in the top division with Birmingham City, and I think the only reason it didn't work out for him was because he didn't have the physical pace to match the sharpness of his mind.

Alan Buckley was one of the two best footballers that I played with during my time at Walsall. The other was Colin Harrison. He was a much better player than people gave him credit for, though he was never undervalued by his team-mates. To this day, I find it difficult to understand why he spent his whole career at Walsall and didn't get a move to a bigger club. He was easily talented enough to have played at a higher level. I played alongside some top full-backs when I was an international for the Republic of Ireland, and he was as good as any of them. That includes such players as Shay Brennan and Tony Dunne, who were the full-back pairing for Manchester United when they won the European Cup in 1968. Colin could play anywhere in defence and midfield and had a tremendous shot on him. Whenever we won a free kick around the opposition penalty area, he would always be dangerous. People talk about Colin 'Cannonball' Taylor's shooting power, but Colin Harrison really wasn't far behind him. Off the field he is one of the nicest blokes you could hope to meet, but once he crossed that white line, he became the fiercest of competitors. Colin had heart, desire and an irrepressible will to win.

Chesterfield absolutely dominated that FA Cup tie. I think their goalkeeper put on weight that night, he had that little to do. We only had one attack, but in the end that was all we needed. In the second half, Miah Dennehy went on a run down the right wing, crossed the ball into the box and Bernie Wright headed it into the net. The goal was greeted with almost complete silence. I don't think the crowd could believe what they'd seen. Walsall had barely been in the Chesterfield half of the pitch all night, but suddenly we were in front.

Our goalscorer, Bernie Wright, was as hard as nails. He was the only footballer I played with who never had the trainer come on the pitch to tend to him if he got injured. I remember him getting battered right in front of the dugout in one match and we all thought he was quite badly hurt. The trainer ran straight on to the pitch and Bernie took great affront. He stood up immediately and told the trainer in no uncertain terms: 'If I require the trainer, I shall come over to you. You *do not* come on to the field for me!'

Bernie also hated it when other players went down and had the trainer come on for them. When Brian Taylor got injured, he would lay flat out on the pitch until the trainer ran on and rubbed some water over him. Then he'd be up and running again as if nothing had happened. He was a bit like a modern-day player in that respect. We had a big communal bath at Fellows Park, and I was in there with Bernie after one match when Brian got in. Bernie said to him, 'Brian, tell me this. We were under pressure in that game. Somebody tackled you and you lay on the floor until the referee brought the trainer on. What was wrong with you?' Brian replied, 'I got a kick on the leg.' Bernie wasn't having any of it. 'Well, you tell me why you were able to sprint 50 yards after having some water sprinkled on you? You weren't bloody injured at all! They might have scored while you were lying on the ground!'

I remember another time we were playing a night match and Bernie went up for a challenge outside the opposition box. The next thing we knew Bernie was on his hands and knees. We were all wondering what was up with him and naturally assumed he was injured. We couldn't have been more wrong. What had happened was that one of his contact lenses had come out and he was looking for it on the ground. You'd think he'd have no chance of finding it, but it glittered under the floodlights and so he was able to pick it up. Without asking the referee, Bernie then ran off the pitch and into the dressing room so that he could put it back in again. We didn't know he wore contact lenses so were all saying to each other, 'Where's Bernie gone?' He was an incredible character, Bernie.

The winger who put the cross in for our goal was Miah Dennehy. He was so quick he could catch pigeons. Strangely, he was at his best when he was under pressure. If he had time and space, his crosses would often end up in the crowd. However, if a ball was played inside the full-back that he had no right to get to, he'd somehow reach it and put a fantastic cross into the box. Like me, Miah played for the Republic of Ireland from time to time. A few months before the game against Chesterfield, I was picked to play in goal against Poland and Miah was brought on as a substitute at the start of the second half. To have two Walsall players in a top international team at the same time was incredible, really. I can't see it happening again.

I was only 19 when I made my international debut. It was a friendly match against Poland in Dublin and Alan Kelly played in goal for most of the game. They brought me on as a late substitute so I could get a taste of what it was like. I was so wound up that when the ball was played back to me, I kicked it all the way up the pitch and it bounced once before flying over the bar. I'd never managed to do that before, and I was never able to do it again. It was pure adrenaline. However, the Irish supporters remembered me doing it, so whenever I played for them, they were always on at me to boot the ball the length of the pitch. That meant every time I threw the ball out, I got booed, even if it landed right at a player's feet!

Playing international football was a bit surreal, and I often had to pinch myself that it was really happening. I'd turn out against France or Spain and then a few days later I'd be back to playing the likes of Gillingham and Rochdale. But it never bothered me that I was at Wembley one week and Spotland the next. Walsall was my bread and butter, and I never forgot that. I played with some incredible players for the Republic of Ireland, such as Liam Brady, Johnny Giles, Steve Heighway, Mark Lawrenson, David O'Leary and Frank Stapleton. They may have been top players, but they never looked down at me because I played in the Third Division for Walsall. I was always just another team-mate to them.

A month before the game against Chesterfield, I played in a World Cup qualifier in Paris. France had some tremendous players in their team, including Michel Platini, Dominique Rocheteau and Marius Tresor. I had an absolute blinder that night. In fact, I think it was the best game I ever played for the Republic of Ireland. Platini was famous for his free kicks and I saved every one he took. They were all destined for the top corner, but I read them without too much difficulty and kept them out. I did get booked in that game, though. David O'Leary went off the pitch with an injury and I tried to waste a bit of time so that he could recover and come back on again. The referee took a dim view of it and showed me a yellow card. We eventually lost 2-0 and, despite beating France back in Dublin a few months later, they qualified for the World Cup in Argentina ahead of us. I won the Irish Sports Personality of the Week award because of my performance in Paris, which was quite a big thing in Ireland at the time. Unfortunately, I couldn't attend the award ceremony as I had a Walsall game on the same day, though they did send it on to me.

Anyway, we managed to hang on to the lead that Bernie's goal gave us and beat Chesterfield. Afterwards, their players were in shock. They just couldn't believe they'd lost, given how one-sided the game had been. What had happened was too ridiculous for words. Meanwhile, everybody involved with Walsall was elated. The players were excited about the prospect of playing at Old Trafford, the fans were thrilled that the Saddlers would be taking Manchester United on again and the directors were delighted because of the money the tie would bring into the club.

There was one amusing incident after the match. In those days, football grounds didn't have media rooms, with press conferences at the Baseball Ground having to take place in a narrow corridor that led to the dressing rooms. The Chesterfield manager at the time was Arthur Cox who, incidentally, had been a coach at Walsall in the 1960s. He was talking to the journalists as I squeezed past on my way to the players' lounge and it soon became evident that he wasn't very happy with me. 'We'd be playing Manchester United if it wasn't for that big bastard!' he shouted as I squeezed past. 'Thank you, Arthur!' I thought as I had a little chuckle to myself.

That match against Chesterfield took place just a few days before Christmas, which was always a busy time for footballers back then. In fact, we played games on two successive days over the break. We were at home to Preston North End on 27 December and then away to Tranmere Rovers just 24 hours later. But that wasn't out of the ordinary. I made my debut for Oxford United on

Good Friday at home to Leicester City. We then played away against Cardiff City the next day and away at Aston Villa on the following Tuesday. That was three games in five days. It amazes me when I hear managers complain these days that their players haven't got time to recover between matches. Whenever they do that, they are just giving their players an excuse for a poor performance. If a manager tries to take his team to task after a defeat, they will simply respond with: 'But gaffer, I heard you say …'. What you need is a manager who says, 'So what if we have two games in three days? We'll just get on with it.'

We played Manchester United early in the New Year, but sadly our FA Cup run came to an end with a 1-0 defeat. The only thing I can remember about that game is the goal. Gordon Hill got the ball on the left-hand side and drilled a hard shot that hit the post and then went in. It could just have easily bounced out, but that's the way it goes sometimes. It's not unusual to play in a big game and not remember all that much about it. I played in an international against England at Wembley and it felt as if we kicked off and then ten minutes later it was half-time. The second half went just as quickly. Time just flies past in games like that.

Walsall continued to struggle in the league and Doug Fraser left the club in March, with the legendary Dave Mackay replacing him as manager. He'd led Derby County to the league title less than two years earlier, so there was a lot of excitement amongst the players about what he could achieve at Walsall. Dave Mackay was the best manager I ever played under at Walsall, bar none. He had an aura about him and was always very calm; there was never any throwing of teacups or anything like that. If things weren't going well, he would talk to us quietly at half-time, identifying what we needed to change and gently putting us right. He was never one for turning a drama into a crisis. As well as being a strong disciplinarian, he was also the hardest footballer I've ever seen. People talk about players like Tommy Smith and Norman Hunter. Well, Dave Mackay would have picked them up and spat them out. He often joined in five-a-side games in training and was easily the best player, which wasn't bad considering he was in his early forties. He also had a will to win like no one else I have ever met. Alan Buckley was our star player, but Dave would still kick him up in the air in training on a Friday, even though he needed him for the following day's game. Sadly, Dave only stayed with the Saddlers for a year and a half before going out to manage in Kuwait. I'm convinced we would have won promotion and progressed as a club if he had stayed.

If Dave Mackay was the best manager I played under, the best captain I ever had was Ron Atkinson. He was captain of Oxford United when I started out and was one of life's natural leaders. Ron was always very confident about his own abilities, despite his tendency to trap a ball further than most people could kick it. He would also frequently give the ball away but that didn't stop him being merciless with anyone else if they lost it. You need to have something about you to be able to behave like that, and Ron did. The team was 30 per cent better whenever he played, and that was because he inspired everyone and got us all going. I could see the qualities he had, and it came as no surprise that he went on to have a long and successful career in management. Ron was, and is, a fantastic bloke.

Results picked up after Dave Mackay joined the club and we finished in 15th place, well above the relegation zone that we'd been in and around for much of the season. I got married towards the end of the campaign, and we played away at York City 24 hours before my big day. To my great surprise, about half a dozen Walsall supporters ran on to the pitch at the end of the match and gave me a stack of wedding presents. I couldn't carry them all and some of the other players had to help me take them to the dressing room, though it wasn't as if they had bought me a fridge or a television or anything like that! That's the sort of thing that could only happen at Walsall. It has always been such a friendly club.

I stayed with the Saddlers for another couple of years before moving to Wolves in the summer of 1979. Their second-choice goalkeeper, Gary Pierce, had left for Barnsley and they wanted me to take his place. In an ideal world I would have liked to stay with Walsall, but Wolves offered to triple my wages. I had a family to look after, so it was a no-brainer really. I was there for three seasons and played the odd game for the first team, though I was largely understudy to Paul Bradshaw. In my first season at Wolves they finished sixth in the top division and won the League Cup, qualifying for the UEFA Cup as a result. It was an enjoyable time to be at Wolves but my main club, and the place where I had all my best times as a footballer, was undoubtedly Walsall.

I played my last international game while I was at Wolves, which was a European Championship qualifier against Northern Ireland in Belfast. It was the height of the Troubles, with Lord Mountbatten and Airey Neave having been assassinated earlier in the year, and so security was incredibly tight for the game. All the players boarded a coach in Dublin, were given an escort by the Irish army to the border and then the British army guarded us all the way to the stadium. There was a lot of shouting and bawling from the Northern Ireland supporters on the day, but thankfully nothing more. We lost the game 1-0 and Pat Jennings had a great game in goal for them. After the match there was no socialising at all. We got straight back on to the coach and were accompanied by the armed forces all the way back to Dublin. It was all quite eerie, but we felt safe. The security that day was fabulous.

I came back to Walsall in 1982 and saw out my career with the club. Playing in the League Cup defeat of Arsenal was one highlight during that period, as was appearing in the same side as my brother Ollie, who had also joined the Saddlers. In fact, there was one game where Ron Green broke his collarbone and Ollie, who was a striker, had to replace him in goal. That would make a good quiz question: name two brothers who both played in goal for Walsall during the same season. People would never get it!

COLIN HARRISON

Colin Harrison
Defender, Midfielder and Winger, 1963–81

Aspiring players are frequently told that football is a short career, but those warning them would never be able to use Colin Harrison as an example. When he played his last game for Walsall there were many in the crowd who hadn't even been born when he first became a Saddler almost two decades earlier. He finally hung up his boots in 1981, not long after Lady Diana Spencer married Prince Charles. As a demonstration of his longevity, the 'People's Princess' had only been a toddler when Colin Harrison started out in football. Back then, even *Match of the Day* was merely a glint in a television producer's eye.

When Colin Harrison made his debut in 1964, sharp suits and a short back and sides were the order of the day. As the years went past, haircuts got longer and lapels grew wider, but one thing didn't change: the dependable Harrison was an ever-present in the team. The man who began playing alongside the likes of Ken Hodgkisson, Jimmy McMorran and Albert McPherson finished as a team-mate of Don Penn, David Preece and Mark Rees. Barely conceivable, but true.

Colin Harrison turned out so many times for the Saddlers that he became part of the small, select band to have played more than 500 games for Walsall. He went on to hold the club's appearance record for three decades before Jimmy Walker finally broke it in 2012. Nevertheless, no other Walsall footballer has played more league games than Colin Harrison, nor have any other outfield players bettered his appearances total.

Three words sum up why Colin Harrison set those records: talent, versatility and loyalty. He played football better than most, he successfully turned his hand to whatever job he was asked to do, and he stayed with the club through thick and thin. The honour of being in a promotion-winning side may have eluded him, but arguably the great FA Cup runs that he was such a key part of were adequate recompense. Will Walsall Football Club ever see the likes of Colin Harrison again? Only time will tell.

Arsenal 4 – 1 Walsall

FA Cup Fifth Round
Saturday, 18 February 1978
Highbury, London
Attendance: 43,736

Arsenal	Walsall
Pat Jennings	Mick Kearns
Pat Rice	Tony Macken
Sammy Nelson	Brian Caswell
David Price	Colin Harrison
David O'Leary	Dave Serella
Willie Young	Alun Evans
Liam Brady	Miah Dennehy
Alan Sunderland	Mick Bates
Malcolm Macdonald	Alf Wood
Frank Stapleton	Alan Buckley
Graham Rix	Jeff King

Managers

Terry Neill	Dave Mackay

Scorers

Frank Stapleton (27, 90)	Alan Buckley (51)
Malcolm Macdonald (35)	
Alan Sunderland (40)	

Referee
John Gow

I SPENT two decades at Walsall Football Club and didn't fall out with any of my team-mates during all that time. I never had a single argument with anyone. I was lucky to play with some lovely lads during my career and it's been a good life, meeting them all. When I joined the club in the early 1960s, I trained with Frank Gregg and we're still friends to this day. One of Walsall's best players when I started out was the left-winger, Colin 'Cannonball' Taylor. I played at left-back behind Colin and would often give him the ball and then watch as he ran on a few steps, before pulling back the trigger to unleash one of his incredible strikes on goal. The power of his shooting was just unbelievable. If you ever made the mistake of getting in the way of one of his shots, you'd be left with the imprint of the ball on your leg for a week!

I grew up in Pelsall and was always out on the Common playing football. We put our coats down as goalposts and then had a kickabout for hours. I don't know if kids still do that these days, or whether they want to have all the gear on before they'll go out and play. When I was young, we just played football whenever and wherever we could. When I got older, I was picked for the Brownhills district team and turned out for them on a Saturday morning. We played our matches in Burntwood and I don't know whether that was where Ron Jukes saw me, but one night he came to our house and invited me to go training with Walsall on Tuesday and Thursday nights with the other amateurs. I would have been 15 at the time. Ron Jukes recruited a lot of great players for Walsall over the years, with Allan Clarke being the most famous of them.

I trained as an amateur with Walsall in the evenings but spent my days working at the GEC factory in Witton.

I caught the coach in Pelsall at twenty past six in the morning, worked there all day, got the coach back again and then raced home so that I could get to training on time. I worked on a bench in the factory with seven other men, and because I was the most junior amongst them, I ended up being the dogsbody. That meant making the tea and running errands all day long. The GEC factory was so big that each of the different departments had their own football team. When the men on my bench found out that I could play football a bit, they wanted me to play for the department's team. I kept telling them that I couldn't play as I had to catch the coach home, but they wouldn't have any of it. One of the men said that he would run me home if I played, so I had no choice in the end. Anyway, we won the first match I played in by six goals to nil and I scored a hat-trick, so I couldn't get out of playing for them after that.

All I ever really wanted to do was play football, and when I turned 17 Walsall offered me a professional contract. I happily left GEC and became a full-time footballer, training alongside other youngsters such as Nick Atthey, Stan Bennett and Dave Tennant. I didn't have to wait too long before making my debut, which came when I was 18. It was an away game at Southend United and I was picked to play on the left wing. They didn't tell me I was playing until the morning of the game, but I was still very nervous beforehand. That never changed throughout my career. I always got jittery before games, though I don't think that's a bad thing as it keeps you on your toes.

When I started out at Walsall, 'Chopper' Guttridge gave me some good advice. He told me to train hard, and always to keep up with Frank Gregg and Alan Roper. Arthur Cox was the trainer at the time, and he made us do a lot of hard running. We were forever doing laps of the pitch and he had us on the clock while we were doing it. I took Chopper's advice on board, making sure I was always just behind or slightly in front of Frank and Alan when we did those runs. As the years went on, I also got into the habit of starting training earlier than the other players. I'd drop my wife, Joan, off at McKechnie's in Aldridge and then get into Fellows Park at around nine in the morning. That gave me an extra hour in the gym before everyone else came in. I used to do a lot of ball work on my own and would often stay behind longer than some of the other players as well. I think that benefitted me quite a lot at the time, and perhaps it also helped to extend my career.

However, there was another good reason for getting into training early at Walsall. I see the young lads at the Banks's Stadium these days and they're all kitted out in the latest sports gear. They look so smart. We didn't have anything like that when I was their age. There was just a bundle of old kit that you had to search through, looking for a pair of shorts that weren't ripped underneath and socks that didn't have holes in them. Back then, getting into training early was the only way of making sure that you had something half decent to wear.

Training was always interesting at Walsall. We often had all sorts of different people come to join us, such as Ron Flowers, who had been a member of England's 1966 World Cup squad. He played in practice matches with us and was a brilliant footballer. The boxing brothers Billy Gray and Ron Gray also came in from Cannock to do some training with us. They were big, strong lads. Then, every Friday, we played a game on the car park. That was going on when I joined the club in the early 1960s, so goodness knows how far back the tradition went. It used to get quite competitive and I suppose it was a bit silly to play on gravel the day before a match. Looking back, we probably ended up on the car park because the groundsman, Roger Johnson, wouldn't let us go on to the pitch. He was so dedicated to that pitch he wouldn't allow pigeons on it, let alone the players!

I played under so many managers during my time at Walsall that I can't remember them all. One that I won't forget in a hurry, however, was Dave Mackay. He took over in 1977 after Doug Fraser got the sack. Dave Mackay had won lots of trophies as a player at Spurs and was the manager of Derby County when they won the league title only a couple of years earlier, so it was a real surprise that he was prepared to come to Walsall. He brought a lot more discipline into the club and would soon put you in your place. He could get quite worked up if we were losing and would come in at half-time and have a good shout at us. His partner, Des Anderson, usually then had to calm things down a bit. I was injured when Dave Mackay arrived, and the first thing he said to me was that I was no good to him while I was in plaster. That knocked me down a little at the time, but he was really good to me once I got myself fit again.

For some reason, Walsall had quite a connection with Nottingham Forest at the time. Dave Mackay had been the manager there a few years earlier while Alan Buckley, Miah Dennehy and Dave Serella had all been at Forest before they came to Walsall. Dave played in central defence and was a bit of a joker, so it was always fun to have him around. Miah was a really quick winger, though he did forget to take the ball with him now and again. Alan Buckley and I were big friends back then. Whenever we stopped overnight for away matches, his wife, Amanda, would come and stay with my wife at our house. Then, when we had the children, we used to go on holiday together to Newquay and places like that. I haven't seen him for a few years now, which is a bit of a shame.

Mick Kearns was our goalkeeper at the time, and he was a really solid presence to have behind you. Looking back, we had some tremendous keepers when I was at Walsall. There was Phil Parkes, a local lad from Sedgley who came up through the ranks at the end of the 1960s. He went on to win the FA Cup with West Ham United as well as play for England. Then a few years later Mark Wallington came to Walsall. He soon left for Leicester City and spent most of his career playing in the top division. Towards the end of my playing days, Ron Green became our first-choice goalkeeper. He was a real torment. If you were standing somewhere, he'd come up behind you and squeeze you to death. I was forever saying, 'Ronnie, put me down! Put me down!'

We had quite a few experienced midfielders in our team when we played against Arsenal in the FA Cup. There was Mick Bates, who had been part of Don Revie's great Leeds United squad that won something nearly every season. He was a very stylish player, though I'm not sure it suited him in the lower divisions where players often relied on their brawn. We also took on Jeff King from Derby County, while Alun Evans joined us from Aston Villa after having been at Liverpool and Wolves. He scored the winning goal when we beat Leicester City at home in the fourth round to set up the tie against Arsenal.

Over the years, I played with quite a few footballers who joined Walsall from bigger clubs. I reckon some of them thought life was going to be easier in the lower divisions, but they often found out that it wasn't. There were still some tremendous players at that level. Ted MacDougall was one. He played up front for Bournemouth and scored nine goals in a match once, which tells you how good he was. Don Rogers was another. He was a winger for Swindon Town and whenever we were due to play them, I'd check the team sheet to see whether I was playing left-back or right-back. If I was up against him, I knew I was in for a long afternoon. He would go inside you. He would go outside you. He would absolutely tie you in knots.

Football didn't really change all that much during my career, but it has done in recent years. Tactics have become much more important. In my day, you got given a job to do, such as stopping on the one player, and you just went out and did it. There's also a lot of tippy-tappy football now, which I haven't got much time for. I played with quick wingers like Miah Dennehy and Mark Rees who would terrorise full-backs with their pace. Raheem Sterling is one of the few modern footballers who can do that, but you don't see many others who are capable of it. I think that's a shame as those are the types of players that fans want to come and see. Football needs more of them, not less.

When Walsall took on Arsenal, Alf Wood played up front alongside Alan Buckley. Alf was a real hard nut. I played against him when he was at Shrewsbury Town and it was never easy. He was one of those footballers you'd rather have on your side than see line up for the opposition. Another tough striker I played with for the Saddlers was Bernie Wright. He was one of the strongest players I ever came across, though his dress sense often wasn't the best. Whenever we travelled away all the lads would have their club suits on, but not Bernie. He'd turn up in a pair of old trousers, his shirt wide open and the soles hanging off his shoes. He never dressed smartly. I remember one time we went away to Spain for a few days when Bill Moore was the manager. We were all sitting around the swimming pool when someone bet Bernie that he wouldn't throw Bill in the water. He went behind Bill, picked him up and I can still hear Bill saying, 'Bernie, no! No!' But Bernie would never have thrown him in the pool. He was a real down-to-earth lad who was just having a bit of fun.

It was really exciting to draw Arsenal in the FA Cup. Most of the lads in the team had spent their whole careers in the lower divisions, playing against the same teams, week in, week out. But when you get a game against a club like Arsenal, it really picks you up and gets you going. In the run-up to the big day you start thinking about what a change it will be and wondering how large the crowd will get. I felt both nervousness and excitement as the game got closer. You want to go down there and give them a game, but there is a bit of apprehension as well. Arsenal had some incredible players and you knew they were going to be tough to play against. Liam Brady and Graham Rix were very talented midfielders, while Malcolm Macdonald was one of the top strikers in England at the time. I had come up against him before when he was at Newcastle United. We played them in the fourth round of the FA Cup a few years earlier and beat them 1-0 on a complete mudbath at Fellows Park. The pitch was a real leveller that day.

It was the first time that Walsall had played Arsenal since their famous FA Cup victory over them in 1933, so the press made a lot of that in the build-up to the game. That match was played at Fellows Park, whereas this one was at Highbury, which was an incredible ground. I remember walking in through the big doors into the marble halls and seeing all the statues. It was a different world compared to what we were used to. Fellows Park may not have been as grand as Highbury, but it was still a smashing little ground. Whenever we played big games there, the top end would get full and the atmosphere was incredible. I loved playing there.

For me, the most memorable moment of the game against Arsenal came quite early on. We had only been playing for ten minutes or so when I went on a long run down the pitch. I remember nutmegging someone and suddenly I was through on goal. I over-kicked the ball and it turned into a race between me and Pat Jennings, who came dashing off his line. Unfortunately, he got there first and booted the ball into the crowd. It would have been tremendous if I could have had a go at goal, but it wasn't to be. If we could have scored, we would have had something to defend and the home fans might have got on their backs a bit. Instead, it became backs to the wall for us which, to be honest, was what we had expected, given the players they had in their team. We held out for half an hour or so and then Alan Sunderland played a wonderful ball that split our defence in two. A cross into the box followed soon afterwards and Frank Stapleton scored with an easy tap-in.

We fell apart a bit after that and Malcolm Macdonald and Alan Sunderland both scored within the next ten minutes or so. It was hard to go in 3-0 down at half-time, but your pride takes over at times like that. You don't want to be on the end of a thrashing, no matter who you are playing, so that galvanised us for the second half. We came out after the interval determined to give it a go, and within a few minutes

Alan Buckley had got one back for us. Arsenal were still the stronger team, but then with about quarter of an hour left to go, Miah Dennehy had a good chance to score. He didn't take it and that was our last hope gone. If he'd scored, that would have probably made Arsenal a bit nervous and we could have built on that. As it was, Frank Stapleton got his second just before the end of the match and it was all over. Arsenal went on to reach the FA Cup Final that year, so at least we lost to a team that got to Wembley.

We had a decent run in the league that season and finished in sixth place, just three points off the promotion places. There were no play-offs back then, so that was the end of our campaign. Dave Mackay was building a good team, but he got offered a lot of money to go out and coach in Kuwait that summer, so he left. I think Walsall would have really pushed on if he had stayed. Because of the name he had in the game, he would have been able to bring in more players from a higher level who would really have strengthened the team.

Personally, I was never tempted to leave the Saddlers. When I signed for them, I could have gone to a host of other clubs instead, such as Aston Villa, Peterborough and Wrexham. But that would have meant leaving home, and I wasn't too keen on that. When I was an established player, nobody ever told me that somebody was looking at me, or that another club wanted to sign me, so I don't know if there was any interest or not. People say to me that I could have played for a bigger club, but I don't know if I would have gone, even if one of them had come in for me. I was too settled at Walsall.

I never moved from the Saddlers and set the club appearance record, which I held for about 30 years or so until Jimmy Walker broke it. I've still got the record for most games played by an outfield player, and I don't know if that will ever be broken. Not many players seem to stop at one club for their whole career these days like I did. But you never know. Liam Kinsella is a good young player who has come up through the ranks and established himself in the first team. Maybe he could do it if he sticks around. I thought for a while that Chris Marsh might break my appearance record. He started out at Walsall like me and was in the team for many years, but he left towards the end of his career with my record still intact. When I joined Walsall there was a forward in the squad called Trevor Foster. He was the first player that I saw do a 'stepover' with the ball when he took someone on. It wasn't something that Chris Marsh invented!

Because of the large number of games I played during my career people may think that I didn't suffer too much with injuries, but I had my fair share. I had to have the cartilages out of both sides of my right knee and was also in plaster for eight weeks when I did my ligaments. I don't ever remember playing through any injuries, though. You had to be fit before they would let you go out on the pitch. I suppose one reason why I made so many appearances for the club was that I was prepared to play anywhere in the team. One week I might be left-back, but then the following week I would replace the right-back if he got injured, or maybe move into midfield. Some weeks I didn't know where I'd be playing until Saturday came around. I didn't like it if I was filling in for an injured player and then ended up on the bench when he got fit again. But I was happy if I was in the first team. I really didn't mind where I played; I just wanted to play.

I wore most of the Walsall jerseys during my time there. I even had to go in goal for the reserves once. That happened towards the end of my career when I coached the youth team for a while. They were a tremendous group of lads, though they used to give me some right stick. We often trained at the Arboretum and would drive down there in five or six cars. I've always taken great pride in my car; I polish it regularly, and I don't like anybody to mess about with it. Anyway, one time we'd finished our training and were driving back to the ground. We got to the big island where the Broadway crosses the Birmingham Road and some of the lads from the youth team drove into the back of my car on purpose, just to wind me up. I was livid. I wanted to have it out with them there and then, but they locked themselves inside their car so I couldn't get to them. They didn't half laugh about it afterwards, saying things to me like 'Colin, you should have seen your face when you got out of the car!' Thankfully they didn't do any damage, but that was the sort of thing they would get up to. They were great fun to be around.

I made my final appearances for Walsall in 1981, but I didn't stop playing football. I turned out for Rushall Olympic for a while and then played for the West Bromwich Albion All-Stars and Aston Villa All-Stars. We would play every week, travelling all over the place for games. There were some fantastic footballers in those teams, such as Cyrille Regis and John Wile. We weren't as fast as we used to be, but the matches were still very competitive and anybody who tried to show off would soon get put right. I kept going until I was in my sixties, but there were others older than me. Once when I played for the Villa All-Stars they had a wing-half who was in his seventies!

I had to have a new knee a couple of years ago, but I'm still quite active. I'm regularly out on my bike, riding around Norton Canes where I live. Martin O'Connor has his football academy there and we often give each other a wave. There's a park near my granddaughter's house, and when I was there with her recently, I spotted a young lad kicking a ball about with his gran. As soon as I saw them, I went over and said, 'Come on then, let me go in goal!' So, there I am, in my mid-seventies, having this kid taking shots at me while I did my best to save them before rolling the ball back out to him. I've always loved playing football and I always will.

PETER HART

Peter Hart
Central defender, 1980–90

It takes an array of talents to make a successful football team. Those that get noticed the most are the headline-grabbers: the prodigious goalscorers, the midfield playmakers or the goalkeepers who save the day. But there are also the unsung heroes who toil away in less glamorous roles, quietly and diligently doing the jobs that frequently get overlooked. One such player was Peter Hart.

A proud Yorkshireman, Hart joined Walsall in 1980 from Huddersfield Town. He stayed at the club for the next decade; a consistent and reliable presence at the heart of the Saddlers defence. An honest, hard-working professional, Hart gave no quarter and asked for none to be given. He never shied away from showing the aggression that his position on the pitch demanded, but his combativeness rarely overstepped the mark. Peter Hart was indeed hard but fair.

Hart's time at Walsall coincided with one of the most exciting periods in the club's history, with a run to the semi-finals of the League Cup in 1984 and promotion to the Second Division in 1988 being amongst the highlights. Hart was a key part of those achievements and was rarely out of the side, missing only six league fixtures during his first seven seasons at the club and playing more than 470 games in total for the Saddlers.

Peter Hart was the team captain for much of his time at the club, doing his utmost every game and leading by example. He retired from football at the relatively young age of 32, though he had still managed to clock up over 700 games by that time. After being a loyal servant to Walsall Football Club, Hart became a committed servant to the Church. He was ordained into the Church of England in 1992 and then returned to Walsall in 1997 as vicar at St Martin's Church on Sutton Road. It's worth noting that the final game played at Fellows Park prior to its demolition was Peter Hart's testimonial. It was an honour he deserved.

Arsenal 1 – 2 Walsall

League Cup Fourth Round
Tuesday, 29 November 1983
Highbury, London
Attendance: 22,406

Arsenal	**Walsall**
Pat Jennings	Mick Kearns
Stewart Robson	Brian Caswell
Kenny Sansom	Kenny Mower
Chris Whyte	Craig Shakespeare
David O'Leary	Colin Brazier
Colin Hill	Peter Hart
Alan Sunderland	Mark Rees
Paul Davis	Ally Brown
Tony Woodcock	Richard O'Kelly
Charlie Nicholas	David Preece
Ian Allinson	Gary Childs

Managers

Terry Neill	Alan Buckley

Scorers

Stewart Robson (31)	Mark Rees (64)
	Ally Brown (84)

Referee
Leslie Burden

THE WALSALL side of 1983/84 was the best team I ever played in. I was fortunate to be part of two promotion-winning sides: the Huddersfield Town team that won the Division Four title in 1980, and then the Saddlers team that won promotion through the Division Three play-offs in 1988. It may appear ludicrous to suggest that a side that failed to win promotion was better than those two teams, but for me it was. The reason I say that is because we had such good players at Walsall at that time. The back four, composed of me, Colin Brazier, Brian Caswell and Kenny Mower was sound, while Ron Green was a very able goalkeeper. Then up front we had Ally Brown and Richard O'Kelly, both of whom were very good strikers.

Arguably, though, the most special part of that team was the midfield four. When Walsall played Arsenal, Gary Childs was 19, Craig Shakespeare and David Preece were 20 and Mark Rees, at the grand age of 22, was the oldest of them all. If you're good enough, it doesn't matter how old you are, and those four were very good footballers. They each had different qualities, but it was David Preece who made the team tick. David was always confident, positive and aggressive, and when I say aggressive, I mean that he had the energy to get hold of the ball, keep it and then make things happen. He left Walsall a year after that League Cup run and spent most of his career in the top division, playing against teams like Arsenal every week. It was where he belonged.

Those young players brought vigour and liveliness to the squad, which really helped us. Craig Shakespeare, in particular, had a wonderful, dry sense of humour that just lit the place up. It was a dressing room that laughed a lot and the value of that should never be underestimated. If a football team is going to be successful it must be united, and it must have a sense of togetherness that can carry it through tough times. That Walsall team had it in abundance. What it also had were some real characters, like Kenny Mower, Richard O'Kelly and Mark Rees, who helped create a great spirit in the dressing room. If you have strong personalities that operate in a positive rather than disruptive way, they can really bring a team together. Those players did that and made the club a great place to walk into every day.

This may sound strange, but another thing that brought us together was the relatively poor training facilities we had back then. We didn't have the fantastic centres that teams seem to have these days. We had to get goals and cones and footballs from Fellows Park, carry them over the bridge and set up a practice pitch on the other side of the railway line. The surface we trained on wasn't the best either. Then, every Friday, we played a practice match on the car park! I can't imagine that Chelsea or Manchester City would allow their multi-million-pound footballers to play in an area littered with ruts and bricks and pebbles and glass, but that's what we did. We'd done all the hard work in the days leading up to Friday, so it gave us a chance to relax a little and get ourselves in the right frame of mind for the following day's game. It was certainly unorthodox, but it was how we prepared, and it worked for us. Clubs wouldn't get away with doing those sorts of things these days, but those experiences brought the players much closer together. Even with all the changes that have happened in football since I played, having a harmonious dressing room and a good team spirit is still as important as it ever was.

I joined Walsall in the summer of 1980, and one of the main reasons I came was because they were a very good footballing team. Alan Buckley was the player-manager at the time, and he was a fantastic striker. He went on to score over 200 goals for the club and you could easily see why. Alan was a very chirpy, positive, confident type of footballer and he took that into his style of management. He wanted his team to play attractive football and he gave us the freedom to go out and do just that. I've no doubt there have been some decent Walsall teams since that 1983/84 season, but I can't imagine that many of them have played better football than that side did. I don't say that because I was instrumental to it; I was simply a defender. It was other players in the team that passed the ball well and made the side so appealing to watch, particularly the young midfield four. The type of football we played made the team a great success and helped Alan Buckley to eventually go on to manage West Bromwich Albion.

I was at Huddersfield Town for eight years before I came to Walsall and had some marvellous times there. We had a very good youth team, which reached the FA Youth Cup Final against Tottenham Hotspur in 1974 and the semi-finals again a year later. I made my first-team debut aged only 16 years and 229 days, which set a club record that stands to this day. The game was against Southend United and I played at centre-half, going up against a striker called Chris Guthrie. He was 6ft 2in tall, compared to my 5ft 10in, so that was certainly an interesting challenge! There was a bit of fuss before the game because I was such a young debutant, and I remember getting a telegram from Roy Ellam, a former Huddersfield Town centre-half who had moved to Leeds United at the same time as Trevor Cherry. One of the reasons why I probably got my opportunity at such a young age was that the club was in freefall. Huddersfield Town were in the top division when I joined them but had slipped down to the Second Division by the time that I became an apprentice. The club then got relegated to the Third Division and only spent two seasons there before ending up in the Fourth Division. Another reason for the early start in my professional career was that Ian Greaves was the manager, and he was someone who liked to give young players a chance.

I played over 200 matches for Huddersfield and was captain when they won the Fourth Division title in 1980, finishing just ahead of Walsall. It was a big decision to leave, not least because it was my first club and I'm a Yorkshireman and love the place. However, I always believed that if you stayed at a club for a long time you tended to get taken for granted. I also felt that Walsall had a better chance of making the step up to the Second Division than Huddersfield did. In the end, Huddersfield got promoted from the Third Division first, but ironically they were one of the clubs Walsall replaced in the Second Division when we won promotion in 1988.

I spent my last year and a half at Huddersfield playing in midfield as they felt they needed some strength and aggression in that part of the pitch. I thought it was only going to be a temporary move, but I stayed there for the whole of that promotion-winning season. Walsall bought me as a midfield player on the back of those performances, obviously believing I was the type of midfielder they needed. My first season with the Saddlers then turned out to be a bit of a nightmare as we struggled in the Third Division, only avoiding relegation by beating Sheffield United in our final match. That result saved us and relegated Sheffield United, which was a bit of a surprise, particularly for them, as I don't think they ever felt they were in the equation to go down.

That season confirmed I could do a job in midfield, if necessary, but showed that I was really a defender. If I'd had the confidence, then perhaps I could have made a better fist of playing in midfield, but being a defender came far more naturally to me. I was a player that liked to compete and tackle, and I enjoyed that side of the game more than any other. So, the following season, I moved to centre-back and that was the start of seven positive, fulfilling years with Walsall during which I barely missed a game. I eventually played over 470 games for the club, which also reflects the fact that I was fortunate never to suffer from a serious injury. I did have to play through little, niggling injuries from time to time as squads were smaller back then, plus there was neither the pressure nor the opportunity to come out if you got a slight knock. My kind of game was never brilliant; it was always steady and at a certain standard. I like to think, therefore, that the manager knew what he was going to get from me. But saying that, even if I experienced a bit of downturn in form, the club just didn't have the players who could come in and replace me.

Compared to now, much tougher challenges were allowed when I played, which makes it even more remarkable that I didn't suffer a serious injury. A lot of the physical contact has been taken out of the game, and perhaps rightly so because we have some quite exceptional football now, particularly in the Premier League. We also have some incredibly talented footballers now who can do wonderful things. I'm not saying that skilful players weren't around in my day, but the pitches weren't as good for a start, plus the kind of tackles that were permitted also thwarted them to a certain degree. The changes in the laws have favoured the talented, flair footballers, enabling them to play without the fear of getting whacked which so haunted their equivalents back in the 1970s and 1980s.

The 1983/84 season was the most exciting of the ten I spent with Walsall, though it didn't start at all well. In September, we lost 8-1 to Bolton Wanderers and 6-3 to Oxford United. It's hard to understand now how a team that could have suffered those heavy defeats could have gone on to beat Arsenal and reach the semi-finals of the League Cup. It may have had something to do with the fact that we were a young team, and perhaps we needed time to settle and to gel. Lee Sinnott was my partner in central defence for that defeat against Bolton, and that turned out to be his last game for the club before he moved to Watford. He was replaced in the back four by Colin Brazier, who had previously been at Wolves. Colin was a good all-rounder and I enjoyed playing alongside him. He had a lot of experience, was composed and passed the ball well. I think he brought something to our team, particularly to the defensive four, that made a difference.

We reached the last 16 of the League Cup by beating Blackpool, Barnsley and Shrewsbury. Walsall were then drawn against Arsenal, away at Highbury. Perhaps inevitably, the press made a lot of comparisons between us and the famous Saddlers side that beat Arsenal in the FA Cup in 1933; Gilbert Alsop and all that. The game also had some particular interest for me, given my previous time at Huddersfield. They had won three consecutive league titles in the 1920s with a side built by the great Herbert Chapman. He then went on to Arsenal and won another couple of championships with them before his premature death. I'd never played at Highbury with Huddersfield, so going there with Walsall was a new experience for me.

The League Cup tie was a huge game for the club but, unfortunately, we didn't have a goalkeeper. Ron Green was out with injury and Tony Godden was cup-tied. Mick Kearns had been involved with the club for over a decade but had recently retired and was working as the steward at Aldridge Conservative Club. Alan Buckley managed to bring him back for the match against Arsenal, and he played in a few league games for the team after that as well. Footballers are largely unshockable, and it was something we just took in our stride. We understood that was how it was and never doubted that Mick could do a good job for us. But it was clearly a sign of the gulf between the two clubs: the great Arsenal, with their marble hallways at Highbury, compared to Walsall who could only field a full team by bringing an ex-goalkeeper out of retirement.

We didn't have any great fear of Arsenal before the game. We hadn't lost a league match for two months and were playing some tremendous football as we climbed up the table. We felt we had a chance, not least because Arsenal were struggling a bit that season compared to their own high standards. I was relishing the challenge of taking on their two strikers, Charlie Nicholas and Tony Woodcock. Arsenal had signed Charlie Nicholas from Celtic in the summer for a lot of money, and he was their big hope. However, he hadn't scored for a while, unlike Woodcock, who had got five goals in a game against Aston Villa a few weeks earlier. Arsenal had some other big-name players at the time, such as Pat Jennings, a very well-regarded goalkeeper within the game, David O'Leary, an experienced Irish international centre-half and Kenny Sansom, England's first-choice left-back.

Highbury was one of those big, old traditional grounds and it was quite an experience to play there. Arsenal may have been the favourites, but Walsall made the better start and Ally Brown had a couple of decent chances to score early in the game. As the half wore on, our stand-in goalkeeper, Mick Kearns, had to make a good save from Tony Woodcock, and then after about half an hour they took the lead. Stewart Robson collected a pass from Charlie Nicholas and then slid the ball under Mick as he came rushing off his line. We were a goal behind at half-time, but there was no negativity or criticism in the dressing room at all. Alan Buckley and the coach, Garry Pendrey, were very upbeat, praising the football we'd been playing and talking up our prospects for the second half. The mood was very much that Arsenal were there to be beaten and that we were more than capable of doing so.

We came out fighting in the second half and Gary Childs went close with a looping shot from outside the penalty area that just dipped over the bar. We kept on pushing forward and midway through the half we got the goal our play deserved. David Preece lofted a pass over the Arsenal defence to Ally Brown, who then played it sideways to Mark Rees, who was unmarked on the other side of the penalty area. Mark trapped the ball and then fired it low past Pat Jennings, who stood no chance. After that, it was all Walsall. Ally Brown had another good chance, but Jennings made a wonderful save from point-blank range. Then Richard O'Kelly twice came close to scoring: once with a shot that was saved by Jennings and then with a header that bounced off the top of the crossbar.

Momentum builds during a game and it was undoubtedly with Walsall in the second half.

We finally got the winner a few minutes from time. David Preece played a bobbling pass into the penalty area and the bounce confused Chris Whyte, with the ball ending up right in front of Ally Brown in the six-yard box. He couldn't miss, and thankfully he didn't. After that, I don't recall Walsall struggling to hang on to the lead at all. There was a clock on the top of one of the stands which appeared to have stopped, but despite that I don't remember us coming under any real pressure. After the final whistle was blown, we went to the corner of the ground where the 2,000 or so Walsall spectators were and celebrated with them. As all Saddlers fans will know, there's now a Morrisons on the site where Fellows Park stood. There's a photograph behind the tills of me and a few other players celebrating with the fans at that Arsenal game, though I don't know whether it was taken after we'd scored or following the final whistle.

Given the performances of the two teams that night, you wouldn't have guessed that there were two divisions between us. It wasn't as if we had defended for 70 to 80 per cent of the game and then scored with two late, breakaway goals. For large parts of that match we were the dominant side and we played some fantastic football. The result may have come as a shock for the wider public, but it didn't surprise us because we knew we were a good team. I don't recall any of the Arsenal players impressing me in that game, really. They were clearly a team that was short on confidence, and it probably didn't help that the crowd got on their backs after we started to control the match. That just emphasised that we were in the game and had a great chance to win it, which was what happened in the end.

I'd say that it was a good all-round team performance against Arsenal. Richard O'Kelly and Ally Brown did a great job up front, while we were tight defensively. The one Walsall player that really stood out for me that night though was David Preece. The match was a big opportunity for him to show his abilities and he certainly did that. He was playing against footballers that he would go on to compete against on a regular basis, and that game showed that he was more than capable of doing so.

There was a lot of press coverage following our defeat of Arsenal, and it should be remembered that the League Cup was a big competition at the time. It had a credibility and a value back then which I think it has since lost. All the big clubs treated it seriously and put out their best teams in every round. We didn't play Arsenal under-23s in the last 16 and Liverpool reserves in the semi-finals; we played Arsenal and Liverpool. I don't recall the Walsall players getting a big bonus for winning that game. Indeed, if it had been huge, I would have remembered it! However, I think the club did take us away for a holiday at the end of the season. Another thing I recall was that Arsenal's manager, Terry Neill, got sacked a couple of weeks after the game. Clearly, losing at home to Walsall played a big part in his downfall.

After beating Arsenal, Walsall drew Rotherham United in the quarter-finals. Initially, I was disappointed that we didn't get a tie against another big club, but on reflection it did give us a great chance to reach the last four. And that was how it turned out. We played them on an icy pitch at Millmoor and won a very tough match by four goals to two.

There was a huge amount of excitement in Walsall when we played the two-legged semi-final against Liverpool.

Indeed, the whole town got interested. To be honest, we were barely in the game at Anfield but, somehow, we managed to score twice and got a good draw. I really fancied our chances in the second leg, but it wasn't to be. We had some good opportunities to score but ended up losing 2-0. The other two semi-finalists were Aston Villa and Everton. I firmly believe that had we played either of them at Fellows Park instead, having drawn the first leg, we would have got to Wembley. But Liverpool were the best team in Europe at the time and they just had a little too much for us.

Nevertheless, to draw against Liverpool at Anfield and then lose narrowly at home to them was no disgrace. In fact, I think it was one of the club's greatest-ever achievements. Famously, Walsall took part in a promotion with British Airways before the beginning of that season, with the billboard poster displaying the team underneath the slogan 'They're only 90 minutes away from a place in Europe'. The idea was to show how quickly you could get to the continent from Birmingham Airport. I suppose that including a team shot of Walsall on the poster was meant to be ironic, but how close we came!

Walsall were top of the table when that League Cup run came to an end, but really struggled in the league after that, winning only five of the remaining 17 fixtures. Before losing to Liverpool we were on track for promotion but ended up finishing in sixth place. There were no play-offs back then, so that meant another season in the Third Division. I've always attributed the downturn in form to the fact that we had such a young team, particularly in midfield. We lost momentum, confidence ebbed away and then we just faded. It was a great shame as that team would have coped in a higher division had we won promotion, given the type of football we played. Having said that, we may well still have lost David Preece and things would have been a lot tougher without him in the side.

We'll never know whether we could have won promotion if we hadn't gone on that run in the League Cup. However, I still view it as having been a positive distraction. If the team had got promoted, we may have spent only a season or two in a higher division before coming back down again, because that's the way it has gone for the club over the last 30 years. A promotion in 1984 may well have been forgotten over time, but those League Cup games, particularly the one at Anfield, are still talked about to this day. So, am I glad that we had the cup run rather than promotion? No, because I wanted to play in the highest division that I could. But no one will ever forget that League Cup run in a hurry.

Many people know that I have been the Reverend Peter Hart for quite some time now. It was just after the semi-final against Liverpool that I became a Christian. My second daughter, Sarah, was born that year and we got involved with St.Thomas' Church in Aldridge when she was baptised. My team-mates at Walsall reacted wonderfully well to my newfound faith. I think they knew that something had happened to me and recognised that I had changed. They were never nasty or aggressive about it, and most importantly they continued to take the mickey out of me. The dressing-room banter was the same as it ever had been, and I was very comfortable with that.

To be perfectly honest, things changed radically for me after I came to faith. As my playing career drew to a close, I started to lose interest in the game. It became obvious that my future lay outside football and I had a genuine sense of calling to be ordained. I knew where I was headed and where I wanted to be. I still did my best out on the pitch, but it's hard when your game has been based on passion and determination and that begins to be redirected in other ways. Something had changed inside me and, frankly, football was no longer god. My life took on a new direction and I've never regretted it.

There have been many things that I've taken into the Church from football. Firstly, there's togetherness, which is so important to a football team if they are to be successful. If a local church is to flourish, it must also be united. Commitment was a very important part of my game as a footballer and it matters just as much in the Church: commitment to God, commitment to one another and commitment to the task. Another great similarity between football and the Church is worship. On a Sunday, I put my gear on, come together with other Christians and we look beyond ourselves to a God who is greater than us. But how different is that to what football supporters do on a Saturday? They wear their religious garb, such as shirts and scarves, they sing their songs, they have a sense of togetherness and they look beyond themselves to something bigger. Football and the Church have more in common than you might initially think.

CRAIG SHAKESPEARE

Craig Shakespeare
Midfielder, 1979–89

There can't have been many football careers that have stretched all the way from Fellows Park to the quarter-finals of the Champions League. In fact, there is surely only one. When Craig Shakespeare arrived at Walsall at the age of 16, determined to carve out a future for himself in professional football, he could only have dreamt of scaling the heights he eventually reached.

An attacking midfielder, Craig Shakespeare was a constant presence during one of the most exciting periods in the club's history. He scored 66 goals for the Saddlers, a total which many strikers have subsequently struggled to match. Indeed, anybody who ever saw one of his blistering free kicks is unlikely to forget it. Shakespeare went on to be a vital part of the team that won promotion in 1988, a well-deserved success for his efforts throughout the decade.

Shakespeare left Walsall at the age of 25 having already played over 350 games; a figure that many footballers fail to reach over the entire course of their careers. His next stop was Sheffield Wednesday, with few Saddlers fans begrudging him the opportunity to play at the highest level. He soon came back to the Black Country, playing for West Bromwich Albion for three years before being reunited with his first boss, Alan Buckley, at Grimsby Town.

As his playing days ended, his coaching career began. Undoubtedly, his finest hour came at Leicester City where he was part of one of football's greatest ever stories. He helped guide the club to the Premier League title and later took over as manager following Claudio Ranieri's dismissal, masterminding a victory over Sevilla that took the Foxes into the last eight of the Champions League.

His achievements have been watched with pride by Walsall fans who still see him as one of their own, though their fondest memories will always be of the stylish young midfielder with an eye for goal and a thunderous shot. The good times that Craig Shakespeare helped bring to the club will not quickly be forgotten, and nor will he.

Liverpool 2 – 2 Walsall

League Cup Semi-Final First Leg
Tuesday, 7 February 1984
Anfield, Liverpool
Attendance: 31,073

Liverpool	**Walsall**
Bruce Grobbelaar	Ron Green
Phil Neal	Brian Caswell
Alan Kennedy	Kenny Mower
Gary Gillespie	Craig Shakespeare
Steve Nicol	Colin Brazier
Alan Hansen	Peter Hart
Michael Robinson (David Hodgson)	Mark Rees
Sammy Lee	Ally Brown
Ian Rush	Richard O'Kelly
Craig Johnston	David Preece
Ronnie Whelan	Gary Childs (Kevin Summerfield)

Managers

Joe Fagan	Alan Buckley

Scorers

Ronnie Whelan (14, 73)	Phil Neal, own goal (42)
	Kevin Summerfield (74)

Referee
Neville Ashley

MY BIGGEST break in football was not getting taken on by Aston Villa. I was with them as a schoolboy but, when I turned 16, they decided not to give me a contract. Within a day of being released by Villa, Walsall's chief scout, Ron Jukes, turned up at my house and offered me an apprenticeship. I jumped at the chance and have never looked back. I made my Walsall debut at the age of 19, and by my 21st birthday I'd played 100 games for the Saddlers. I'd never have got the chance to make anywhere near those number of first-team appearances if I had stayed at Villa Park.

I had dreamt of being a footballer when I was young, but I soon learned that it didn't pay very well. My first wage at Walsall was £16 a week, plus a bus pass on top, which was a big help as I didn't drive at the time. I lived in Great Barr and so would either catch the number 51 bus to Perry Barr and get the train from there to Bescot, or else take the same bus into Walsall town centre and then get another one out to Fellows Park. After establishing myself in the first team I renegotiated my contract with the chairman, Ken Wheldon, but ended up worse off as he withdrew the bus pass! These days young players have agents to look after them, but I remember being sat in a room with the chairman on my own and being told that I couldn't leave until I'd signed a new contract. It was a different world back then.

My youth team coach was Colin Harrison, who held the club appearance record at the time. He was a genuine guy who had a good ethos about how the game should be played and he instilled good habits into all the youngsters. I got on very well with him. I spent my first week at Fellows Park cleaning the stands of weeds, and over time I built up a good relationship with the groundsman, Roger Johnson.

As an apprentice, I had Colin as my gaffer in the mornings and Roger in the afternoons. Roger always treated the youngsters with respect and I always sought him out whenever I returned to Walsall in later years. He was a very conscientious groundsman and the Fellows Park pitch was a credit to him. It always played well, even though it had to accommodate all the first team, reserve and youth team games each season. Colin taught me well, but there was also a good group of older players at the club who didn't let you get away with much. Indeed, just playing alongside them was an education.

Training was also quite an experience. We had to carry the goals from Fellows Park to the pitch on the other side of the railway bridge, one player holding each corner. Whoever lost the practice match would then have to lug them back. A canal ran alongside the training pitch and if you accidentally kicked the ball in you would have to wade in and fetch it, regardless of whether you were a first-team player or an apprentice. On Fridays, we always trained on the car park outside the ground. It was a ritual. The surface was covered with potholes and there were countless times when someone either turned their ankle or injured themselves some other way and couldn't play the following day. It was incredibly competitive, with no one wanting to be amongst the losers that had to go to the shop across the road and buy the sandwiches for the winners. Many things have changed in football since those days, but not the desire to win, which was there in abundance.

Fellows Park may not have been all that easy on the eye, but like many old grounds, it had a wonderful atmosphere. Before I started driving, I took the bus there on matchdays. I remember walking through Walsall town centre, carrying my boots over my shoulder, with one group of people after another wishing me luck for the game. Then, afterwards, I'd walk around the ground, trying to find someone who could give me a lift back into town. Nothing like that would ever happen now. Saying that, I wouldn't change the times I lived through even if I could. Those experiences helped to keep my feet on the ground and were the making of me as a person.

Alan Buckley was player-manager when I arrived at Walsall in 1979. He had a reputation for fielding teams that played attractive football, as well as for giving youngsters an opportunity if he thought they were good enough, all of which suited me. I shall always be grateful to him for giving me my debut and for helping to get my career off the ground. I even had the privilege of playing alongside him as our careers overlapped for a couple of seasons. By the start of the 1983/84 season he was 32 and you could see that his yard of pace had gone. What he hadn't lost, however, was his eye for goal.

Alan played around a dozen games that season, and though we knew he was after one of the club's goalscoring records, he never put himself in the team for selfish reasons. He played when he knew he could contribute something to a game, and we all appreciated his presence on the pitch. You could still see his ability in the five-a-side games we played in training. He would be extremely annoyed if he wasn't picked first and his desire to contribute to those sessions was never in doubt. Alan also had a very able assistant in Garry Pendrey, who could give him a nudge during a game and tell him to get ready to come on for the last ten to 15 minutes. The players never baulked when Alan brought himself on as a substitute because we knew he could help get us back into a game, or even win it.

For the 1983/84 season, I was part of a young midfield trio with David Preece and Gary Childs. When we played at Liverpool, I was 20, David was 20 and Gary was only 19. David was a free spirit and one of the finest midfielders I ever played with, while Gary was a wonderful technician. I'd known Gary for years as I had played against him when I was with Aston Villa and he was a schoolboy at West Bromwich Albion. We even used to share lifts into training together. There was a good connection between the three of us and we each had a drive and determination to do well for the football club and for ourselves. Alan's training sessions were always intense, which was important for the three of us as they really helped to develop us as players.

That season may have turned out to be one of the most memorable in the club's history, but it started terribly. In early September, we played away against Bolton Wanderers and got thrashed 8-1, with Tony Caldwell scoring five goals. Then a couple of weeks later, we played Oxford United at the Manor Ground and got beaten 6-3. Sadly, both of those games are still etched in my memory. It's hard to pinpoint now what went wrong, but something clearly did. There were no sports psychologists to talk to back then; you were just expected to roll your sleeves up and get on with it. To be honest, there's not too much wrong with that philosophy as it helped me to grow up fast, both as a footballer and as a person. What all the players knew, however, was that we were a much better team than those two results suggested.

We proved that soon enough in the League Cup by beating Blackpool, Barnsley, Shrewsbury Town, Arsenal and Rotherham United on our way to the last four. I can remember precisely where I was when the draw for the semi-finals was made. As soon as I heard the date of the first leg, a light bulb flashed on in my brain. I knew it was important for some reason, and then I realised why: it was the day I was due to take my driving test! I was booked in to take it at half past ten in Birmingham and the coach was due to leave for Anfield at two o'clock in the afternoon. It would be a rush, but I was confident I could get back home to Great Barr after the test, get changed, put my tracksuit on and be at Fellows Park on time. I really didn't want to cancel my test as it was going to be my second attempt. I'd failed the first one for driving too slowly!

I had to go and see Alan Buckley and tell him about my plans. Inevitably, he asked me what frame of mind I'd be in for the game if I failed the test. I told him that I looked at it positively, that I'd pass and so would be in a great mood for the match. Thankfully, I managed to convince him and duly took my test as planned. At the end of it the driving examiner asked me several questions, which I must have answered reasonably well as he told me that I'd passed. My first reaction was to ask him if I could leave as I'd got a game that night. He asked me what I meant, and so I told him that we were playing Liverpool in the semi-finals of the League Cup. He then looked silently at me as if to say: *what? really?* Anyway, it all worked out fine. I made the coach on time and all I had to worry about after that was the small matter of playing against the best team in Europe.

It was the second time the team had travelled to Liverpool as we'd been there shortly before to watch them play in the league. It was a smart move by Alan Buckley as we were a young team and he didn't want us to be overawed by the occasion. I'd never been to Anfield before and that trip allowed me to sample its unique atmosphere, watching the household names that I'd soon be up against.

One of the things I had to do before the game was get tickets for my family. These days clubs have player liaison officers to help with that kind of thing, but there was nothing like that back in the 1980s. You had to buy the tickets yourself, hand them out to your family and then make sure they knew where they were going. There wouldn't be any car parking spaces reserved for them at the ground either; they had to leave their car in one of the nearby streets and make the rest of the way on foot like everyone else.

Confidence was high amongst the players prior to the game. We'd already beaten Arsenal at Highbury and knew we deserved to be in the semi-finals. I didn't feel any nerves or trepidation at all, just excitement. I learned later as a coach that each player's emotions are different just before the start of a match; some may be too eager to get out there while others can be under-aroused. It's all about finding the right balance and Alan was excellent at helping players to do that. He was never too bothered about the opposition. He wouldn't give us detailed dossiers on each of their players or big presentations on how they would play. His focus was always on you as an individual, making sure that you were in the right frame of mind and ready to do yourself justice. For him it was all about playing to our strengths, rather than worrying about how we were going to stop the other team from playing to theirs. That said, we weren't completely in the dark about Liverpool. We knew that Alan Hansen liked to bring the ball out from the back and initiate attacks, while Craig Johnston would pop up all over the pitch and be very hard to mark. We knew how they played. We were ready for them.

The Liverpool player I was most looking forward to taking on was Kenny Dalglish. He was my favourite footballer as I was growing up, but he missed the match through injury. I was gutted about that, but also a little bit pleased. Liverpool wouldn't be quite the same force without him. We started the game strongly and Ally Brown almost scored with a header from a corner. Even without Dalglish, they still caused us plenty of problems and it took a well-timed tackle from Brian Caswell to take the ball from Ian Rush's feet as he bore down on our goal. The game wasn't quite 15 minutes old before we went behind, with Ronnie Whelan scoring after latching on to an overhead kick from Rush. It wasn't the start we wanted but we had been here before. Arsenal had taken the lead against us, but we had come back to win, and we knew we had the character and resilience to do it again.

My most vivid memory of the first half is giving away a penalty. Well, it should have been a penalty. Craig Johnston made a run into the 18-yard area and I felt I could win the ball, but all I got was his legs. To this day I don't know why the referee didn't give it. As is usual in those circumstances, I pleaded innocence as the Liverpool players appealed for a spot-kick. The referee shook his head and I carried on as if nothing had happened. Thank goodness we didn't have VAR back then or I would have been in real trouble. It was something I got away with and something the team got away with. We could have gone two goals behind if a penalty had been given, and it would have been difficult to have come back from that.

Inevitably, Liverpool had a lot of the ball and they spent long periods of the game in our half of the pitch. Strange as it may sound, that actually played to our strengths. We were able to use Mark Rees's pace on the counterattack and he absolutely tormented the Liverpool left-back, Alan Kennedy, that night. Mark had had a similar start in football as me, having been released by Aston Villa before coming to Walsall. He was one of the stars of that League Cup run and the problems his speed caused Liverpool helped to get us back into the game. He pressurised Sammy Lee into making a poor back pass to the goalkeeper, which Richard O'Kelly intercepted before rolling the ball along the goal line. There was then an almighty mix-up, with Gary Gillespie attempting to clear the ball off the line, but all he succeeded in doing was hammering it at Phil Neal. The ball then ricocheted off him and into the back of the net. To this day Richard maintains that it was his goal, but, having witnessed it, I can honestly say that it wasn't. I reckon Richard knows that really, too.

We got that goal back just before the break, and it was good timing on our part. It gave us a slightly different outlook to go in level at the interval, plus a bit more confidence for the second half, knowing that we'd be starting it all square. Alan was very encouraging at half-time, praising us for holding our own against one of the best teams in the world and telling us that we were still very much in the game. He wanted us to carry on playing our football, getting the ball forward to Mark and counterattacking whenever the opportunity arose.

Ron Green was in goal for us that night and there were several times when he had to keep us in the game. He often pointed that out to us afterwards, but we would just remind him that he was a goalkeeper and that was his job! Halfway through the second half Alan decided to make a substitution, bringing Kevin Summerfield on for Gary Childs. He obviously felt that he needed more of a threat at the top end of the pitch and Kevin provided that. I don't recall how he switched the team around to accommodate Kevin, but he would have had plenty of options as myself, Richard O'Kelly and David Preece were all quite versatile.

Looking back at the game now, I can see that the Liverpool players started to get a bit frustrated when they couldn't get the better of us. You see that a lot in cup games, when the so-called bigger teams don't get a goal that they believe their play deserves. It's just human nature, really. Their irritation was reassuring for us because it showed that we could compete at their level. The game was an end-to-end cup tie, with both teams creating chances, but it was Liverpool who scored the next goal. Craig Johnston fired a cross into the penalty area and Ron Green got a hand to the ball, but it only went as far as Ronnie Whelan who headed it into an empty net.

Their second goal gave us a bit of a conundrum. On the one hand we wanted to attack because that was our DNA: playing through the thirds, spreading the ball wide, getting it to the strikers' feet and playing off them. But, just as importantly, we didn't want to concede a third goal. That was vitally important. We were only one goal down and still had the second leg to come, so taking a small deficit back to Fellows Park wasn't too much of a worry. But sometimes in football you don't have much time to think those sorts of things over. Within a minute of Liverpool going in front we were level again. David Preece attacked with the ball, but Steve Nicol nicked it from under his feet and looped it back towards Bruce Grobbelaar. Fortunately for us, he hadn't spotted that Kevin Summerfield was lurking on the edge of the penalty area. Kevin latched on to the ball and lobbed it neatly over the goalkeeper, to the evident delight of the Walsall fans behind the goal.

My immediate reaction to the goal was to think, 'Wow! This is happening! This is terrific!' My next response was to swivel my head towards the linesman as I wasn't sure whether Kevin had been onside when the ball was played. His flag stayed down, so we all celebrated with Kevin and got the ball back to the halfway line before the referee had the chance to change his mind. The Liverpool players protested, but to no avail. So, was Kevin's goal offside? Absolutely no chance!

After the final whistle we went to the Walsall fans, who had been magnificent that night, getting right behind us throughout the game. Around 10,000 of them had made the trip, which was a phenomenal level of support. When we turned to walk off the pitch, we saw that the Kop was applauding us as well. I think they appreciated the effort we'd put in and the contribution we'd made to a real humdinger of a game. It was a very rewarding sight as it's rare to play away and have the home crowd cheer you off the pitch at the end of the match.

When the game was over, I didn't feel euphoric at all. Strangely, it was quite the opposite. I remember getting back to the dressing room and being pleased with the effort that the team had put in, but I was disappointed with my own performance. It was Garry Pendrey who came to me first and I told him I should have contributed more: that I should have done this, and that I should have done that.

I'd been given the opportunity to play on a big stage and showcase my talents, but I didn't feel I had done myself justice at all. It's only when I had put my boots away and reflected with a wiser head that I realised what I had achieved. I had contributed to the team's performance and we had got a good draw against one of the best teams in Europe, if not the world. Often only time can give you that sense of perspective.

There were no over-zealous celebrations, either in the dressing room or in the coach on the way home. The mood amongst the players was that we were pleased to have got a good result, but we knew that there was a second leg to come, and as the cliché goes, it was still only half-time. The reaction from the media was a bit different, but it was all very low key within the club, considering we had just secured one of the greatest achievements in the club's history.

Looking back, I think the greatest strength of that team was its togetherness. There were no big egos; we all knew what our jobs were, and we just got on and did them. Alan drilled us in his philosophy of how the game should be played, but it took the characters in the team to really bring it out. I'm a big believer that if you get the right environment, the right culture and the right people then you've every chance of being successful. Walsall had all that, which was why we did so well. There was a good bond between the players and that came from training hard and playing hard together, though occasionally we pushed the boundaries a bit.

The sports reporter, Tom Ross, often came to Fellows Park on a Friday to interview the manager. One week, Mark Rees and Kenny Mower came and told me that Tom was in with Alan and that he'd left his car keys out on the side. It was too good an opportunity to resist. We found his car, jacked it up, took all four wheels off and then left it standing on piles of bricks. We then put his car keys back and waited around the corner for Tom to come out. When he saw what we'd done, he was simply aghast. He went back into the ground and they had to come out and find us so that we could put the wheels back on his car. That was the type of skulduggery that went on in those days and it really reinforced the togetherness between the players. Playing tricks like that was second nature to us, but I don't think you could get away with doing something like that now.

I was never a great one for nightclubs, but I loved the company of the other players and the banter that came with being part of the group. Young players these days have a lot more trap doors to fall through than we did back then. If I went out, then my mom, or later my wife, had no idea where I was until I came back. That was probably a blessing, given the type of lads who were at Walsall, but I never took it too far. I'd worked hard to be able to do something that I'd always wanted to do, and I was never going to put that at risk. Football was the real pull for me.

A week separated the first and second legs of the League Cup semi-final and we played Southend United on the intervening Saturday. A crowd of over 8,000 came to Fellows Park and we gave them a real treat, hammering the visitors 4-0. The team was on a high, but we never became over-confident about our chances in the next game against Liverpool. There was no talk of going to Wembley and getting measured for suits, or anything silly like that. Alan and Garry simply wouldn't have allowed that to happen. We'd fired a warning shot over Liverpool's bow at Anfield and they knew the second leg wouldn't be a walkover. As for us, we knew that we were in for a tough game against some very good opponents.

I don't have too many memories of the second leg, just a few that I'd like to forget. It was a great occasion and it was wonderful to see Fellows Park full. There were almost 20,000 fans packed inside and the atmosphere was something to behold. Liverpool won by two goals to nil, with Graeme Souness being the difference between the two sides. He'd missed the first leg but, unluckily for us, was back in their team for the second. Souness had an aura about him and was a player that all midfielders admired at the time. As well as being able to battle and scrap, he could also play. He's particularly well remembered in that game for carrying a fan off the pitch after the wall collapsed at the Laundry End following Liverpool's second goal. Losing that game was a huge disappointment as we knew we would never get the opportunity to play in the semi-final of a cup again for Walsall. We had earned our chance to be 90 minutes from Wembley but were beaten by the better team on the night, so there are no regrets in that respect.

Our league form came off the rails after that defeat to Liverpool. We had won game after game before that tie and had been top of the table for over a month. Following our exit from the League Cup, we suffered three straight defeats, dropped out of the promotion places and struggled to put a decent run together for the remainder of the season. We eventually finished in sixth place, which would be good enough for the play-offs now, but they didn't exist back then, so that meant another season in Division Three. I still think we should have won promotion that year, given the team we had. To my mind it would have been a much greater achievement than reaching the League Cup Final because it would have been accomplished over the course of a whole season. It's hard to put my finger on what went wrong. It was probably a culmination of several factors, including the 'after the Lord Mayor's show' effect of not getting to Wembley, some loss of form and injuries to one or two players.

I was fortunate with injuries that season as I didn't miss a single game, either in the league or the three cup competitions we played in. I once had a run of 100 games or so without a break which only ended when I kneeled to wash the car. I got housemaid's knee and had to have it drained before I was fit to play again. In terms of the types of challenges that were permitted, football was a much tougher game then compared to how it is now. You can't tackle from behind these days, but that was part and parcel of the game when I played. You knew that if you were coming up against someone who was renowned for his physicality, you were likely to get an elbow from him at a corner or stud marks down your shin. Only one substitute was allowed as well, which meant that if you got injured after he'd entered the fray you just had to soldier on until the end of the game.

In the 1980s, I played game after game after game. Forty-eight-hour recovery periods hadn't even been dreamt of, so on a Monday I would be running up hills, pushing myself to the limit all over again. We didn't have sport science departments to advise us how best to manage our fitness. Everything moves on, but that intense training and constant playing gave me a mental toughness and resilience which shouldn't be undervalued. Your body is often capable of a lot more than you think it is. Undoubtedly, all that effort put a lot of strain on me, but I look back at those times with fondness as I attained a much greater level of fitness than I would ever have thought possible. Having said that, it's good there is so much more expertise in football nowadays. If someone suffered a head injury or was concussed when I was playing, they'd simply be told 'you'll be all right son, just carry on'. It's frightening, really, what used to happen.

I sustained my first serious injury when Walsall played Notts County in the first leg of the play-off semi-final in 1988. I hurt my foot during the game and went to hospital to have it X-rayed. They told me I'd broken a metatarsal, which wasn't great news as we had some important games coming up. The physio and I went to see the manager, Tommy Coakley, who I really enjoyed playing for. We discussed the option of having my foot injected with a painkiller so that I could play, which was what I did. We got past Notts County and then had a two-leg play-off final against Bristol City, which then went to a replay. That meant that I ended up playing four games with a broken foot when I should have been in a cast. Why did I have those injections? I did it because I was desperate to play.

In the end, I asked for a transfer from Walsall because I wanted to better myself and move on. It wasn't because I didn't like the club any more or didn't enjoy playing for them. The opportunity to come back later in my playing career never arose, but if Walsall had shown an interest after I'd left West Bromwich Albion and gone to Grimsby Town, I would have jumped at the chance. But the club moved on, and so did I. Personally, I don't think you should have many regrets in life, and I don't have too many in mine.

I visited the Banks's Stadium in late 2018, and it was the first time I'd really been back. I did the guest lounges with Mick Kearns and was made to feel so welcome by the fans. When you spend a decade at a club, as I did with Walsall, it creates an affinity and a fondness that never goes away, particularly as it was my first club. I always look for their results and genuinely wish them well. Over the years, I have naturally lost touch with most of those I played with at Walsall, but I still see Richard O'Kelly from time to time, as well as Peter Hart. I also have a coffee with David Kelly now and again. I can honestly say that my happiest memories and most intense times as a footballer came during my time at Walsall. There were a lot of local lads in that team and it had one of the finest team spirits I've ever encountered. The camaraderie was simply incredible. That League Cup run was probably Walsall's greatest ever achievement in a cup competition, and I'm very proud to have been a part of it.

RICHARD O'KELLY

Richard O'Kelly
Midfielder and Striker, 1979–86, 1988

Good things always seem to happen for Walsall when Richard O'Kelly is at the club. He arrived from non-league Alvechurch in 1979, just after the Saddlers had been relegated to Division Four for the first time in their history. The club won promotion that season, with O'Kelly making his first-team debut at the start of the following campaign. His elegance and versatility made him ideal for Alan Buckley's style of football and he was rarely out of the side for long as a result.

Richard O'Kelly was an important part of the buccaneering team that reached the semi-finals of the League Cup in 1984, scoring in the victory over Rotherham United in the quarter-finals. Arguably, his finest moment in that cup run came at Anfield when his rolled cross into the Liverpool goalmouth caused so much confusion that Phil Neal ended up bundling the ball into his own net.

The following season was O'Kelly's most prolific at the club, with his total of 18 making him the side's top goalscorer. He moved on to Port Vale in the summer of 1986, but a knee injury limited his appearances and he returned to Walsall in January 1988. The Saddlers were pushing for a long-overdue promotion from Division Three and he was a vital addition to the squad that eventually won the play-offs.

After 254 appearances and 65 goals for Walsall, O'Kelly became one of Alan Buckley's first signings for Grimsby Town. A productive season followed but he broke his leg towards the end of it and never played competitive football again. A career in coaching then beckoned for the thoughtful O'Kelly, with his peripatetic career taking him far and wide, including spells at Aston Villa, Bournemouth, Brentford, Bristol City, Doncaster Rovers, Hereford United and West Bromwich Albion. During that time, he returned to Walsall for one last time, working with Dean Smith to create the best side seen at the Banks's Stadium for a decade. Richard O'Kelly has devoted his life to football, and it seems only fair that the game has given him a lot in return.

Coventry City 0 – 3 Walsall

League Cup Second Round Second Leg
Tuesday, 9 October 1984
Highfield Road, Coventry
Attendance: 9,214

Coventry City	**Walsall**
Steve Ogrizovic	Steve Cherry
Andy Spring	Paul Jones
Micky Adams	Kenny Mower
Kenny Hibbitt	Craig Shakespeare
Ian Butterworth	Colin Brazier
Trevor Peake	Peter Hart
David Bennett	Ian Handysides
Micky Gynn	David Kelly
Nicky Platnauer	Richard O'Kelly
Terry Gibson	David Preece
Peter Barnes (Brian Kilcline)	Gary Childs

Managers

Bobby Gould	Alan Buckley

Scorers

	David Kelly (53, 75)
	Richard O'Kelly (65)

Referee
Alf Buksh

ALLEGEDLY, THE things that you regret most in life are the things you don't do. I was 22 when Walsall came in for me and I had a good job at the time. I'd just finished my apprenticeship and was a fully qualified process development engineer. I was also playing part-time for Alvechurch, and so was earning two wages, but I had always wanted to be a professional footballer. The way I saw it, the worst that could happen was that I failed to make the grade at Walsall and would have to go back to engineering. So, I decided to give it a go with the Saddlers and I have never regretted it.

I had trials with Arsenal and Leeds when I was a youngster, as well as with local clubs, including Walsall. It didn't work out, but I carried on playing because I just loved the game. I played for my school on a Saturday morning and then for a local works team in the afternoon, who later gave me a job. Then I'd turn out again on Sunday morning for another side and got paid £3 a game for doing that. I started to play men's football when I was about 16 or 17, which turned out to be a good apprenticeship. I went around the non-league circuit, starting off at Oldbury United, then Dudley Town and finally Alvechurch. There was no coaching at all; it was simply 'learn on the job'. No one told me when I should turn this way or that, or how I should position myself for a challenge. I found out all about the importance of awareness when an opposition defender told me that he was going to break my legs. I suppose I had a different upbringing in the game from most professional footballers, but it worked for me.

It was Alan Buckley who signed me for Walsall. He was coming towards the end of his career and was player-manager at that time. 'Buck' would train lightly because of problems he had with his knee and I remember him having fluid drained off it before he could play. He was still one hell of a striker, though. Everything that I look for as a coach these days in a goalscorer, Buck had. He was constantly alive to situations and you always knew he had a goal in him. He was a bouncy, bubbly, loud character whose enthusiasm for the game constantly shone through. He did have a bit of a side to him, which not all the players welcomed, but I found it most invigorating. I like a good discussion, and Buck could certainly give you a good discussion!

You take something from everyone you work with, and what I picked up from Buck was a certain style of play. I've always enjoyed a passing game and that was at the heart of his philosophy. He was always talking about the right way to play, but he was never a dictator. There were times in games when it was right to kick and chase the ball, and he wouldn't stop us from doing that if we felt we needed to. He would tell us how he wanted us to play but also gave us a degree of freedom once we'd crossed the white line. As long as we backed each other up when we changed things, he allowed us to make decisions on the pitch.

It's fair to say that Buck wasn't a traditional coach. He never told us to move this way or that, to turn left here, or turn right there. There was none of that. What he did was create an environment in which players could learn, educate each other and thrive. We would play 8 v 8 games on different-size pitches and it was either two- or three-touch football, with lots of movement. As a coach, that was one of the most important things I learnt from him. In any training session you put on you should always try to create an environment, and then let that environment teach the players. On a Friday before a game, we would play on the car park at Fellows Park, just in front of where the turnstiles were. The surface was full of potholes, there were pieces of concrete here and there and you would often get smashed up against the fence because it was such a small area. Even though we were playing on a car park, Buck still demanded that we passed the ball, rather than just kicked it anywhere. You had to have incredible awareness to play that game, and that was another thing he gave us.

The training facilities we had in my day certainly left a lot to be desired. A few years ago, I was on 'garden leave' from Doncaster Rovers and I bumped into Dean Smith at a charity game when he was managing Walsall. I wasn't working and was bored, so Dean invited me to come down to the club's new training ground at Essington. I just couldn't believe it when I saw it. To be honest, I never thought I would see the day when Walsall would have their own training facilities like that. The place is very well equipped and is something that a lot of clubs would be proud of, regardless of what division they're in. As a coach, I think it's vital you have somewhere like that you can go and work in.

We do a lot of tactical work on shape and structure these days, which was never something we spent any time on when I was a player. I've watched a couple of Walsall games on video from the 1980s and I am amazed at how organised we were when we lost possession, even though it was something we never practised in training. Part of it was due to our knowledge of the game, but it was also because of the incredible togetherness we had in the team. If one player made a mistake, then everyone else immediately tried to put it right.

Players were very close in the non-league football culture that I grew up in, particularly at Alvechurch. It was more like a social club than a football club. After a game, we would get together for a drink and the directors would put some money behind the bar. We would sit there as a group, digesting the game and talking about what had gone on. The camaraderie was exceptional. I remember once we played a midweek game away at King's Lynn and I went to work in the morning, leaving around midday in order to catch the coach. We travelled all the way over there, played the game, won, and then came back home again. It was about half past ten at night and we had to stop at a set of traffic lights, somewhere in the middle of Leicestershire. Suddenly, one of the directors jumped off the bus, dived into a pub, and then came back a minute or two later saying, 'Come on lads, we've got afters!' So, everybody piled off the coach and went into the pub, even though we all had to go into work again the next morning. It was just like that at Walsall. It might have been a professional football club, but it still had a bit of a non-league culture as well. And I say that as a compliment, because the togetherness amongst the players was a huge part of the success Walsall had in those days. We all had each other's back.

After I joined Walsall, I was always knocking on Buck's door and asking when he was going to give me a game. He must have got fed up of it, but I never gave up and kept on going back. I eventually made my debut at the start of the 1980/81 season and played for a lot of that campaign. Neil Martin came in the following summer and became joint manager alongside Buck. He didn't seem to like me for some reason, and I was out of the team for a while, but then something happened, and I was brought back in again. One of the first games I played after that was at home to Newport County. I scored all of Walsall's goals in a 3-1 victory and was in the team a lot more after that. I remember the match well because it was almost surreal; it was as if everything was moving in slow motion. People talk about being 'in the zone', and I certainly was that day. It was almost effortless.

One of the goals I scored that afternoon was a penalty. I didn't have a specific technique for taking them, but I did whatever research I could on opposition goalkeepers. I remember looking at football programmes because they often had photographs of goals being scored, including penalties. Most goalkeepers tended to dive to the right, so if there was a picture of one of them doing that, I would try to stretch him on his left-hand side. On other occasions, I would strike the ball with the middle of my laces and give it some power. What was important was not to do the same thing every time. I always volunteered to take penalties because it was another opportunity to score a goal. It was a free shot from 12 yards, so why not give it a go?

In saying that, things didn't always go according to plan. I remember taking a penalty against Derby County in a home game over Easter and their goalkeeper, Eric Steele, making a fantastic save, turning the ball around the post with his fingertips. We got another spot-kick later in the match and Nicky Cross grabbed the ball, so I said, 'OK, I've missed one, off you go.' Nicky ran up, kicked the ground and the ball just bobbled along in a straight line. Eric Steele had already dived, so it simply rolled into the net and we ended up drawing the match 1-1. A few days later we played away at Cardiff City and won another penalty. Crossy picked the ball up, put it down, walked back, ran up and duffed it again. The ball bobbled along the ground once more, but this time the goalkeeper just stood there and picked it up. Then, just a few minutes later, we were awarded yet another spot-kick. All the other Walsall players stood there, looking around at each other, so I picked the ball up and had another go. I smashed the ball down the middle of the goal, and even though the keeper dived towards one of the posts, it somehow managed to strike the underneath of his backside. The ball bounced up, hit the crossbar, came back down again and then rebounded over the bar. That all happened just before half-time, and when we went in at the interval Buck was furious. He'd missed penalties over the years, but that didn't stop him from having a right go. I don't think I slept for three nights after that. It wasn't that I was a worrier, but I knew I could have done a lot better.

By the time we played Coventry City in the League Cup in 1984, Buck had been in charge for a few years and had put an excellent side together. He was quite astute in recruiting players who would add to the group, such as the goalkeeper he signed that summer, Steve Cherry. Steve was a larger-than-life character who commanded the penalty area like Peter Schmeichel used to do. He was aggressive, driven and demanded 100 per cent from everybody around him. Steve was also quite a fit lad, which made him stand out a little from other keepers at that time as their diets often weren't the best. He took over in goal from Ron Green, who was a great lad, but you'd never look at him and say he was an athlete.

The two centre-halves in front of Steve were Peter Hart and Colin Brazier. 'Harty' signed for Walsall at a similar time to me and we ended up spending a lot of time together. We bought houses near to one another and car shared each time we went to the ground. He was a midfield player when he first came to the club but moved back to play in defence after a season or so. Harty always chides himself that he wasn't all that good on the ball, but he was technically better than he thought he was. He was a calm, composed player who never got flustered, and you need people like that in your team. Harty was a good tackler and, despite being one of the best friends I've made in football, he would still kick lumps out of me in training. The only way to improve your game is to play with and against better footballers, and Harty tested me all the time. I had to become a more intelligent player just to get a touch on the ball. He was also very loyal. I remember we played Everton once in a pre-season friendly and they began to get frustrated because they couldn't get the better of us. A couple of their players started to kick David Preece and Harty was on to them like a shot, holding them up in the air by the fronts of their shirts. I've always believed that if you have good people in your team then you have a great chance of being successful and Harty was, and is, a good person.

Colin Brazier was a very talented footballer. He might not have been the quickest player you'd ever see, but he could read the play really well. If he came up against someone stronger, he would just outthink him, perhaps giving him a nudge before nipping round the front and taking the ball from his feet. Colin was a good lad, but he could wind people up on occasions. I remember once when we played Brentford in the final match of the season and there wasn't anything hanging on the outcome. It finished 1-1 and Buck was not at all happy with the effort we'd put in. He always demanded enthusiasm from us because that was how he was himself, and he had a right rant at us afterwards. He went on for about a quarter of an hour, telling us we were all a waste of time and that he shouldn't be paying any of us; that we hadn't done this, and how we should have done that. When he'd finally finished, the room went quiet for a moment and then Colin said, 'Well, it was the last game of the season, gaffer.' Buck just exploded. He then went off for another ten minutes or so, while we were all shaking our heads and whispering, 'Colin, no, no …'

The full-backs on either side of Harty and Colin in that game against Coventry were Kenny Mower and Paul Jones. Kenny was a skilful footballer who should have gone on to play at a higher level than he did. He was a great athlete who would race up and down the wing and get attacks going. Kenny was voted into the PFA Third Division Team of the Year at the end of that season, and again two years later. It was an honour he deserved. Paul Jones played at right-back in that match, although he eventually established himself in the team as a midfielder. He was a good distributor of the ball and was so adept with both feet that you couldn't tell which was his best. 'Jonah' wasn't all that quick, but he had this languid style that enabled him to go past people and, despite being a skinny lad, he also had a bit of steel in him.

The four midfielders in that team had barely left their teens but that didn't mean they were looked upon as being young, inexperienced players. David 'Mini' Preece, in particular, was mature beyond his years. I remember when we played Liverpool in the semi-final of the League Cup we were under a bit of pressure at the end of the game, with the score level at 2-2. He managed to get hold of the ball and knocked it all the way up to the far corner flag and out for a throw-in. That showed incredible presence of mind for someone so young. Mini was, without a shadow of doubt, the best footballer I ever played with. He could do things with the ball that you could only imagine. Whenever we played on the car park, you wouldn't dare get near him because he'd nutmeg you every time. One of his finest moments for Walsall was when we beat Arsenal 2-1 in the League Cup. They had recently bought Charlie Nicholas from Celtic, but Mini so outshone him that night you'd have thought he was the big money signing.

Like me, Mini went into coaching after he'd finished playing. We used to keep in touch, and he rang me once because he needed to get a player on loan. I mentioned someone, but he wasn't keen. When I asked why, he explained, 'Well, he's not all that big, is he?' I couldn't believe it. Here was 'Mini', all 5ft 5in of him, saying he didn't want a player because he wasn't tall enough! It was so sad that he passed away at such a young age, leaving behind a wife and a young family.

Mini joined Luton Town a couple of months after the game against Coventry and it was a real loss for the club. His place in central midfield was taken by Craig Shakespeare, who had tended to play out wide before then. 'Shaky' was my apprentice when he started out and there wasn't much of him in those days. He needed to build himself up and so spent one close season doing weights with his brother, who was in the army. He came back looking like the proverbial outhouse and was a far more robust player from then on. Shaky had a wonderful left foot, great technical skills and could also look after himself on the pitch. He wouldn't react or get riled if he was on the receiving end of a bad challenge; he'd just bide his time and wait for an opportunity to get his own back. Shaky was also a great striker of the ball. Whenever he pulled his left foot back to shoot at goal, I would go straight in for the rebound. Even if a goalkeeper managed to save his shot, nine times out of ten it would be too strong for him to hold.

The other central midfielder in that team was Gary Childs. He joined us from West Bromwich Albion to improve what was already a very good side. Gary was a David Silva-type of player who had a superb range of passing, as well as a great ability to run at people with the ball. You probably wouldn't say that he was the bravest in the tackle, but he didn't need to be as he had the courage to get on the ball and make things happen. Gary also had an exceptional burst of pace. I remember when we played Rotherham United in the quarter-finals of the League Cup, he flashed past one of their players in a blur to set up Ally Brown for our third goal.

Gary was a quiet lad, like our other midfield player, Ian Handysides. He was signed from Birmingham City, and even though he came into a side that was quite established, he fitted in so well it was as if he'd always been there. Ian had the ability to find little gaps in the opposition defence and had a real eye for goal. He wasn't a conventional winger as he would often come inside, making good use of the change of pace that he had over two to three yards. Ian was a busy, bright little footballer and it was terrible that he died so young. What happened to him was a real tragedy.

I played up front with David Kelly in that game against Coventry. Like me, he joined Walsall from Alvechurch, and I took him under my wing a little because of that.

I remember telling him, for instance, never to go in goal in training, even for a laugh. We only had one goalkeeper in the match squad in those days, which meant if he got injured one of the outfield players would have to take his place. It wasn't something any of us would ever want to do, so the last thing you should do is get yourself earmarked for the job.

It was during the season when we played Coventry that Dave first broke through into the first team, and he was a real breath of fresh air. He was bubbly and inventive and had this infectious enthusiasm that reminds me of how Jack Grealish is now. If a game was drifting a bit, he would give it a spark by either chasing the ball down, putting a defender under pressure or producing a sublime bit of skill. I can imagine that, for a centre-half, he was a real pain to play against. As well as being a top footballer, he was also a cracking lad to have around. He never changed a bit after he left Walsall for West Ham; he knew where his roots were, and he stayed grounded.

Dave was the striker I most enjoyed playing alongside during my time at Walsall, but the partner I had greatest success with was Peter Eastoe. He came to us on a month's loan from West Bromwich Albion and went back shortly before we played Coventry in the League Cup. By the end of his spell, he'd scored two goals, while I had got six. Up until then I had always played as a 'number 10', just behind the centre-forward. Peter took that role and so I was able to get into the six-yard box much more. He had a lot of presence on the pitch and I learned a huge amount from playing with him.

The first forward I played with at Walsall was Don Penn. He came through at the same time as Ian Paul and they were both Premier League quality. Ian had the ability of Steven Gerrard, while Don was the bravest lad I'd ever seen. There would be situations where you would worry about putting your foot in, but Don would just dive in and head the ball. He had exceptional talent. Another good striker from those days was Ally Brown. He had played in the top division with Leicester City and West Bromwich Albion and came to Walsall towards the end of his career. Despite his age, Ally was still a strong athlete and the team really missed him whenever he didn't play.

We had two wingers in our squad that season, and they each had different qualities. Mark Rees was one of the fastest players I've ever seen. When we played Liverpool at Anfield in the League Cup semi-final, I remember him knocking the ball past Alan Kennedy at the start of the game and chasing it down the pitch. Kennedy's face was an absolute picture. It was like he was saying, 'What the hell …'. The only problem with Mark was that he could often be too quick for the rest of us. He'd race down the wing and fire a cross in before we'd all had a chance to catch up! Even if he was having a bad day with the ball for some reason, you could still guarantee that the opposition left-back and left-midfielder wouldn't get a kick. Mark would work them so hard that they would find it difficult to get into the game.

Our other winger, Willie Naughton, was a much more mercurial player. He wouldn't hunt the ball down; we had to get it to him if he was going to work his magic. On his day he could beat defenders for fun and they simply wouldn't be able to get the ball off him. Willie could have gone all the way to the top with the ability he had, but he lacked consistency. It's not easy being a winger as they are expected to beat people, get into the box and score goals, which is the most difficult thing to do because there are ten players trying to stop them. By contrast, it's much easier for a midfield ball-winner to get into their stride as they're always in the thick of things. For some reason, Willie didn't always seem to have the 100 per cent belief in himself that he should have had, given the talent he possessed.

Walsall drew Coventry City in the second round of the League Cup after knocking out Swansea City. We must have enjoyed playing Swansea that season because we beat them four times, scoring ten goals in the process. Coventry were an established top division side back then, having been at that level for almost 20 years. However, they were struggling a bit when we played them and were in the relegation zone. The first leg was played at Fellows Park and Coventry won 2-1, with Shaky getting our goal. I don't remember much about the first leg because we lost, but I do recall that we were always in the game.

Buck made a key change to the team for the second leg, opting to play David Kelly up front with me instead of Dave Bamber. Ironically, Dave had joined us from Coventry towards the end of the previous season. There were high expectations of Dave when he arrived as he was 6ft 3in and a wonderful athlete, but it didn't really work out for him at Walsall. The problem was that our style of football didn't suit him at all. We never adapted to him as much as we should have done.

Our mindset for the second leg was that we could beat Coventry. We had a lot of energy in our side and great belief in ourselves and how we did things. Our attitude was 'we'll play how we play, do what we do, and they'll have to cope with it'. That may have showed a bit of naivety, which is possible as we were a young group, or perhaps the confidence came from having played them once and not having been knocked off the park. Buck was in and around us before the game, full of enthusiasm as always. He would build us up, telling us to go out there and show the opposition how to play football.

And we did. We dominated both halves of the game and our football was free-flowing. It was almost like we were playing against mannequins. I always loved evening games at that time of year because the lights were on and the surface was slick. We moved the ball quickly, found each other easily, frequently broke their lines and got at the heart of their defence. Coventry had some good players, but we were very energetic around the ball and never gave them time to settle and build attacks. Gary Childs was exceptional that night. He caused them huge problems by running at their back four from the centre of midfield, and that was how our first goal came about. A few minutes into the second half, Gary ran at their defence and shot at goal. Their goalkeeper could only parry his strike and Dave Kelly was on hand to knock in the rebound.

You can smell blood at times like that. We had got the first goal, levelled the tie and you could sense the atmosphere starting to change. Coventry's support wasn't all that vocal, while the Walsall fans were making a lot of noise. It reminded me of when we played Arsenal at Highbury and how they came under pressure when we equalised and got a bit of momentum. They had taken the lead in that match and celebrated as if that goal was going to be the first of five or six. That certainly fired us up a bit.

About ten minutes later, Paul Jones broke away on the right wing with the ball. I was in the centre of the pitch and I remember sprinting towards the far post while Dave Kelly made a run to the opposite side of the goal. The ball was played across and I slid in and put it into the net. I was probably only a yard out, but to me those were the best goals. Then, with about quarter of an hour to go, Dave Kelly put us three goals up on the night, lifting the ball over the goalkeeper after Paul Jones had put him through. Dave was still only 18 that night, which was incredible really.

We eventually beat Coventry by four goals to two on aggregate, and I thought we were going to have another good run in the League Cup. We had got to the semi-finals the previous season and I didn't see any reason why we couldn't do as well again. We always felt like we could win every game. That's how we were. I have lots of great memories from that time, such as when all the Walsall players were on the British Airways poster under the banner 'They're only 90 minutes away from a place in Europe'. I remember driving into Birmingham and seeing my face on the billboard, which was a bit surreal.

I also recall that, before we played Liverpool at Anfield in the semi-final, we wanted to practise with an Adidas Tango ball because that was what they used. We only ever played with the old Mitre ball. Those Tango balls cost a lot of money and we had to get special permission from the chairman to go out and buy one. We trained with it once on the grass and then we made the mistake of taking it on to the car park. It soon got ripped to shreds, so that was the end of that ball! I remember both matches against Liverpool very well. For the second leg at Fellows Park, the pitch was like rolled mud because we'd had a lot of bad weather beforehand. Even though we lost 2-0 on the night, we were always in the game and had chances to score. Mark Lawrenson was outstanding for them, as were Graeme Souness and Ian Rush.

After beating Coventry, we got a home draw against Chelsea. I didn't play in that game for some reason, but we put in another good performance. Walsall twice took the lead: the first time through David Preece and then Shaky scored with a screamer from the left wing to put us 2-1 up. We got the ball in the net a third time, but it was disallowed, and then they managed to get an equaliser six minutes from the end of the game. That meant a replay at Stamford Bridge, which they won 3-0. Another League Cup run had come to an end, but it had taken Liverpool and Chelsea to stop us over the course of two seasons, which is something we can be proud of.

I stayed with Walsall for a couple more years after that and then moved on to Port Vale. It was only because of money that I left. Back then players had to negotiate their contracts directly with the chairman, Ken Wheldon. It was like dealing with Don Corleone. You'd knock on his door and go in and he'd look up from his newspaper. 'All right, ma lad,' he'd say. 'You want a new contract, then? Humm, well you haven't done all that well this year, have you?' 'I was top scorer, Mr Chairman,' I'd reply. 'OK, I tell you what, I'll give you so-and-so.' 'That's ten pounds a week less than I was on last year, Mr Chairman.' 'Oh, is it?' he'd respond. It was like pulling teeth.

Tommy Coakley took over as Walsall manager while I was away, and I asked him once if he would take me on if Port Vale didn't want me any more. He said he would, which was helpful, because I got injured later and Port Vale didn't want to keep me. I came back to Walsall in 1988 and I remember walking into Fellows Park to get changed for training. Roger Johnson, the groundsman, was there when I came in. 'All right, Rog,' I said. 'All right, Rich,' he replied. It was like I'd never been away.

Trevor Christie and Dave Kelly were the first-choice strikers in that side, so I was only going to play up front if something happened to one of them. I ended up playing in several different positions for Walsall including full-back, central midfield, wide midfield, and even once as a centre-half. That was never a problem because I always felt I knew what was going on all over the pitch. We got into the play-offs that year and I was in the team for the first three matches against Notts County and Bristol City because Andy Dornan was injured. It was a great feeling to finally win promotion after missing out so many times when Buck was in charge. I joined him at Grimsby Town that summer and finished my playing career up there.

I had already taken my coaching badges in readiness to move into another phase of my life, which included attending any football seminars and coaching courses I could in my thirst for knowledge. It has been hard work but enjoyable for the majority of my career and I am very grateful for all the opportunities that have come my way. I returned to Walsall for the final time in 2013, as assistant to Dean Smith. I shall never forget when we drew with Preston at the Banks's Stadium a couple of years later to reach the final of the Football League Trophy. After having got so close to Wembley as a player, helping the club to finally get there after so many years of trying was simply amazing. That was a very emotional night for me.

DAVID KELLY

David Kelly
Striker, 1983–88

David Kelly was the finest young striker to emerge from Walsall Football Club since Allan Clarke had come to the fore in the 1960s. Alan Buckley gave him his chance in the professional game, but it was under the tutelage of Tommy Coakley that Kelly really prospered. The effervescent Scot put the 20-year-old striker into the first Walsall team that he selected, and Kelly remained a regular starter for the next two seasons. Never once did he warm the bench as a substitute during Coakley's tenure.

Initially, Saddlers fans watched with excitement as the young Kelly developed, and then with a nagging sense of foreboding, knowing in their hearts he would soon outgrow the club that he had first called home. The goals flowed, the scouts came to watch and the inevitable soon came to pass. Kelly left the Black Country for the bright lights of London, with West Ham United winning the race to sign Walsall's favourite son.

Kelly made his debut for the Republic of Ireland while still a Walsall player, scoring a hat-trick in a 5-0 win against Israel. He went on to appear another 25 times for his country, scoring six further goals, as well as making an appearance in the 1994 World Cup finals in the USA.

Both Kelly's and Walsall's fortunes took a dip after he left in the summer of 1988, with the Saddlers struggling to adapt to life in Division Two and Kelly finding goals harder to come by at his new club. Walsall were embarking on one of the darkest periods of their history, but Kelly came back fighting, first rebuilding his reputation at Leicester City and then becoming a folk hero at Newcastle United. Spells at Wolves, Sunderland, Tranmere Rovers and Sheffield United followed and he continued to score goals aplenty. Ultimately, David Kelly was a gun for hire; a guaranteed goal-getter wherever he played. To this day, Walsall fans remain thankful they were there to hear the starting pistol.

Walsall 4 – 0 Bristol City

Football League Third Division Play-off Final Replay
Monday, 30 May 1988
Fellows Park, Walsall
Attendance: 13,007

Walsall	**Bristol City**
Fred Barber	Keith Waugh
Mark Taylor	Andy Llewellyn
Andy Dornan (Mark Jones)	Rob Newman
Craig Shakespeare	Glenn Humphries
Graeme Forbes	John Pender
Mark Goodwin (Paul Sanderson)	Steve McClaren
Phil Hawker	Ralph Milne
Peter Hart	Steve Galliers
Trevor Christie	Carl Shutt
David Kelly	Alan Walsh
Willie Naughton	Joe Jordan

Managers

Tommy Coakley	Joe Jordan

Scorers

David Kelly (12, 17, 63)
Phil Hawker (19)

Referee

George Courtney

I SHALL always be grateful to Walsall for giving me a chance to become a professional footballer, but I had to accept a pay cut to join them. I was working in the returns department at Cadbury's at the time, which was a pretty soft place to be. All the guys in there had suffered injuries or illnesses and all I had to do was look after them while they opened the boxes, threw the rejected chocolates away and recycled the silver foil. Cadbury's were paying me £75 a week, but all the Saddlers could offer was £50 a week and a £7.50 bus pass on top. That bus pass was a godsend as I could hardly afford to run a car on my wages.

As a teenager, I trained at West Bromwich Albion's centre of excellence, down on Spring Road. They told me I wasn't quite good enough and so I joined Cadbury's after leaving school. I played in Alvechurch's youth team for a while and was eventually invited for a trial at Wolves. At the same time, Steve Joesbury asked me to play in a few reserve games at Walsall, which went well. I duly signed for the club shortly before Christmas 1983, despite the pay cut.

I played under Alan Buckley for the first few years of my career and retain a huge amount of respect for the man that gave me my chance in football. In 1986, the club was bought by Terry Ramsden, who announced his presence by arriving in a helicopter, which was unheard of back then, particularly in a town like Walsall. It was Hollywood stuff, really. Ramsden brought his own people in and that meant that 'Buck' was out of a job.

The new manager was Tommy Coakley, who had previously been in charge at Bishop's Stortford. His non-league background was initially a subject of discussion amongst the players, but I liked him from the first moment we met. He was excitable and bubbly and evidently loved his job. The new coach was Gerry Sweeney, who'd been a defender at Bristol City. He was easily the fittest person at the club, even though he was in his forties by then. His fitness levels were an eye-opener for the players, and he gave me a different outlook on training. I was already in pretty good shape as I was skinny and held no weight, but I soon realised that if Gerry could be as fit as he was at his age, then I needed to get a lot, lot fitter.

Buck had been at Walsall for quite a few years and, inevitably, training sessions became a bit repetitive towards the end of his tenure. By contrast, Tommy and Gerry were a breath of fresh air. They only changed little things, such as the time of day we trained, but the new regime woke everybody up. They made for a strong partnership and Tommy had excellent man-management skills. He soon realised that he had a lot of strong characters at the club who knew how to dig each other out and look after the dressing room, so he let us get on with it. Tommy would nip things in the bud if he saw trouble brewing and was canny at making sure that everyone's opinion was heard, or so we thought!

As far as coaching was concerned, we didn't need much guidance from Tommy and Gerry on that front either. We were fortunate to have a wealth of experienced players at the club who must have played thousands of games between them. Senior professionals such as Peter Hart, Mark Rees and Kenny 'the greatest coach never to have coached' Mower taught us youngsters all we needed to know about playing the game. Richard O'Kelly and Trevor Christie were particularly helpful to me. Richard took me under his wing when I arrived at the club and looked after me on the pitch. He is still my oldest friend in football. In later years, Big Trevor did the same thing. By then I'd scored a few goals, and as those were the days when you could kick each other, I soon became a bit of a target. Big Trevor was great at helping and supporting me through that, as well as taking some of the knocks for me. He was an old-timer who'd had a good career, played at the top level and was also a thinker about the game. I learned a lot from him.

Another of Tommy's astute moves was to bring Graeme Forbes and Andy Dornan down from Scotland. Not only did they strengthen the defence, but their arrival also helped to shake the dressing room up a bit, which was no bad thing. 'Forbsie' was the most fearless defender I've ever seen. He'd quite happily tackle with his head if that would help him win the ball. Tommy also brought in goalkeeper Fred Barber, who used to run on to the pitch wearing a rubber mask. You wouldn't get away with anything like that now, but it was funny at the time.

Tommy undoubtedly had a talented group of players at his disposal, but that team's greatest strength was its togetherness. We didn't only work together, we played together. Every Tuesday afternoon, without fail, we'd head to the King George opposite Fellows Park, not that I had much choice in the matter. I used to tell Mark Rees and Kenny Mower that I didn't drink, but they just told me I was coming anyway! They were senior players, so I could hardly refuse. I even spent my honeymoon with Craig Shakespeare, not that we planned it that way, though. Bizarrely, 'Shaky' and I and our new wives just ended up staying at the same resort. It was just a complete coincidence.

Walsall finished in eighth place at the end of Tommy's first year in charge and we started the following season well, going top of the table in mid-September. We were rarely out of the top three and were gunning for promotion. It therefore came as a bit of a surprise when Nicky Cross was sold to Leicester City halfway through the campaign. 'Crossy' was a great finisher. Indeed, he was much stronger than me and Big Trevor in that regard. He was very similar to John Aldridge, who I played with for the Republic of Ireland, as both could somehow find themselves a split second of calm before shooting at goal. By contrast, I was quick and agile and would try to nip in front of defenders, snatching and snapping at any balls I could get my toe on to. Crossy's departure might not have gone down well with the fans, but it was happy days for me and Big Trevor. We were both more likely to be in the team as a result!

As the season came towards an end, we guaranteed ourselves a place in the play-offs, but automatic promotion still remained a possibility. April was a great month for us; we won all four league matches, the last of which was a 2-1 home victory over Notts County in front of nearly 12,000 spectators. That put us in second place with two games to go and our destiny was in our own hands. But then we blew it, losing away at Bristol Rovers and drawing at home to Gillingham. Brighton and Hove Albion sneaked past us and we were consigned to the lottery of the play-offs.

Our opponents in the semi-finals of the play-offs were Notts County (again) and they didn't pose us too much of a problem. We beat them 3-1 at Meadow Lane, courtesy of two goals from me and one by Shaky, and then drew 1-1 with them back at Fellows Park. That set up a final against Bristol City, though it wasn't played at Wembley back then. It was a two-legged tie instead. Again, we were away from home in the first leg and we won again as well. Bristol City were 1-0 up at half-time, but Big Trevor got one back in the second half and I scored two late goals to give us a decent lead to take back to Fellows Park. To be honest, we thought the job was done after the win at Ashton Gate. We weren't complacent; it was just that we had a decent record at home that season and were confident of getting at least a draw. But then we messed it up again. Rob Newman scored in the first half and Carl Shutt added another in the second to level the tie.

If away goals had counted double then we'd have been promoted, but they didn't and so a replay was needed. There was a penalty shoot-out to decide where it would be played, which was a bit odd as I don't remember Tommy telling us that there would be one if the tie ended in a draw. That may have been the rule, but it wouldn't surprise me if they only decided that after the match had finished. Football was a bit like that back then ('Shall we toss a coin? Nah, let's take penalties …'). I wasn't all that good at spot-kicks, but I still took them all the time. I was never too bothered about missing as I knew I'd get other chances to score. Thankfully, I put the winning penalty away and so we got home advantage for the replay. The Walsall fans ran on to the pitch afterwards and in the melee, somebody nicked my boots. If it was you and you're reading this, I'd like them back!

The dressing room was fairly quiet after the game, with just a few players swearing at each other, which was normal if you'd lost. Then, out of the blue, Tommy said, 'Right, everybody in tomorrow!' Everyone looked at each other, completely aghast. We then protested, saying things like 'Tomorrow's a day off, boss!' Back then, no one came into a football club on a Sunday. It was supposed to be a day of rest! Football is a seven-day-a-week job now but coming in on a Sunday was unheard of then, even if you'd just been hammered 9-0. It was typical of Tommy to do something different like that; he was a bit ahead of his time.

Anyway, we all went in and there was a big urn of tea on the treatment table in the middle of the dressing room, along with plates of sandwiches and biscuits. Tommy spoke for about an hour or so and everybody had their chance to have their say about what had happened. We were all a bit apprehensive about coming in, but it enabled us to discuss what had gone wrong and how we were going to rectify it. Instead of us all mulling the defeat over individually, the meeting got everything out in the open, banished the disappointment and lifted the mood. The meeting started out as a post-mortem, but we soon realised that no one had died and that we still had a great chance to get promoted. We'd beaten Bristol City once already and we could beat them again. We were ready to go and that was all down to Tommy getting us in for that meeting. His rather odd decision turned out to be a masterstroke.

We'd blown two good chances to win promotion, but we weren't going to throw away the third. It wasn't going to be easy, though. On paper, Bristol City were a better side than us. Up front they had Carl Shutt, who I thought was one of the best strikers in the league at the time, as well as Joe Jordan, who was still a phenomenal player, despite being at the end of his career. He was big pals with Tommy, which I thought a bit odd at the time as they were going up against each other for promotion, despite being friends. On the wings they had Alan Walsh, who'd been around for years, and Ralph Milne, who'd played in a European Cup semi-final and would later move to Manchester United. Then, in defence, they had Rob Newman, who really impressed me whenever I played against him. He just used to get in the way all the time and I was forever wishing that he would just leave me alone! It's only in looking back at the game that I have discovered that Steve McClaren played in midfield for them that day. I don't remember him from the game at all, but then I could hardly have known that he would go on to manage England.

I don't remember any words of wisdom from Tommy before we went out on to the pitch, but then he'd said everything he needed to when we'd had the tea and biscuits. He kept the same team that had lost 48 hours before, which I suppose was a vote of confidence in us. The only change I remember him making was playing Andy Dornan on the right wing, instead of at right-back, and Mark Taylor taking his place in defence. Other than that, it was the standard 4-4-2 formation we played every week, with me and Big Trevor up top.

The replay took place on a Bank Holiday Monday and every side of Fellows Park was absolutely rammed. I remember the noise of the crowd hitting me as we ran out at the corner of the ground and it didn't die down during the warm-up. It had been 25 years since Walsall had last been in the Second Division and there seemed to be a feeling in the air that we were finally about to return. It felt like this was our moment. I used to enjoy warming up back then as it gave me the chance to mess about a bit on the pitch. There wasn't any stretching or drills or anything like that; I would just boot the ball at the goalkeeper as hard as I could and try to score!

Walsall's performance in the first 20 minutes of that match must have been amongst the finest ever seen at Fellows Park. We were all over them from the start and never let up. Early on, Big Trevor had a decent shot at goal that Andy Dornan nearly got a toe on to, and we scored not long afterwards. The ball was played into the penalty area and one of their defenders tried to push it back to the goalkeeper, but it bounced off him and fell right into my path. I just couldn't miss.

Five minutes later, Mark Goodwin played a wonderful pass forward and I raced in behind their defence to collect it before slotting the ball beneath the goalkeeper. No sooner had Bristol City kicked off than we were on the attack again. Big Trevor challenged the goalkeeper for a high ball, and it bounced across to Willie Naughton whose effort was cleared off the line by a diving header from the covering defender. Shaky took the resulting corner, which was knocked out of play by Bristol City, and then 'Goody' took the next one. Phil Hawker came storming in as the ball came over, climbing above everyone to head it into the net. Of those first three goals, it's Phil's that I remember the best. As we ran back to the centre circle, I was thinking to myself, 'We're 3-0 up in 20 minutes here, the job's done, we're going to get promoted!' I almost scored again before the interval, but my shot went narrowly wide.

We were exuberant in the dressing room at half-time and Tommy had to calm us down, reminding us that if Bristol City got a goal back, they'd be right in the game. He was right, of course, but I couldn't see us getting beaten. Besides, being the selfish striker that I was, all I could think about was scoring a hat-trick! It can't have been easy for Joe Jordan in the other dressing room, particularly with him being a player-manager. I mean, how do you sort out problems on the pitch when you've been part of the problem yourself?

We ran out for the second half full of purpose and intent, but not so the Bristol City players. They sloped on to the pitch, their body language telling us that they thought the game was already over, which is just what you want to see. Nevertheless, they did try to stage a comeback and Fred Barber had to make an excellent save from an Alan Walsh free kick. But then came the goal that finished them off for good.

My third goal is often described as the best I scored that day. From where the cameras were positioned it looked as if I got hold of the ball, fell under the weight of a tackle, got back up, took a touch to my left and then blasted it into the far corner. I can reveal now that the reality of it was far more prosaic. What really happened was that I took the ball down just outside the penalty area, half tripped over, got up, hit the ball and then watched as it took a huge deflection off the back of the defender in front of me before looping into the net. The poor goalkeeper had no chance.

Even though the score was 4-0, we didn't shut up shop and try to kill the game off. That just wasn't the type of team we were. Tommy would never have brought on an extra centre-half to help protect a lead. It wasn't that we were a gung-ho team; we just had good players that knew how to attack and how to close out a game once we were in front. Fair play to Bristol City; they didn't give up and Fred Barber had to make another fine save to keep them out. Then, a couple of minutes before the end of the game, Carl Shutt got sent off for taking a swing at Fred. It was just frustration as 'Shutty' wasn't that type of player at all. We lived in a different world back then. There were no fourth officials, or videos or VAR. If the referee hadn't seen it happen, Shutty would have got away with it. He just did it at the wrong time!

The match was moments away from ending and we could see that the Walsall fans were getting ready to run on to the pitch; only they came on too soon. The referee blew for a foul and they mistook it for the final whistle. I got out of the way, but I remember Big Trevor shouting at 5,000 people, yelling at them to get off the pitch. I'm not sure what he thought he was going to achieve single-handedly! The fans did retreat, but only to the edge of the playing area, and they were on again a minute later when the referee blew his whistle for the final time. I was immediately surrounded by thousands of delirious Walsall fans, all of whom wanted my shirt. All I could give them, though, was a rather Anglo-Saxon response. We only had two shirts in those days: one home and one away. There were no spares. If you ripped your kit, you had to go to the club shop and buy yourself another one.

It was great being amongst the Walsall fans as we'd won, but it would have been quite intimidating for the Bristol City players. When I was at Newcastle United, we played Leicester City at Filbert Street in the last game of the 1991/92 season. They were going for promotion and we were trying to avoid relegation. Newcastle won and stayed up and there was a huge pitch invasion by the home fans after the end of the game. I jumped into the stands with the Newcastle fans and had to stand there for ten minutes, getting mobbed by them, before a steward arrived to guide me back across the pitch and into the safety of the dressing room. It wasn't much fun walking back through those Leicester City fans.

There was no way I could get back to the dressing room at Fellows Park as my path was barred by thousands of jubilant Walsall fans. I had no choice other than to climb into the stand above the dugouts and try to get back that way. My girlfriend, mom and sisters were all sitting up there, so people assumed that I was going to celebrate with them. However, I wasn't trying to do an Andy Murray at all: I was simply taking the quickest route to safety! My detour even took me through the directors' box, which I had to walk through with my kit on! It took me about a quarter of an hour to reach the dressing room and it was bedlam in there. It was jammed with players, coaching staff, apprentices, the press and even television cameras. The celebrations went on for hours afterwards and everyone involved with the club joined in, including the physios and even the girls who worked behind the bar. We went to a little club down the road and savoured the moment, happy that we'd finally won the promotion that our season deserved.

I was given the match ball, as I'd scored a hat-trick, and it's now at the Banks's Stadium. I'm glad the club have got it as it should be kept for posterity. Most footballers are only sentimental for a short period of time, and sadly all your shirts and memorabilia eventually end up in a suitcase in your loft, or down at your mom's house.

The greatest game that I played for Walsall also turned out to be my last for them. I got an agent over the summer and he introduced me to a host of managers who were keen on signing me. I was hot property at the time, having scored 56 goals over the previous two seasons. I even went on a trial at Bayern Munich, which was an incredible experience. I played in a game between the first team and the reserves and scored a couple of goals, which wasn't bad considering that players like Klaus Augenthaler and Stefan Reuter were on the pitch. I went over there with my girlfriend and it was a bit surreal, the two of us standing in the middle of Munich on our own. I was only 22 at the time and the prospect of relocating to Germany was quite daunting. They offered me a contract, but the rules at the time stipulated that they could only have two foreign players. They already had their full complement, so they wanted to loan me out to another German club. That wasn't for me, so I let the opportunity pass.

In the end, I opted for the Happy Hammers, but looking back I should have gone to Spurs. I went to West Ham because I thought I'd get a game there. Terry Venables was signing players like Gazza and Paul Stewart and the more I spoke to him, the more convinced I became that I would only be a sub if I went to Tottenham. I've only ever wanted to be a first-team player. I couldn't be in the reserves, which is why I've moved clubs a few times during my career. As soon as I thought I was going to be on the bench, I was off to somewhere where I'd be guaranteed a game. Hindsight is a wonderful thing, but that doesn't mean I have regrets. Every decision I made as a player was the right decision to make at the time.

When the Saddlers finally reached Wembley in 2015, I just had to be there. I'm a fan of all the clubs that I've played for and I shall be eternally grateful to Walsall for giving me my start in the game. A whole load of us went down and my sister drove the minibus. We were all so excited because we thought Walsall had a good chance of winning, but what an anti-climax it was! It took Bristol City nearly 30 years, but they finally got their revenge against us. They did to us what we had done to them back in 1988: they got an early goal, went in ahead at half-time, got another in the second half and then saw out the game. It was hard to take, but that's football. Maybe next time, it'll be our turn again.

MARTIN O'CONNOR

Martin O'Connor
Midfielder, 1993, 1994–96, 2002–03

Born and bred in Walsall, Martin O'Connor is the archetypal local lad made good. It appeared initially that a life in football was going to pass him by, with the term 'late developer' barely appearing adequate for someone who didn't make his league debut until the age of 25. O'Connor soon made up for lost time, helping the Saddlers to reach the Division Three play-offs in his first loan spell at the club. He came back on a more permanent basis in 1994, put on the captain's armband and duly led the team to promotion.

Seeing O'Connor's name on the team sheet would always lift the spirits of Saddlers fans, for his presence guaranteed Walsall wouldn't go down without a fight. A bustling, all-action, no-nonsense midfielder, O'Connor was every central defender's dream; his never-say-die attitude often halving their workload. Many may see N'Golo Kante as the quintessential holding midfielder, but to Saddlers fans he is simply a poor man's Martin O'Connor.

After helping Walsall to establish themselves in Division Two, O'Connor moved to Peterborough United and a transfer to Birmingham City followed soon afterwards. He became the backbone of their repeated assaults on the Premier League and, though promotion eluded them, the Blues did reach the 2001 League Cup Final, losing narrowly to Liverpool on penalties. O'Connor captained Birmingham City that day, just as he led most of the teams he played for. 'Skip' was not merely a nickname; it was a badge of office.

O'Connor returned to Walsall in 2002, joining a side that was struggling to avoid relegation from Division One. To Saddlers fans, it was like seeing the cavalry coming over the hill. It didn't take long for results to improve and survival was secured with a game to spare, a barely conceivable outcome prior to his arrival. True local heroes are rare in the modern game, but Martin O'Connor is undoubtedly one.

Walsall 1 – 1 Leeds United
FA Cup Third Round
Saturday, 7 January 1995
Bescot Stadium, Walsall
Attendance: 8,619

Walsall	**Leeds United**
Trevor Wood	John Lukic
Wayne Evans	Gary Kelly
Stuart Ryder	David Wetherall
Charlie Palmer	John Pemberton
Colin Gibson (Darren Rogers)	Nigel Worthington
Chris Marsh	Carlton Palmer
Martin O'Connor	Gary McAllister
Charlie Ntamark	Lucas Radebe (Phil Masinga)
Scott Houghton	Gary Speed
Kyle Lightbourne	David White (Rod Wallace)
Kevin Wilson	Brian Deane

Managers

Chris Nicholl — Howard Wilkinson

Scorers

Chris Marsh (30) — David Wetherall (87)

Referee

Jeff Winter

I'VE BEEN lucky to have made football my life, but it nearly didn't turn out that way. I had trials with Aston Villa when I was young and wanted to make a career for myself in the game. They decided not to take me on, and so I didn't kick a ball for two years after that. I left school and became a train driver instead, working shifts in the company of miserable old men who clearly didn't want kids around. It wasn't much fun driving trains around in the cold at three o'clock in the morning, but that experience taught me a lot. I learnt the value of self-discipline, maturity and a work ethic: virtues that were the backbone of my success in football. Ironically, I don't think I would have lasted the course if I had become an apprentice at Villa; I just didn't have what it took to be a professional footballer back then. I had to get my hands dirty before I would be ready.

I grew up in Goscote in the 1970s: a rough, dark, cruel place back then, particularly if you didn't have a white face. But the experience hardened me. I only realised how much when I played away at Millwall for Crystal Palace reserves in the early 1990s. The black players in our side were called all the names under the sun and many of them were shocked by the level of abuse, but not me. I'd heard it all before.

School was a bit of a trial for me as I wasn't much of an academic. All my friends chose to go to Forest or Manor Farm, but I opted for TP Riley as their sports department had a strong reputation. The sports master was a black guy called Mr Walker, and he had a huge influence on me. I was good at sport, but that still brought about its own pressures. The school wanted me to be in every team they'd got, so I ended up playing cricket, rugby, football and, even though I wasn't the tallest of kids, basketball. Football was my first love, though the school wouldn't let me play for their team unless I agreed to turn out for their rugby side as well. That led to me being scouted for the county rugby team, but the first game I was due to play for them clashed with a soccer match. I opted to play football that afternoon instead, so that was the end of my rugby career.

The opportunity with Villa came and went, and after a couple of years away from the game I drifted back to play for a side called Afro-Caribbean, who were a team of Rastafarians run by my friend's dad. My first game was against the HM Prison Swinfen Hall side who, incidentally, fielded another of my mates. Unsurprisingly, the match was played at their place. My performances got me noticed and I soon moved on to Bloxwich Town. I hadn't been there long when Bobby Hope, manager of Bromsgrove Rovers, came to watch me play. To be honest, I didn't even know where Bromsgrove was at the time, but I went for a trial and was offered a contract. I started playing for them, but my attitude was still wrong. The training was too frequent and too hard, and I was fed up with not being allowed to go out on a Friday night. Just two months into the season my frustration boiled over, and I had a big bust-up with Bobby. I threw my pay cheque at him and drove home thinking, for the second time in my life, that I was done with football.

But Bobby didn't give up on me. He got me back at the club and made me realise what I could achieve if I knuckled down, got fit and applied myself. I listened because Bobby knew what he was talking about, having played for West Bromwich Albion and Scotland. It was Bobby who switched the light on for me. He even looked after me when I got injured and had to have the first of my nine knee operations. Bromsgrove Rovers soon got promoted and the scouts started to come and watch me play. Bobby advised me to go to the biggest club I could, and that was how I came to sign for Crystal Palace. I wasn't the only one in the division to get a big move that season. Ian Taylor and David Busst also got their big chance, moving on from Moor Green to play in the Premier League for Aston Villa and Coventry City respectively.

The first time I saw Kenny Hibbitt and Paul Taylor was when they watched me play in the Crystal Palace reserves side, away at Southampton. The following day, Steve Coppell indicated there'd been some interest in me and asked me whether I wanted to go out on loan. I'd just bought a house in Walsall so the idea of going back home really appealed. The only problem was that it was Chesterfield who were showing the interest! I went up to their ground to have a look around and spoke to their manager, John Duncan, who was keen for me to join. Over the weekend, I went to watch Rushall Olympic play and mulled the offer over, but the following week I told Steve Coppell that I wanted to stay at Palace. Then he said that Walsall were asking after me as well. Now, there was a club I was prepared to leave London for.

To be honest, Walsall came as a bit of a culture shock, compared to what I was used to at Crystal Palace. They were a Premier League club and each player had his own bundle of training kit, all washed and ready to use. When I arrived at Walsall, all Tom Bradley could give me was a load of old, leftover kit, a T-shirt here, the odd sock there. I went straight into the first team and all my family and friends wanted to come and watch me play. I needed about 30 tickets, but each player was only allocated two free ones. I managed to get some from team-mates who didn't need theirs, but still ended up buying a load of them myself. In the dressing room at Palace, I had seen first-team players throw up before games or spend all their time on the toilet. I never got nervous and my debut, a league match at home to Shrewsbury Town, was no different. The game ended in a 1-1 draw and my professional career was up and running.

Kenny Hibbitt was sacked early in the 1994/95 season and it came as a real shock to the players. We hadn't seen it coming at all. There were murmurs about who his replacement was going to be, but we were in the dark until Tom Bradley came in one day and said that the new manager was on his way to see us. Then this mean, angry-looking figure marched into the dressing room and his first words were simply, 'I want promotion.' Chris Nicholl had arrived.

The new gaffer was intense, right from day one. Training sessions were simple and focused on the basics, but if we didn't get it right, we had to stay behind until we had. What mattered most to him were attitude, determination and desire: the things that summed up Chris Nicholl as a player. I wasn't the greatest at training back then and I felt that he was always on my back, banging on at me about raising my standards. It finally came to a head during an away game against Blackpool. The score was 1-1 at half-time and I walked off the pitch feeling pretty pleased with my performance. It soon became obvious that Chris Nicholl thought otherwise. He absolutely slaughtered me in the dressing room, getting right in my face. I had a go back and thought he was going to sub me there and then, but he didn't. I went back out in the second half, scored the winner and took great delight in giving the boss the fingers as I celebrated. Back in the dressing room, he came over to me and I wondered what was going to happen. But all he said was, 'Well done, Mart,' and then he walked off. That was a guy who knew how to get the best out of his players.

Chris Nicholl and Paul Taylor put together a solid team that had just the right mix of experience and youth. In the centre of defence were Charlie Palmer and Stuart Ryder: the old hand and the England Under-21 player. The left-back, Colin Gibson, had won the league with Aston Villa and played for Manchester United, while Scotty Houghton put in some unbelievable performances on the wing, plus Chris Marsh had a great season too. Then, up front, we had Kevin Wilson, an ex-Chelsea and Northern Ireland international, alongside Kyle 'Killer' Lightbourne. Kevin helped Killer to become a much better player, and he and I got into the PFA Division Three Team of the Year that season, so we can't have been all that bad a side.

Chris Nicholl wasn't one for fancy tactical systems. He just told us to keep it solid at the back, not take risks, and to play in the opposition half as much as we could. We all had our jobs to do and he made sure we knew what they were. Scotty Houghton and Chris Marsh were our wingers, so they had to focus on staying out wide and getting crosses into the box. He absolutely loved it if we won by one goal to nil. In fact, that was his favourite result. I remember when we beat Torquay United 8-4 in an FA Cup replay, he hammered us in the dressing room afterwards for conceding four goals. He didn't once mention the eight goals we'd scored! The reason why Chris Nicholl prized a 1-0 win was that it showed we could get a lead and then hold on to it. That was perfection for him.

What Chris didn't have time for, though, was injured players. I had continual problems with my knee that season and was forever in the treatment room. If he saw you in there, he would just ignore you, even if you'd won a game the day before. In fact, he would blank you until you returned to training. It was hard to take, but I understand now why he did it. Players that couldn't play were just no use to him.

We beat Doncaster Rovers a week before we were due to play Leeds and my knee injury flared up again. I was getting treatment the following day when Chris Nicholl came and asked me whether I'd be fit for the big game. I told him I wasn't sure, and we must have discussed it for at least an hour. The more we talked, the more I realised how much I wanted to go up against players like Gary McAllister, Carlton Palmer and Gary Speed. He made me grasp how much I would learn from competing against them and how much the experience would help me improve as a player. To be honest, I spent a lot of time worrying about my knee back then. I found out that Walsall had drawn Leeds when I was having Sunday lunch with my wife at the Bescot Stadium and someone came over and told me. It was interesting news, but I was still thinking about my knee.

Unusually, we didn't do much training in the week before the Leeds game. Chris Nicholl even gave us a couple of days off, which was unheard of. Looking back, I think he wanted us to be full of energy, ready to chase and harry for a ball we hadn't seen all week. You could feel the excitement building up as the game got closer, but there was no pressure on us at all. The objective that season was promotion and few people expected us to beat Leeds, so we treated the FA Cup as a bonus. It was simply a chance to go out and show what we could do against the best. It didn't do any harm that we were also in good form, having won eight and drawn two of the last ten games.

We had a team meeting on the day before the game and Chris Nicholl wound us all up, telling us that the Leeds players were better than we were and that they drove bigger cars than we did. He was laying down a challenge for us, daring us to go out and prove that we could live with a team that had won the league title only a couple of seasons earlier. There was even a promise of a holiday, all expenses paid, for the Walsall man of the match. On the day itself, the stadium was packed, and you just couldn't move. The *Match of the Day* cameras were there, so clearly even the BBC sensed that an upset could be on the cards. I remember standing in the tunnel and hearing the crowd outside. They were loud, the atmosphere was electric, and I thought to myself: 'Yes, let's have it!'

The game itself was a bit of a scrap. Back then, the pitch at the Bescot Stadium got very poor in the winter and it acted as a leveller, forcing Leeds to play direct football instead of trying to pass the ball through us. In a way, that played to their strengths as they were a much taller side than us, and we struggled to match them in the air. Leeds had the better of the opening chances, with Trevor Wood having to save a header from Lucas Radebe before stopping a Gary Speed shot with his legs. Then, half an hour into the game, we broke swiftly out of defence and Killer fired a raking pass across their penalty area. Nigel Worthington let the ball run, seemingly thinking it would go out of play, not realising that Marshy was steaming in at the far post. He managed to get to the ball and slid it past John Lukic at his near post. It may have been the first chance we'd created, but unlike Leeds, we'd made it count.

Normal service was quickly resumed as Leeds peppered our goal for the remainder of the first half. Brian Deane headed the ball powerfully at goal from just outside the six-yard area and Woody somehow managed to tip it over the bar. From the resulting corner, Deane won the aerial battle again and his header ricocheted off both bar and post before bouncing out to safety. A few minutes later, Deane won another header and the ball bounced off the post with Woody well beaten. We were relieved to go in at half-time still in the lead, but the second half brought no respite. Deane fired a fierce shot at goal, which Charlie Palmer got a touch to, deflecting the ball into the side-netting. Then Deane won yet another header, bringing out a brilliant save from Woody, who pushed the ball on to the post before throwing his body on top of it.

It might sound like Brian Deane was the only player troubling us, but that was far from the case. They had top footballers all over the pitch. Gary McAllister was the one who impressed me the most. His touch was first-rate, his movement sublime and his decision-making faultless. He almost scored when he got on to the end of a Gary Speed header, but Woody denied him with another stunning fingertip save.

To be honest, I didn't touch the ball much in that game at all. I spent most of it screening and blocking and trying to win second balls, though I did create a great chance for Killer in the second half. I burst forward on the left wing and the Leeds defence were wide open. I knew I had to cross the ball into the box quickly or the chance would go, so I didn't even look up. I just hit a pass and it went straight to Killer's feet. He only had the goalkeeper to beat and was in great form that season, so I'd have put money on him scoring. But it wasn't to be. He tried to dink the ball over John Lukic, but he just got a hand to it, forcing it away from the goal. If that shot had gone in, Walsall would have gone 2-0 up and I don't think Leeds would have come back from that. We were so close.

Leeds continued to batter us after that. Carlton Palmer was the first on to a Gary Speed cross and Woody had to make another good save. A few minutes later, Speed went on a great run, beating two players before shooting at goal. His strike beat Woody but struck the far post, and then Palmer connected with the rebound, only to see his shot hit the other post. We were hanging on, but Chris Nicholl had instilled resilience into us, and we were only a few minutes away from glory. Phil Masinga thought he had finally broken us when he headed in a cross from Brian Deane, but the referee immediately ruled it out for a push on Wayne Evans.

Leeds were getting closer and closer, and just 200 seconds from full time they finally found a way through. They won a free kick on the left-hand side of the pitch, 20 yards from goal, and all their players packed into the penalty area. McAllister fired in a pinpoint cross and David Wetherall got on to the end of it, directing his header past Woody, who couldn't save us this time. The goal was scored in front of the Leeds fans who came running on to the pitch, their jubilation in complete contrast to our disappointment. The referee blew the final whistle soon afterwards, but we weren't downhearted at all, despite having come so close to winning. Leeds might have created a lot of chances, but we knew we'd done enough to get a draw. We deserved a replay. Chris Nicholl didn't say much to us after the game, but then he never did. It was just the usual, 'day off tomorrow, fellas, come in on Monday'. He never wanted to talk about a game until he'd had chance to think it over for a day or two.

The Leeds players were brilliant after the game. They came into our dressing room, shook everyone's hands and told us that they'd see us back at their place. No big heads, no arrogance, just class. I was up for a good night out, but no one else wanted to know. To be fair, the lads were just drained. Leeds had taken everything out of us. Woody won the holiday, but he'd earned it so none of us complained. Saying that, I don't think he ever played as well as that again. In fact, he lived off that performance for the next three seasons!

We didn't do much training on the day before the replay, which was a bonus as my knee was in a bad way. I had to have it aspirated and was having jabs to control the pain. I had an ice pack on my knee for the entire journey up to Leeds and it was touch and go as to whether I'd be fit to play. Chris Nicholl came over to me on the coach and gave me the option of playing or not, which was rare for him. It was Leeds at Elland Road and I didn't want to miss that, so I told him I'd play. If it had been a normal league game, there was no way I would have done that. The gaffer seemed pleased, but he never asked about my injury again. Everything was black and white with him. If you said you were fit, then he'd expect you to give 100 per cent. If you were injured, then he'd send you to the stands and you wouldn't hear anything more from him. Chris Nicholl had many qualities, but he certainly wasn't the cuddly type. Football's a man's game and he only ever wanted men in his team.

Stuart Watkiss was brought back into the team to give us some much-needed height and we launched into Leeds straight from the kick-off. Killer went close twice and then it all went dark when the floodlights failed for about quarter of an hour. That gave Leeds a bit of a breather and they scored not long after the lights went back on. We battled away and won a penalty when Killer was bundled over by John Pemberton. Kenny Hibbitt had made me the team's penalty taker, but I don't remember why. I think it was because I was captain and he wanted me to take responsibility. I didn't have any specific technique for taking spot-kicks, other than switching sides from time to time. Anyway, I didn't miss many and I didn't slip up that night. I put it away in front of the Walsall fans, which was great, but I don't remember my celebration being all that elaborate. It was just a wave, really. What I do remember is that, just as the ball hit the back of the net, I felt pain in my knee for the first time that night.

I had an ice pack on my knee again at half-time and it was sheer adrenaline that kept me on the pitch. We were a goal down at the break as David Wetherall had scored with a header a few minutes after my penalty, though not everything went his way in the second half. With 20 minutes to go, Kevin Wilson's shot at goal took a big deflection off Wetherall and ended up beating John Lukic. We held on for extra time, but the boys had nothing left to give. I was pretty much immobile by then and the gaffer soon took me off. Leeds brought Phil Masinga on at the start of extra time and he went on to score a hat-trick to put the tie beyond us. It was a defeat, but we had lost with dignity. We were proud of having taken a Premier League side to both a replay and to extra time. In the end, their class (and our exhaustion) was the difference.

Chris Nicholl didn't say much to us after the final whistle, just 'bad luck, fellas. Let's go again in the next match.' He was never one for big speeches. Once again, the Leeds players were great to us after the match. They invited us into their dressing room and Carlton Palmer signed his shirt for me. That experience really fuelled my ambition. It made me want to be where they were, signing shirts for players from the lower leagues. A few cans of lager were left out for us on the coach, but no one touched them. We were too shattered. It had been a great ride, but in the end, we just weren't quite as good as they were.

I used to enjoy a night out after a game back then. My motto was that if you worked hard, you could play hard, though I was a bit naïve initially. It took me a while to realise that I couldn't go to all the places I used to as stories would somehow find their way back to the gaffer. Most times, I would have a few beers, but nothing heavy. It always gave me a buzz to have a drink with Saddlers fans on the night after a game and then see them in the crowd the following week. There was a tight group of us that went out regularly, including Marshy, Killer, Jimmy 'Wacka' Walker, Charlie Ntamark, John Keister and Scotty Houghton. One of the big strengths of that Walsall team was our togetherness, and part of that stemmed from the nights out we shared.

Not that we always saw eye to eye, though. Our final game that season was away to Bury, and we needed a draw to win promotion. Two days before, we had beaten Scarborough and, unusually, the club had put us up in a nice hotel there rather than bringing us back home. There wasn't a huge amount to do, so we played table-tennis and it ended in a big fight for some reason. We were all competitive athletes and we couldn't just switch that instinct off, even if we were only playing ping-pong. I remember that Chris Nicholl didn't intervene at all. He just watched it all unfold. I think he liked us to have that bit of edge; to see us stand up for ourselves when we had to.

We stopped at another hotel the night before the Bury game and quite a few Walsall fans were staying there as well. Being around them helped remind us how much promotion meant to them. There were Saddlers fans everywhere as we drove to Gigg Lane and they were simply magnificent that night. I saw my mom in the crowd before the game and she was crying, even though nothing had happened yet!

The game was 0-0 at half-time, so we were doing fine, but the gaffer tore into us in the dressing room. I remember him ripping his tracksuit top off and throwing it down, before going around each one of us individually and telling us in no uncertain terms what we had to do in the second half. It was all '*you've* got to do this' and '*you've* got to do that'.

We kept it tight in the second half and Wacka made an unbelievable save late on to keep the game goalless. Woody had played in goal throughout that season but was injured during the previous game against Scarborough and Wacka had come on to replace him. He might have been Chris Nicholl's second-choice goalkeeper, but all the players had total confidence in him. We'd seen what he could do in training and knew he wouldn't let us down. I think the gaffer preferred Woody at the time because he trained well and was always professional. Wacka could be a bit of a joker at times and his attitude didn't always go down well with the boss.

For once, my knee felt all right, but I went into a 50-50 tackle late in the game (to be honest, it was more like 40-

60) and got my shin ripped open. I didn't want to go off, but Tom Bradley told me I had to. I was raging in the dressing room, roaring at Bury's doctor to get me fixed up so that I could get back on to the pitch. Then I found out that I'd already been subbed! Anyway, I was lying back on the treatment table, getting stitched up, when the door burst open and Chris Nicholl came rushing in and started shaking me, yelling in my face that we'd won promotion.

It's fair to say there was plenty of celebrating that night. Bottles of champagne were uncorked in the dressing room and I joined in the party as best I could, even though I was still hobbling about. I saw my mom again after the game and she was still crying! The celebrations continued on the coach on the way back home, though the gaffer didn't drink beer with the rest of us. He sat quietly at the front of the coach, sipping a glass of wine, no doubt reflecting on what he'd achieved in his first season at the club.

Charlie Palmer and Kevin Wilson stayed at my house that night and we all went into the ground the following morning a little worse for wear. The chairman, Chris Nicholl and Paul Taylor were waiting there to tell us that we'd be going on a trip to Tenerife, not simply as a reward for promotion but for everything we'd achieved that season. Everyone went, without exception, and we all had a marvellous week. The gaffer beat Paul Taylor at tennis and bragged about it all week, while some of the players almost drowned poor Tom Bradley in the swimming pool. The Port Vale team were at the same hotel as us, so we had a few beers with them as well. It was a smashing way to round off what had been a great season.

I left a year later for Peterborough United and then played for Birmingham City for six seasons, before coming back to Walsall in 2002. The Blues were going well at the time, but I fell out with Steve Bruce after a game and he told me to go and find myself another club. That was more easily said than done as he wouldn't let me leave for a side that was also pushing for promotion, and those were the ones showing an interest! Then I heard that Walsall wanted to take me back. I met with Colin Lee and Paul Taylor at The Belfry one Sunday and was impressed by how much they wanted me. The conversation was going well, but then I had an urgent phone call from my wife, who told me that our daughter had been taken ill. I gave my excuses and rushed off, but Colin Lee phoned me three times that day to ask how she was. He didn't mention football once. I liked that, so I decided to come back and play for him.

Some things had changed at Walsall in the six years I'd been away, while some hadn't. The club was in the Championship and had a lot more financial clout, but the kit situation hadn't improved any. On my first day back, it was still an old pair of shorts here, the odd sock there. The Saddlers were in the bottom three when I arrived, so I was expecting the mood to be a bit subdued. I couldn't have been more wrong. Training was really lively, with tackles flying in everywhere. Colin Lee told me he had a group of good players, but they just lacked a bit of experience and needed a leader, which is why he had brought me in. That was music to my ears.

It took a few games for performances to improve but we finished the campaign strongly, winning three of our last four games. Survival was ensured with an away victory over Sheffield United and the club took the players to Ayia Napa as a reward. While we were away, we found a bar so we could watch Birmingham City take on Norwich

City in the Championship play-off final. The Blues won on penalties so, inevitably, all the drinks were on me that night. Both teams I'd played for that season had achieved their goals, which was very satisfying.

While I was at Walsall, Colin Lee started to give me more responsibility. He would ask me to speak to the players for five minutes at half-time before he came in to give us a few tactical pointers. He also encouraged me to take some of the training sessions and that was a real eye-opener. I found that not only could I do it, but that I enjoyed it as well. That put me on the road to becoming a coach, and in 2009 I came back to Walsall for a third time as assistant manager to Chris Hutchings. Mick Halsall was the head of youth when we arrived, but he soon left for Wolves and I told Chris that we should get Dean 'Smudge' Smith in to replace him. I'd heard good things of him at Leyton Orient, and I knew the fans would appreciate having another ex-Saddlers captain back at the club. Smudge made a name for himself at Walsall and has never looked back, though to be honest, when I played with him, I didn't see anything to suggest that he would go on to manage a huge club like Aston Villa. But good luck to him. He deserves his success.

I'm as busy now as I've ever been, running my football academy. Football is what people know me for and football is the only thing I know. I feel lucky to have had the career I've had and privileged to still be working in the game. Football has been good for me, so I'm glad I gave it another go. I'll always be a Saddler.

SCOTT HOUGHTON

Scott Houghton
Winger, 1994–96

There are some footballers who spend their whole career with one club, with the relationship between them and the fans eventually developing the feel of a marriage. Scott Houghton was destined not to be a long-standing partner. Rather, he was the torrid love affair; the exhilarating one-night stand that leaves behind wonder and regret in equal measure. In quieter moments, all would later reflect on what would have happened if they had stayed together for longer. Perhaps it would have ended in the clinking of champagne glasses, ringing bells and vows of never-ending loyalty. Maybe it would have made for a messy divorce. We shall never know.

In a sense, the Saddlers and Scott Houghton were made for each other. He was the exciting young winger with the world at his feet. FA Youth Cup glory with Tottenham Hotspur and under-20 appearances for England promised a glittering career, but he somehow got lost along the way. The club he ended up at had also lost their way. The 1980s had seen Walsall appear in a League Cup semi-final and win promotion to the second tier of the league, but consecutive relegations had dumped them back at the bottom of the pyramid. What the two of them had in common, however, was a desire to rise again.

And rise they did. Scott Houghton joined Walsall only a few weeks before Chris Nicholl was recruited: the manager who would finally lead the club out of darkness. It was perfect timing, with the diminutive winger becoming a key part of the well-organised team that won promotion from Division Three in 1995. He then stayed for another season as the club consolidated themselves in Division Two, before falling for the rather more dubious charms of Peterborough United.

Saddlers fans have been fortunate to see a succession of marvellous wingers over the years, from Colin 'Cannonball' Taylor, to Miah Dennehy, Mark Rees, Willie Naughton, John Hodge and Pedro Matias. 'Super Scotty Houghton' is part of that fine tradition. He may only have been at Walsall for two seasons, but he's remembered because he made an impact. A casual fling perhaps, but one never to be forgotten.

Walsall 8 – 4 Torquay United

FA Cup Second Round Replay
Tuesday, 12 December 1995, Bescot Stadium, Walsall
Attendance: 3,230

Walsall	**Torquay United**
Jimmy Walker	Ashley Bayes
Charlie Ntamark	Ian Gore
Darren Rogers	Lee Barrow
Adrian Viveash	Chris Curran
Chris Marsh	Alex Watson
Derek Mountfield (Stuart Watkiss)	Russell Coughlin
Martin O'Connor	Rodney Jack (Jose Mateu)
Darren Bradley	Mark Hall (Tony Bedeau)
John Keister (Kyle Lightbourne)	Richard Hancox
Kevin Wilson	Mark Hawthorne
Scott Houghton	Ian Hathaway

Managers

Chris Nicholl	Eddie May

Scorers

Chris Marsh (14, 93)	Mark Hawthorne (36)
Kevin Wilson (58)	Lee Barrow (53)
Darren Bradley (71)	Ian Gore (65)
Kyle Lightbourne (96, 119)	Jose Mateu (101)
Martin O'Connor (97)	
Scott Houghton (104)	

Referee

Dermot Gallagher

WHEN I arrived at Walsall in the autumn of 1994 my career was on the slide. Even though I was only 22, many people in the game thought that my best years were already behind me. And I can't blame them for thinking that. I had a reputation for being ill-disciplined and it was drinking that was the root of all my problems. Chris Nicholl was the first manager I ever had who wouldn't let me do what I wanted to do, which was go out drinking seven nights a week. He was the one who told me that I wouldn't get drunk the night before a game. He was the one who told me to stay at home. He was the one who gave me the discipline I lacked. It's no exaggeration to say that Chris Nicholl saved my career.

I started off as a schoolboy at Luton Town and David Pleat was the manager there at the time. I was on the verge of signing for Arsenal, but then one morning my mom and dad got a call from him. He told them he was moving to Spurs and that he wanted me to go with him. I still believe that I was his first signing for the club. There was a good set-up at Spurs, and I was part of the team that won the FA Youth Cup in 1990. There were some good players in that side including Ian Walker, who went on to be Tottenham's first-choice goalkeeper for several years, as well as Stuart Nethercott and Ian Hendon, both of whom had decent careers in the game.

I was lucky enough to play for England from under-15 through to under-20 level. My swansong was the World Youth Championship, which is what the Under-20 World Cup used to be called. It was held in Portugal in 1991 and I played in all three of England's matches, which were against Spain, Syria and Uruguay. There were a lot of players in that side who went on to have incredibly successful careers, such as Andrew Cole, who won a Champions League with Manchester United, Steve Harkness, Scott Minto and Alan Wright. To get into that team I had to keep out wingers like Steve McManaman and Darren Anderton, which gives some idea of the competition that I was up against. At 20 years of age I wasn't far off being one of the best wide players in the country, but within a couple of seasons I had slipped a long, long way down the pecking order. Ultimately, I found it very difficult to recover from the damage I did to myself in the early days.

I made my way into the Spurs first-team squad for the 1991/92 season and trained alongside players such as Gary Lineker, Vinny Samways and Paul Stewart, which was an incredible experience. I made ten league appearances for Spurs, albeit I came off the substitutes' bench for all of them. The most memorable of those games was a 4-1 victory in which I scored twice. Ironically, it was against Luton Town, which was not far away from where I grew up. The highlights from that game are on YouTube, so when my youngest son grows up, I will be able to show him that his dad could play some decent football and hasn't always been a fat layabout!

To be honest, at that time I didn't really comprehend where I was or what I was doing. I know now that I was a real loose cannon. I couldn't stay out of the pub and was going completely off the rails. Terry Venables was the Spurs manager by then and the number of times he had me in his office to warn me about my drinking was ridiculous. He tried to guide me, but I thought I knew better. I remember playing in a pre-season friendly for Spurs against Sheffield Wednesday. Frank Barlow was their assistant manager and he told me that they were looking to sign me, but he had two burning questions: did I have a weight problem, and did I have a drink problem? I replied that I didn't. Unfortunately, both teams were staying at the same hotel and that night I got completely blotto. I fell over in the toilet, cracked my head open and, unsurprisingly, that was the end of that deal. If I had my time again, I would train much harder, as well as drink less. There are countless footballers who have natural ability but go nowhere, and then there are players who perhaps aren't so talented but absolutely work their socks off. They are often the ones who go on to have better careers. Some young players think that ability counts for everything, but it doesn't.

Terry Venables was always clear with me that I had the ability to be a first-team player at Spurs, but I had a stinking attitude and so he eventually let me go. The next stop was Luton Town, and that was when I really hit rock bottom. I found it hard to come to terms with leaving Spurs after being there for five years or so. In fact, it was a bit like breaking up from a long-term girlfriend. I started off quite well at Luton, but then we lost 2-0 at home to Bolton and I was interviewed by a reporter after the match. Luton had several young players in the side at the time, so I explained that we were inexperienced, and that people should accept that we would make mistakes from time to time. But the article that came out was really damning of the club. David Pleat was back in charge of Luton by that time and I got called into his office to explain myself. I told him that I hadn't said what had been printed, but he wasn't having any of it and I didn't start any of the next eight league matches.

Not being in the first team just served to fuel my drinking habit. I was out every single day, without fail, and started to put on weight. Unsurprisingly, my fitness really started to suffer. I remember in one game, when I finally managed to get back into the team, I was stood by the post for a corner. Three or four Luton fans suddenly shouted out, 'Fucking hell, Houghton, how come you're not in the Old Oak today?' That was the pub I used to drink in, so the supporters clearly knew what I was up to. Eventually, the penny dropped, and I spent the whole of the summer of 1994 in the gym. I lost a lot of weight, got myself into good shape and did really well in pre-season, winning every single run. I played in Luton's first match of the season, but then David Pleat called me into his office and told me that I was no longer in his plans because of how I'd behaved the previous season. My reputation had finally caught up with me.

During that summer, Wayne Turner, who was the reserve-team manager at Luton, told me that the gaffer had arranged for me to play in one of Walsall's pre-season friendlies as they were interested in taking me on. My initial response was: 'Where the hell is Walsall?' He told me it was up near Birmingham, so I agreed to give it a go. The game was against Halesowen Town and I did well. I really liked the look of Walsall; the lads were great, there was a buoyant spirit in the dressing room, and they got the ball down and passed it. That was important to me as I didn't want to play in a kick and rush side. After having been at Spurs and then slipping down a division to play for Luton, I thought I was making a big step down to go to Walsall, but I was absolutely amazed by the standard of players they had.

I went back to Luton for a bit but had no hesitation in signing for Walsall when a deal got sorted out. I could see that it was a team that was going places. The money they offered me was awful, but that wasn't what mattered at the time. I was trying to resurrect a career that I'd almost set fire to and Walsall were prepared to give me one last chance. Kenny Hibbitt, who was a real gentleman, had been the manager when I'd been at the club during pre-season, but he got sacked just before I signed for the club in September. It was a bit of a strange time to join, but it was harder for those players who'd been there longer and had known Kenny well. It was different for me as I wasn't really one of Kenny's players; I was just a nomad.

I played my first four games for Walsall during the short period between Kenny being sacked and Chris Nicholl taking over. The last of those matches was a league game at home to Fulham, and I remember it well. I had played against Fulham in the first round of the League Cup that season when I was still at Luton. We drew 1-1 and I thought Fulham were a decent side. In fact, I think they were one of the favourites to get promoted from Division Three, but Walsall absolutely demolished them. We were 3-0 up at half-time, and the final score was 5-1. Kyle Lightbourne scored a hat-trick, but I still picked up all the cans of beer for winning man of the match. It was probably as good a game as I played during my entire time with the Saddlers.

There is one funny story from that match. Walsall's club doctor was sat next to Jimmy Hill in the stands, who was Fulham's chairman at the time. Fulham had come in for me at the same time as Walsall but had backed off because Don Howe had told Jimmy Hill that I couldn't defend. I think I had a hand in all five of Walsall's goals that afternoon, and every time we scored Jimmy Hill kept saying, 'Bloody Don Howe! Bloody Don Howe!', which the doctor found really amusing. It was just one of those games where most things

I tried came off for me. I underachieved in my career and should have done more than I did, but that game showed what I was capable of.

I remember the moment when Chris Nicholl first walked into the dressing room at Walsall because he was wearing a blazer that was three times too small for him! After he finally managed to wedge it off, he told us he wanted promotion and that if any of us didn't think it was possible, or that we didn't want to be there, then he made it clear where the door was. Chris quickly made his presence felt and there was no doubt who the boss was. British football is in a real state these days, with managers getting forced out by players all the time. Well, there was no way that man would have been forced out of a club by anyone. He had complete control of the dressing room and didn't tolerate any messing about. Chris instilled discipline into the players, changed the dynamics of the squad and the rest, as they say, is history.

Some of his training sessions were hard, though. We did a lot of one-to-one exercises, where you played directly against someone else for an hour or so. That was tough because no one wanted to lose and so wouldn't give an inch, which made the training quite intense. At the same time, Chris had his head screwed on. If he knew the players were fatigued, then he'd lay off us. But if he thought the players needed to be pushed a bit, then he'd make us do extra running sessions. He would also bring some fun into it now and again. After a defeat, we'd turn up expecting to do a lot of running but he might take us go-karting, or out somewhere to play a game of cricket. Chris would keep us guessing by doing things like that. I had no grumbles about the training as a lot of it covered patterns of play, which I think is incredibly important, especially in the lower reaches of the league. If a team doesn't have that platform to build from then it's always going to struggle.

Walsall played a rigid 4-4-2 formation under Chris Nicholl and he drilled that structure into us. In some training sessions we were physically tied to each other, which meant that if you got into the wrong position you would get pulled over. You couldn't do something like that now, with the way that health and safety is, but it worked. Regardless of who the left-sided central midfielder was, I would know exactly where they were and where I needed to be in relation to them. Chris made the team defensively solid and set us up to counterattack. The ball would go up to Kevin Wilson and he would then feed it out wide to either me or Chris Marsh. Our job was to get the crosses in for the boys to finish off. The system worked a treat, and I think the gaffer was ahead of his time in that regard. Back then there weren't many teams that counterattacked with pace like we did. Now everybody does that when they play away from home, though we would do it wherever we played. That was the Walsall way. But what we didn't do was boot it. We passed the ball to feet and played one- and two-touch football whenever we could. It was a real pleasure to play in that team.

Chris Nicholl was great for me. My previous managers would just drop me if I went out drinking the night before a game, but he made it clear to me that my career was at stake and gave me the discipline I'd lacked. If I had played under a manager who allowed me to get away with what I had been doing previously, then I'm in no doubt that I would only have lasted a season at Walsall and the next stop would have been a non-league club. Chris gave me a lot of confidence in myself and I was hardly ever out of the side during my two years with Walsall. My performances as a young wide player had tended to be a bit inconsistent, but I became much steadier and more reliable under Chris. I also got a lot fitter and lost weight, though he did make it known on a few occasions that I could still do with losing half a stone!

There was a great camaraderie between the players at Walsall. Whenever we did a running session, we never had someone off in front and someone else two miles behind. We all ran together and stayed together. We also had good senior players who were a calming influence in the dressing room. If you had a bad game, Charlie Palmer would be the first to put his arm around you, telling you that you'd just had an off day and reminding you how well you'd played previously. As a young player, that really helped me. I played in front of Colin Gibson in my first season at Walsall and he was an absolute legend, having been at Manchester United and Aston Villa. He was 34 and his legs had gone a bit, but his mind was in overdrive and he was phenomenal to play with. 'Gibbo' used to talk me through games, and if he came up against a winger who was a bit on the sharp side, I'd do his running for him.

A lot of the Walsall players had young families, so after a game we'd stay behind, have a few beers and the kids would play together. The wives would also all sit as a group; there were no WAGs in those days. Most weeks the players would go out or have barbecues and be around at each other's houses. We were probably one of the worst-paid teams in the whole league, but because we were all on peanuts that meant that there were no big-time-Charlies. We also helped each other out, so if I couldn't afford something I needed, then one of the other lads would lend me money and vice versa. There were no bad apples who would upset the dressing room, and everyone just mucked in for each other. Without a shadow of a doubt, that was the best team spirit of any club I played for during my career. We were like a family.

Paul Taylor brought a lot of decent footballers to Walsall. He assembled a good mix of experienced players and young, upcoming talents who had the potential to push on and achieve more in the game, such as myself, Kyle Lightbourne and Martin O'Connor. Stuart Ryder was also a cracking young defender until he got injured. It didn't take long for Chris Nicholl to gel us all together and then we really got on to a roll. Promotion came at the end of my first season at the club and it was well deserved.

Chris Nicholl reworked the defence for my second season at Walsall, though that was forced on him a bit because Gibbo retired and Stuart Ryder and Charlie Palmer both got injured. Darren Rogers took over at left-back and he was quite a different player to Gibbo. He was strong and quick, but not so comfortable on the ball as Gibbo had been. That meant I didn't have to do so much defending, but I also became a bit isolated as Darren didn't demand the ball the way that Gibbo had. Charlie Ntamark often played at right-back, though I don't think anybody knew what his best position was, so he ended up filling in here, there and everywhere. He was a cracking lad to have in the dressing room as he could be very funny. Charlie had a lot of skill, but sometimes he would baffle even himself, never mind the opposition.

The new pairing in central defence was Adi Viveash and Derek Mountfield. Adi was a marvellous player who had a wand of a left foot, was strong in the air and was a good leader. The only thing he lacked was a bit of pace. If he'd had that, there's no doubt in my mind that he would have been a Premier League defender. Derek was a great signing for Walsall as he'd played at the top level for Everton and Aston Villa, winning a league title and an FA Cup. He came to Walsall at the back end of his career, which wasn't so unusual for a top player back then. That was because they didn't earn the money that footballers do now, plus the difference between what they would get at a big club and a smaller club was nowhere near as great as it is now.

Like Adi, Derek was a powerful leader and excellent in the air, though he also lacked a bit of pace. Saying that, I don't think they got caught out too often because they had Jimmy Walker sweeping behind them. He was one of the best footballing goalkeepers I ever played with and was ahead of his time in that regard. If 'Wacka' was still playing now he would be worth £15m to £20m, without a shadow of a doubt, especially if he grew a few inches! I wasn't at all surprised that he went on to have the fine career that he had.

Ian Roper made his debut that season and was there as backup to Adi and Derek. Many people would have looked at him, thought him cumbersome and overweight, and showed him the door. But Chris Nicholl saw something in him. He worked hard with 'Ropes' and turned him into an excellent defender, which shows that you can mould players if you give them time and attention. We had several other young players coming through at that time, such as Martin Butler, who went on to become a fine striker, and Dean Keates, who looked after my boots. He was a Walsall boy through and through.

The aim that season was to consolidate our place in Division Two after having won promotion. We achieved that and went on a decent run in the FA Cup as well. We drew Burnley away in the first round, which was always a tough place to go. It was 1-1 at half-time, but we went in front after the break and then I got the winner. Darren Bradley played a long pass forward which put me one-on-one with the full-back, who I then went around and scored. Next up were Torquay United, and we were drawn away from home again. We went 1-0 down in the first half from a free kick that got deflected off me. The gaffer wasn't best pleased about it, to put it mildly, and made his thoughts known at half-time. That led to a skirmish which pretty much became a 14-man brawl. But that was just one of those things that would happen back then. Passions were running high, Chris wanted to make an impact, and if that was what it took to get a result, then so be it. Nobody got injured.

Anyway, we got an equaliser in the second half and earned a replay back at the Bescot Stadium, which proved to be the craziest game that I ever played in. Kyle Lightbourne was recovering from an injury, so he started on the substitutes' bench, while Martin O'Connor was pushed up from midfield to partner Kevin Wilson in attack. Martin could do that because he had absolutely everything. He was strong, quick, could head, could pass and was an extremely consistent performer. Like myself, he arrived at Walsall as a bit of a misfit. He had previously been at Crystal Palace, but it hadn't quite worked out for him there. He was probably the best footballer I ever played with throughout my career, and he'll always be 'Skip' to me. I just can't speak highly enough of him. He wasn't too good on a stretcher though, but that's another thing!

Skip had a hand in our first goal that night, laying the ball off to Chris Marsh, who then tricked a defender with his infamous stepover before firing a shot between his legs that bobbled past the goalkeeper. I loved that stepover. 'Marshy' was 'Mr Popularity' in the dressing room, so no one was bothered about him doing his party trick now and then. We would only give him a hard time if he fell over while doing it! Marshy was a good all-rounder and he scored a lot of goals from the right wing in the two seasons I was at Walsall. He and I would work in conjunction on the wings, so if I was marked man-to-man that would usually free up some space on the other side of the pitch and Marshy would make good use of it. That would usually throw the opposition, and I would often get a bit more freedom from then on.

Torquay equalised about ten minutes before half-time when a deflected shot deceived Wacka, and so it was all square at the break. Chris Nicholl was always constructive in the dressing room. He would tell us where we were going wrong and how we could improve, though you knew you'd have to buck your ideas up if he gave you 'the look', or else you'd be sat next to him in ten minutes' time. He certainly wasn't happy with us at the start of the second half. Wacka had to make two good saves just to keep the scores level, and then he conceded a goal when he came off his line to punch a corner away but didn't get there in time. Thankfully, we managed to get back into the game five minutes later when Kevin Wilson got on to the end of a free kick and flicked the ball past the goalkeeper.

Kev was another of those players in the squad who had played at a higher level and was coming towards the end of his career. He kept himself immensely fit and was a tremendous professional. Kev was probably the key to my success at Walsall as he was adept at holding up the ball before playing it out to me on the wing. When I was at Spurs, my coach would always tell me to play off the front man. That's all well and good but there's nothing worse for a winger than waiting ten minutes to get the ball, playing it up to the striker and then watch him lose it. It was soul-destroying. But it wasn't like that with Kev as he had an incredible first touch. When you passed the ball up to him, he would keep it before playing it back out again, either into midfield or wide on to the wings. Arguably, Kev made that Walsall team tick.

Unfortunately, it wasn't long before Torquay went back in front again. They scored another goal from a corner, and that was probably the catalyst for Chris Nicholl bringing Kyle Lightbourne on. That substitution restored the normal balance of the team as 'Killer' went into attack, while Skip dropped back into the centre of midfield where he normally played. The player that made way for Killer was John Keister, who was a fearless little lad. John was only about 3ft 4in tall and made me feel like a giant! His tackling was legendary, though even he would admit he wasn't the greatest of footballers. Most times his first touch would end up with a throw-in for the opposition. However, John wasn't in the team for what he could do with the ball. He was there to break up play, win the ball and pass it on to someone more creative. John knew his limitations and did a great job for the team.

It didn't take long for Killer to make an impact. Within a few minutes of coming on he played a delightful little pass to Darren Bradley, who raced into the penalty area before lofting the ball into the roof of the net. 'Bradders' was a fine midfielder whose passing ability was second to none, particularly over long distances. Defenders can always get close when a team is making short passes, but if you've got someone who can hit a ball accurately over 50 yards or so then you can run at the opposition, which was great for a winger like me. The score stayed at 3-3 for a while and we were preparing for extra time when Torquay nearly finished us off. The ball came across our penalty area and one of their players fired it past Wacka, only for it to hit one post, roll across the goal line, hit the other post and then bounce out to safety. There comes a time when your luck is in, and ours was clearly in that night. That incident happened well into stoppage time, so if they had scored, we wouldn't even have had time to kick off again.

Torquay had been in front three times in the tie – once in the first game and twice in the replay – but we finally overpowered them in the first period of extra time. We scored three goals in five minutes and they just had no answer to that. The first was a good volley by Marshy after he got on to the end of a cross from Killer, while I had a hand in the second. Skip played a ball out to me on the wing and I raced shoulder to shoulder with the full-back for 30 yards or so, tussling with him before crossing the ball into the penalty area. Killer tapped it in at the far post, getting the glory after all my hard work! Skip scored the next goal, racing out from midfield, taking the ball around the goalkeeper and then sliding it into an empty net.

Inevitably, given the type of game it was, Torquay soon got a goal back. They scored from yet another corner, but we weren't to be denied. Three minutes later I finally got my name on the scoresheet, cutting in from the left-hand side and hitting a shot with my right foot that went past the full-back and bent away from the goalkeeper at the far post. That was something I had practised since I was 16 years old and it was a bit of a trademark for me. It worked because I was two-footed and so could either go to the left of the defender and put in a cross with my left foot, or else cut inside and shoot with my right. That goal came in the 104th minute, which was quite something for me as I usually ran out of steam after 60!

I should have had a second just before the end of the game, but Killer nipped in as I was about to tap the ball into the net. But that's strikers for you, they just love scoring goals. Killer formed a great partnership with Kevin Wilson and the two of them scored over 80 goals between them in the two years I was at Walsall. Looking back, the fact that we scored five goals in extra time reflects well on our fitness and on how hard we trained. Clearly, the Torquay boys just couldn't last the pace like we could. I can't pick out any one Walsall player as being any better than the rest that night, but that was how it always was to us. We won as a team and lost as a team. If we won then we were all heroes, and if we lost then we were all the fall guys, which is how it should be.

Chris Nicholl was pleased that we'd won, but he wasn't happy about the four goals we conceded. Clean sheets were everything to him and he prided himself on the work that he did in training with the defence. We finished in 11th place in the league that season but only four teams conceded fewer goals than us, which tells its own story. Saying that, to play in a game in which there were 12 goals was just incredible. The crowds would soon come back if it was 8-4 every week!

Next up in the cup were Wigan Athletic at home. We beat them 1-0 and that earned us an away trip to Ipswich Town in the fourth round. I'd spent two months there on loan in 1991, when John Lyall was the manager. They wanted to sign me but couldn't agree a fee with Spurs, so nothing more came of it. I was fond of the club and really wanted to go back there and do well. Unfortunately, I had a poor game by my standards and was substituted midway through the second half. We eventually lost the game by a goal to nil, which was disappointing as we were a good team and quite capable of beating Ipswich on our day.

At the end of that season I left Walsall for Peterborough, which I regret doing now. However, I had good reason to go at the time as we were so poorly paid at Walsall. In fact, I had mates who were working on building sites that earned more than me. When we got promoted a year earlier all I got was a £25 rise in my weekly wage. I had two young kids and a mortgage and life was a struggle at times. I used to have to borrow money from my grandad to make ends meet, which I didn't like doing as I'm a proud man. I must say, though, that I could often be my own worst enemy. I still went out boozing from time to time and was frivolous with what little money I had. Barry Fry offered me an increase which was almost double what I was getting at Walsall, though I would have stayed if they'd paid me just a little bit more. It's a shame that's what it came down to in the end, but I needed to pay the bills and stop taking money from my family.

I stayed in the game for another six years and by 2002 was playing for Stevenage Borough in the Football Conference. By that stage I wasn't enjoying my football any more; I was just picking up money for the sake of it and my legs had gone. The police were advertising for officers, and I thought they could give me the self-discipline that I had lacked throughout my football career. My application was successful, and I've never looked back. It's a hard job, but it can be rewarding, particularly when you see lads that have got themselves into trouble become rehabilitated. Working in the police keeps me on the straight and narrow, just as Chris Nicholl helped me to do all those years ago. I am still very fond of the Saddlers and am thankful to the club, players and supporters for the wonderful two years I spent there.

CHRIS MARSH

Chris Marsh

Defender, Midfielder, Striker (and Occasional Goalkeeper), 1986–2001

Not many footballers can boast of a career that spans three decades at one club like Chris Marsh can. He was signed as a trainee by Alan Buckley in 1986, experienced the highs and lows of the Tommy Coakley era and then the dark days under John Barnwell and Kenny Hibbitt. That was followed by Chris Nicholl's enlightened renaissance, the curious Jan Sorensen interregnum, and finally the glory years of Ray Graydon that stretched into the new millennium. It was certainly not a dull time to be a Saddlers player, with Marsh witnessing three promotions and three relegations during that period.

A native of Sedgley, Chris Marsh was one of the handful of players who graced both Fellows Park and the Bescot Stadium. He played for Walsall in three different divisions of the Football League and looked comfortable at every level. Opportunities to play at the very top of the English game came and went, but one suspects that he wouldn't have embarrassed himself had one of the big clubs taken a punt on him.

The depth of Chris Marsh's talent was demonstrated by his ability to play in almost every position in the team. At various times in his career he was a striker, a midfielder, a defender and, when circumstances demanded, even a goalkeeper. The phrase 'Jack of all trades, master of none' simply didn't apply to him, for he looked at home wherever he played. Except perhaps, it must be said, in goal.

During Chris Marsh's time at the club, no trip to watch the Saddlers would be complete until you'd seen him do his stepover; a party trick that the fans knew was coming but the opposition never seemed to. His time with Walsall came to a premature end in 2001, when he left for Wycombe Wanderers after playing nearly 500 games for the club. It was a sad loss, and for some time afterwards fans would walk into the ground on matchdays and instinctively feel that something was missing. Chris Marsh had gone, but he would never, ever be forgotten.

ADI VIVEASH

Adi Viveash
Central defender, 1995–2000

They say that the best things in life are free, and that's certainly true when it comes to Walsall's acquisition of Adi Viveash. He started his career at hometown club Swindon Town in 1986, spending nine years there before being deemed to be surplus to requirements. Walsall FC know a good deal when they see it and it didn't cost them a penny to sign the released player. Viveash made his way up the M5 and into Saddlers folklore, with the West Country's loss undoubtedly becoming the Black Country's gain.

Viveash went straight into Walsall's first team and remained a fixture there for five memorable seasons. He made an immediate impact, winning Walsall's player of the season award in both his first and second years with the club. Viveash's first manager was Chris Nicholl: a hard taskmaster who knew from personal experience what it took to be a top centre-half. The fact that Viveash was rarely out of his side tells its own story.

Adi Viveash was one of those relatively unique figures in English football: a central defender who was just as comfortable spraying long cross-field passes as he was scything down opponents and thumping the ball away with his head. A master of the dead-eyed stare, Viveash was an uncomfortably fierce presence on a football pitch. Indeed, it was never quite clear who was most afraid of him: opposing strikers, or team-mates who didn't give their all.

The undoubted highpoint of his time with Walsall was the promotion he helped to win during Ray Graydon's first year in charge. The step up to Division One football was a tough one for the club and no one fought harder than Viveash to keep them there. His call to arms, complete with clenched fists and lung-bursting roars, remains the stuff of legend. Even though Viveash knew he would be moving back home to the West Country after the end of the season, he never stopped giving his all for the Saddlers. Sadly, his last game for the club ended with the confirmation of relegation, but never once was his ardour diminished. Walsall's very own 'Braveheart' remained defiant until the end.

Walsall 3 – 1 Oldham Athletic

Football League Division Two
Saturday, 1 May 1999
Bescot Stadium, Walsall
Attendance: 9,184

Walsall	Oldham Athletic
Jimmy Walker	Gary Kelly
Chris Marsh	Scott McNiven (Matthew Tipton)
Neil Pointon	Andy Holt
Nick Henry	Shaun Garnett
Adi Viveash	Stuart Thom
Ian Roper	Lee Duxbury
Darren Wrack	Mark Allott
Rob Steiner (Siggi Eyjolfsson)	John Sheridan
Andy Rammell (Richard Green)	Paul Beavers (Ryan Sugden)
Dean Keates (Bjarni Larusson)	Paul Rickers
Jason Brissett	Paul Reid

Managers

Ray Graydon	Andy Ritchie

Scorers

Darren Wrack (22)	Lee Duxbury (56)
Chris Marsh (34)	
Siggi Eyjolfsson (76)	

Referee

Rob Styles

Chris Marsh: I had some great times in my 15 years at Walsall and have lots of wonderful memories, particularly of playing at places like Old Trafford, Maine Road and Stamford Bridge. However, my most memorable match was when the Saddlers beat Oldham Athletic to win promotion in 1999. It was the third time I'd been part of a promotion-winning side at Walsall. The first came over a decade earlier when the club beat Bristol City in the final of the Division Three play-offs. When we played the first leg at Ashton Gate, I was one of the two apprentices that took the skips down. We won that game 3-1 and only needed a draw at Fellows Park in order to go up. In fact, even a 1-0 defeat would have been fine.

Before the second leg, Tommy Coakley asked me if I was up for being on the bench, to which my reply, unsurprisingly, was 'Yeah!!!' Unfortunately, we lost 2-0 and I didn't get on to the pitch. Tommy came to see me again before the replay, and this time it wasn't good news. He told me he still had faith in me, but it was going to be a big occasion and he wasn't sure whether it would be too much for an 18-year-old. Some of the older players were also fit again after having been injured. He decided to go with experience and the rest is history. David Kelly scored a hat-trick, we won promotion and I have great memories of being in the dressing room that day.

Alan Buckley had signed me as an apprentice in the summer of 1986, two years before that play-off final. Previously, I'd been with the club on schoolboy terms, playing on a Saturday morning in the reserves and then in the Midland Intermediate League. I had arranged to go on holiday before I signed as an apprentice, and the club let me go as I'd already paid for it. The club would never have allowed me to go once I was on their books as it meant missing ten days of pre-season training. So, I went away and when I got back Alan Buckley had been sacked and Tommy Coakley had been unveiled as the new manager. It was all a bit unsettling, given that I was 16 and had only just joined the club.

Tommy Coakley turned out to be great for me. He gave me my debut a couple of weeks before my 18th birthday, bringing me on for Nicky Cross in a 5-2 home victory over Rotherham United. Nicky had just scored a hat-trick, and understandably wasn't very happy at being taken off. I'd only been on the pitch for a few seconds when Phil Hawker played the ball upfield to Willie Naughton, who held it up, swivelled and put a cross into the middle. David Kelly went as if to hit the ball but dummied it, and it came to me instead. I trapped the ball, cut inside the defender and hit it past the goalkeeper with my left foot. Trevor Christie was standing in an offside position and had seen that I was going to hit the ball. He started running back, but it was too late. The 'goal' was ruled out for offside, though it would be given these days as Trevor wasn't interfering with play in any way. It would have been the fastest-ever debut goal at the time, so it was heart-breaking for it to be disallowed. But, at the same time, it was just great to be on the pitch and to be involved in such incidents. I remember thinking, 'I *love* this!'

I started out as a striker but ended up playing all over the pitch. I could kick with both feet, so I played left-back, right-back, left-wing, right-wing, central midfield and even as an emergency centre-half. The club loved my versatility, but presumably only because it saved them money! I enjoyed filling in all over the pitch, and it did help me to learn the game more thoroughly, but with hindsight it probably held me back a little as it prevented me from focusing on playing in one position.

I even played in goal three times for Walsall. Every now and then I used to join in Mick Kearns's goalkeeping training sessions, telling him how easy it was, just to wind him up. He'd get his own back by working me really hard. Goalkeeping training is genuinely tough; all that getting down and getting back up again soon wears you out. Anyway, after a while, Mick told me I wasn't all that bad a keeper and that I could do a job in goal, if it was needed. I should have known better because I got called on eventually.

I remember going in goal away at Northampton Town after Jimmy Walker got clattered. 'Wacka' didn't know what day it was and so had to go off. We ended up losing that game 3-2, but my worst experience was at home to Barnsley in 2000. We were fighting to avoid relegation from Division One and really needed the points, so it was a huge blow when Wacka got sent off after about ten minutes. We didn't have a goalkeeper on the bench, so it was me again. I really didn't fancy going in goal that day. It's hard enough at the best of times, but we were playing against a good side with only ten men and were up against it. At times like that you start thinking: 'Why does it always have to be me? Can't it be someone else for a change?' You can get away with things in training, but it's different in a real game. Playing in goal is hard, and against Barnsley I just wanted it to be over as soon as possible. We ended up losing that match 4-1, and thankfully I was never called on to be a goalkeeper again.

We got promoted a few months after I made my debut and then spent the following campaign playing teams like

Chelsea, Leeds United and Manchester City. I was only a young kid and I thought it was going to be like that all the time. I didn't expect us to get relegated twice on the bounce! That was a good learning curve for me, a real wake-up call. Tommy Coakley went and then John Barnwell came in, but he didn't fancy me at all. I was in and out of the side and he wasn't prepared to offer me a new contract. Then, one Friday night, we played against Tranmere Rovers and had so many injuries that John had no choice other than to put me in the team. Their best player was a great little winger called John Morrissey and I played against him at left-back. I marked him out of the game, which pleased the gaffer, so I got a bit of a run in the side after that, as well as a two-year contract.

There's a lot of luck in football and I could easily have gone out of the game at that point in my career. I always thought I was a good player, but different managers have different styles and sometimes your face just doesn't fit. Stan Collymore was an apprentice at Walsall at the same time as me, but he got released and it was only when he went to Stafford Rangers that he blossomed. He went on to play for Liverpool, and three years after almost being shown the door by John Barnwell I nearly signed for them myself. Like everything else in life, you need a bit of luck now and again.

Adi Viveash: I joined Walsall in 1995 from Swindon Town. I had been there since leaving school, was in my mid-twenties and at the peak of my career. Unfortunately, I couldn't agree a new contract with the club and so had to go on a week-to-week deal. Some Division One teams came in for me during the summer, but I couldn't get anything sorted out. Then, in October, Steve McMahon, who was the manager at the time, called me in and said that the club was letting me go. My son was only a few months old at the time and I'd got a mortgage to pay, so it was hardly great news. By that point in the season all the clubs had got their squads sorted out and I remember thinking that I was done for. Graham Roberts, the ex-Spurs centre-half, was manager of Yeovil Town and he offered me a joint player and community officer role. Even though they were a non-league club back then, I was seriously considering that option, or else signing on the dole. Then I got a call from Walsall.

Chris Nicholl was the Walsall manager and he asked me to play in a trial game at the Bescot Stadium. They mixed the sides up and I played centre-back against Kyle Lightbourne and Martin Butler. My team won 2-0 and I kicked both of them into the stands. Darren Bradley was on my side in that game and he gave those two some real stick afterwards, telling them they never got a kick, which they hadn't! I signed a one-month deal and my third game for Walsall was a 2-0 away victory over Bristol City. The club took me on until the end of the season after that match, and then I signed a longer deal in the summer.

To be honest, I wasn't Chris Nicholl's ideal type of centre-half. He wanted his defenders to be big and strong and make tackles, so I gave him that, but I played a bit too much for his liking. Whenever I started spraying passes around, he would just ask me what I was in the team for. Clearly, he didn't think it was for that. He thought it was a bit risky for central defenders to start playing football, so we had a bit of a love/hate relationship in many ways.

Nevertheless, Chris Nicholl undoubtedly improved me as a defender. He taught me how to handle myself as a centre-half, to understand where my space was on the pitch and how not to let strikers invade my territory. The gaffer was very skilled in the art of defending and was forever making me play head tennis against him. Chris Nicholl was one of the top 50 tennis players in the country for his age and so knew all the angles. He had a good touch for a big guy and would completely tie you in knots.

One thing Chris Nicholl demanded of us was that we didn't concede a goal in the final 15 minutes of a game. If we ever did, he would make us run for miles the following week. It didn't matter if the goal should have never been given; that had no impact on him at all. He would simply say that his teams didn't let in goals in the last 15 minutes, and that was that. It certainly made the players switch on and focus towards the end of a game. Indeed, I remember whenever we played away, you'd always look for where the scoreboard was and then keep an eye on the time. Psychologically, it was a very shrewd move.

Chris Nicholl left in 1997 and then Jan Sorensen came in, though he only lasted for one season. I was on holiday the following summer, painting my lounge, having just moved to a house in Worcester. The phone rang and at the other end of the line was a voice I didn't recognise, though he had a West Country burr like myself. He asked whether he was speaking to Adrian. I thought that was rather formal as only my mother, God rest her soul, ever called me that. So, I replied that this was Adi and the mystery voice simply asked again whether I was Adrian. Reluctantly, I relented and said yes, and then he announced that he was my new manager, Ray Graydon. I offered him my congratulations but before I could catch my breath, he asked me where I lived and how far I was from the ground. I told him I was half an hour away and he instructed me to be there within the hour. And then he put the phone down. I was absolutely livid!

Anyway, I drove up to the Bescot Stadium and Ray Graydon was waiting there for me, wearing a shirt, tie, blazer and shoes you could see your face in. He looked me up and down and told me he'd given me an hour so that I could get changed, which I deliberately hadn't done. In fact, I still had paint on my face. Clearly, this wasn't the look he was after from his players. He then explained that he was getting some of the senior players in and wanted to hear what we had to say. We talked for an hour, but it was one of those conversations where we discussed things and then agreed that he was right and would do things his way. Ray then started going through some of his rules, and I thought I'd joined the army. It was obvious that it was going to be a strict regime, though that was probably what was needed, compared to how things had been under Jan. Ray Graydon was evidently a man who meant business.

Ray was particularly keen that players kept on the right side of referees. He fined us for getting booked in matches and was just as strict in training. If a decision was made, you had to get straight back into position and there was no answering back. He would even go and see referees after a game and ask what we'd been like, taking great pride if he was told that we'd been exemplary. Being on the other side of the game now I can see that Ray was trying to avoid losing players through suspension, which can happen if you get silly bookings. We only had a squad of 15 or 16 first-choice players, and then it was either kids or players who were Division Three level. It was a bit infuriating for me though, as I couldn't make sly little kicks at opponents any more. He certainly moulded those out of my game.

***

Chris Marsh: For Ray Graydon, backchatting the referee was the worst sin you could commit on the pitch. He would frown on you getting booked for tackling someone hard, or catching them too high, but talking back to an official would cost you a week's wages. It was in your contract, so he could do you for it if he wanted to. It meant that you soon learned to bite your tongue as Walsall never paid enough money for you to be able to lose any of it. Back then, I couldn't see the logic of what he was trying to do, but I can now. Once a referee has made a decision, you're never going to turn it by arguing with him. You're better off walking away and maybe next time, if it's a 50-50 decision, he will sway towards the side that gives him less grief.

It was a very regimented regime under Ray Graydon. We had to wear a suit, collar and tie, just to go into training. We also had to be clean-shaven, and we'd be fined if we weren't. Swearing wasn't allowed either. He kept a very close eye on our weight as well. At the start of the season, he decided how much he thought each of us should weigh, and then he got the scales out every Monday and we had to hit the target he'd set. He docked £10 from our wages for every pound we were overweight, which might not sound much but it soon added up, particularly as we didn't earn all that much to start with.

I remember one time I'd been out all weekend and knew I was going to be way over my target when Ray got the scales out. There was a hotel near the ground, and we had free membership of their facilities, which included a sauna. So, at six o'clock on Monday morning, I went in to sweat some of the pounds off. I sat down, and as the mist cleared, I realised I was not on my own. 'Morning, Marshy' said a voice. It turned out to be 'Wacka', and Ian Roper was in there as well! Poor 'Ropes' always struggled to meet his weight because Ray had set it way too low. He got fined a fortune and I eventually had to get involved as I was the PFA representative for the club. They helped me to sort it out, but it took a lot for Ray to agree to increase Ropes's target to something that was reasonable.

I'd already come across Ray Graydon before he took over as Walsall manager. He was pals with Chris Nicholl and the gaffer used to bring him in now and again to do some coaching sessions with us. Ray was one hell of a coach, but we had no inkling of what he'd be like as a manager. For his first pre-season, he took us on a tour of Scotland. Normally we'd have 25 to 30 players on a trip like that, with trialists coming in as well, but we barely had enough to make up a team. In one of the games Wacka came on to play in midfield in the second half; that's how bad it was. The bookies had Walsall as favourites to go down, and to be honest, at that point in time, we agreed with them. It didn't help that there were some really big clubs in Division Two that season, such as Manchester City, Kevin Keegan's Fulham and Stoke City.

One of the players that left us early on during that season was Jeff Peron. I've played with some great footballers at Walsall over the years, like Willie Naughton, Martin O'Connor and Craig Shakespeare, but Jeff was the best of the lot. He was an outstanding talent. Preparation was everything for him, and we'd often take the mickey when we saw him eating apples and bananas in the dressing room. We'd ask what he was doing, and he'd tell us that was what they did in France. He just couldn't believe it when we went down to the pub. To be fair, that was why we were finished at 32 and he was still playing at 40!

Things began to settle down as Ray started to bring new players in, slowly adding in different pieces of the jigsaw. One of the new arrivals was Andy Rammell. By his own admission, 'Rams' hadn't been a regular goalscorer during his career, but he was a great target man and scored plenty of goals for us. Richard Green was also brought in to play in central defence. He was one of those hard players you want in your side; the sort that would kick his own grandmother to win the ball. I remember him going right through people, even in training. Another experienced recruit was Neil Pointon, a left-back who'd played for Everton and Manchester City. I learned a lot from him, and he was a great lad to have around. For one of his birthdays he took all the players and their wives to Manchester for a slap-up meal at a Chinese restaurant. There was even a singing Elvis! He also booked us all into hotels, which was an incredible gesture and sums up what kind of guy he was.

Adi Viveash: Ray's decision to bring in several experienced players was vital to the success we had that season. Walsall only had a small squad, which meant that youngsters such as Dean Keates, Ian Roper and Michael Ricketts had to be developed through the season. You need to have good role models if you're going to integrate young players into a team, and the players Ray brought in were perfect for that. To get Neil Pointon on a free transfer, even though he was in his mid-30s, was a masterstroke. He had bags of experience, a wand of a left foot and he brought a lot of calmness to the team. It wasn't just about what those players did on the pitch, however; it was also about what they contributed off it. The new players bought into the togetherness we had in the squad straight away, though they must have wondered what was going on when we could barely put a full team out in that pre-season tour of Scotland. There were also people at the club who had been there a long time, such as Marshy and Wacka; they knew what the club was about, and they helped the new players to understand its identity. The camaraderie amongst the players that season was exceptional. If we went out, then everyone went. Not a single player missed anything we did. We all bonded and had a genuine affinity with the club, and that can take you a long way.

Things changed very quickly under Ray, compared to what they had been like when Jan Sorensen was in charge. Jan gave us the freedom to play and encouraged us to attack, which made us into a brilliant cup team. The 2-0 FA Cup victory over Peterborough United, which got us a game at Old Trafford, was as good a Walsall performance as I was ever involved in. But, over 46 league games, we just weren't good enough. In fact, we should have gone down that season. Ray's approach was very different. We worked on team structure and shape every day in training, as well as on roles and responsibilities. He drilled what we had to do into each of us and left us under no illusions that he would bring others into the team if we didn't do what he expected. There was always someone ready to take your place if you didn't follow Ray's instructions to the letter.

Ray was massive on the details. He worked with each unit of the team separately and covered everything that could possibly happen in a game. He coached us on how he wanted us to defend in wide areas, how to defend from throw-ins, how to take throw-ins and how to move the ball from one side of the pitch to the other. It so became second nature to us that at any point during a game everyone knew where they had to be on the pitch. It took a huge amount of strength and determination for Ray to achieve that. The only others I've worked with who were also able to do it were Glenn Hoddle at Swindon Town and Alan Pardew at Reading. They both went on to become Premier League managers, which shows just what a good coach Ray was.

As good as Ray's work on the training ground was, it was getting results that made the players really buy into what he was doing. Once you start winning matches regularly and experienced players like Neil Pointon start to endorse the gaffer's methods, everyone else soon follows suit. Our first game of the season was away to Gillingham. They had Tony Pulis in charge, had spent a bit of money and were one of the favourites to win promotion. We defended really well as a team, kept our structure and there was a lot of pride in the shirt that day. Gillingham had a few opportunities but Wacka made some great saves and we nicked a 1-0 win. That match really set the tone for the rest of the season as we put in a lot of similar performances after that.

Chris Marsh: I remember that game against Gillingham because we won it with an own goal that I tried to claim! I pumped the ball into the penalty area from the halfway line and their centre-half jumped up to head it away. Unfortunately for him, it skimmed off the top of his head and looped into the back of the net. We didn't play that well, but we scrapped for a result and came away with a 1-0 win. I've played at Gillingham quite a few times since then, but I don't think I've ever won there again. We got a draw in the next game, followed by another couple of wins, momentum slowly started to build, and then we really got going.

The players that Walsall had that season were nowhere near as good as those that the likes of Manchester City and Fulham could field. If you look at the team that started against Oldham, I don't think the club paid a transfer fee for any of us. We either came through the youth system, like me, Dean Keates and Ian Roper, were loan players, or else came in on free transfers. But what we did have was an incredible team spirit. We often went on days out, doing things such as go-karting and the like, and it's amazing how little things like that brought us together. We fought for each other in games, worked as a team and scraped 1-0 wins, which was what got us promoted that season. I know it's a cliché, but if I was going to war, it would be those guys that I'd want with me. They would be up and over the trenches and fighting. We loved each other like brothers.

Wacka got the club's player of the season award, but to be fair half a dozen of the team could have won it that year. Neil Pointon was knocking on a bit, but he had real quality, while Adi Viveash and Ian Roper were outstanding in the centre of defence. 'Ropes' often didn't get the credit he deserved as people looked at him and just thought he was a big lump. He was surprisingly quick and would win everything in the air. I never enjoyed playing against him in training.

Darren Wrack joined us at the start of the season, and he was a talented player. He scored a lot of goals for a winger and was an excellent crosser of the ball. We played together on the right-hand side of the pitch and our partnership developed really quickly. Ray devised this system where 'Wracky' attacked on the wing and I had licence to go and help him. The two centre-halves and the other full-back would then come around and keep a solid defensive line. It was a very attack-minded approach as it enabled one of the central midfielders, the other winger and the two strikers to get into the penalty area when the cross came in. If the pass got intercepted, then we had a regimented approach for quickly getting back into position. It was a really difficult system for other teams to play against.

Nick Henry was like a little machine in midfield, while Dean Keates was always busy, getting around people and snapping at their heels. I often like to remind 'Keatesy' that he was my boot boy when he started out! Jason Brissett played out on the left-wing and had a lot of pace. Ray liked 'Briss', but he had to put his foot down with him a few times as he got sent off three times that season. Andy Rammell led the line well and formed a good partnership with Rob Steiner when he came in on loan towards the end of the season. I remember Rob's first training session because he quickly fell foul of Ray's 'no swearing' rule. Breaking it cost you a fiver every time and Rob was cursing throughout that session. He must have lost about £85 that day!

Adi Viveash: Andy Rammell was a great front man for us that season, though he had to play alongside a succession of different strikers. First it was Briss, who was an exceptionally gifted footballer, and then it was Walter Otta, Andy Watson, Colin Cramb, Rob Steiner and Siggi Eyjolfsson. Looking back, that was clearly the one position in the team where Ray was looking for the missing ingredient. Those forwards were different types of players and had quite diverse skill sets, so Ray did well to integrate each of them into the team and ensure they knew what they had to do. That process was made a bit more difficult by the fact that some of them came from abroad and weren't all that familiar with the English game. Walter was an Argentinean, for example, while Rob was Swedish and Siggi came from Iceland. I suppose Ray kept trying alternatives because he was looking for the right balance in his team. To be fair to him, he wasn't afraid to keep looking until he found what he wanted. Nevertheless, we had goals throughout the team that season, with Marshy flying in from right-back and Wracky scoring goals from the wing. That meant we always felt we could get something out of a tight game, and it would come from within the structure Ray constructed for us.

Walsall had a great defence that season, and Wacka was a big part of it. He was agile, calm and quick on his feet, though what really marked him out was his ability to make incredible saves in key moments in big games. But it wasn't all about the saves. Wacka's kicking was excellent and he could pick out Andy Rammell with a pass every time. There just weren't any weak areas in his game, though he could have done with being a few pounds lighter! But, to be fair to him, there weren't many of his height who could do what he did as a goalkeeper. That was why he went on to sign for some big clubs later in his career.

My partners in central defence were either Ropes or Richard Green. Ropes and I both made our Walsall debuts in a match against Fulham, and I enjoyed coaxing him through his early games. He was quiet and shy off the pitch, but a real warhorse on it. Ropes was one of those old-fashioned types of centre-half who would do whatever it took to keep the ball away from our goal. Saddlers fans just loved his wholehearted approach to thc gamc. I'll never forget them cheering him on as he raced down the channel with an opposing striker before cleaning him out with a last-ditch tackle. Ropes went on to become a Walsall legend, and rightly so. The only thing that stopped him from playing at the highest level was that his distribution of the ball wasn't as good as that of the best centre-halves.

It was Chris Nicholl who gave Ropes his debut, and he absolutely loved Ropes to bits. In fact, we used to call Ropes 'number-one son', because that was what he was to Chris! I think he saw a lot of himself in Ropes, which is why he gave him his chance. The only time Chris ever criticised him was when he tried to play. I still remember Chris shouting in training: 'Ropes! Know what you are, son!' I think Chris was really proud of the work that he did with Ropes, and so he should be. He made him into an outstanding centre-half.

Richard Green was one of the hardest players I ever met. Like Ropes, he was quiet and reserved off the pitch, but a strong and aggressive character on it. If you ran into him, it was like hitting granite; strikers would just bounce off him. 'Greeny' was calm on the ball, could use it well and was a better footballer than many people gave him credit for. We'd play the game quite differently, depending on whether Ropes or Greeny was alongside me. We could defend higher up the pitch if Ropes was in the team, as he had youth and pace and could protect the space behind us. If it was me and Greeny then we had to give ourselves another ten yards, using our experience to keep us out of trouble. Ray would always work it out in advance and make sure that we knew exactly what we had to do, depending on who was playing.

The momentum built through the season, but we never got ahead of ourselves. We only ever took it one game at a time. Even after losing 3-1 away to Manchester City and getting spanked 4-1 at Fulham, we just kept going. The only big disappointment that season was losing in the Southern Area Final of the Football League Trophy to Millwall. It was heart-breaking at the time because we missed out on going to Wembley, and you don't know if you're going to get a chance to play there during your career. It would have been a great experience and I don't think it would have distracted us from trying to win promotion. We would have needed to fit another league game in at the back end of the season, but that wouldn't have been a problem. We were playing too well to allow ourselves to become destabilised by a big day out.

Chris Marsh: I was lucky because I got to play at most of the big stadiums with Walsall, but one of my biggest regrets is that I never got to Wembley. Three times in my career I was 90 minutes away from playing there, and each time it didn't happen. It was gutting to lose to Millwall and the memory of it haunts me even now, because we nearly won. But, with the benefit of hindsight, it might have been for the best that we lost, as far as the league campaign was concerned. If we had beaten them, it would have been the club's first-ever trip to Wembley. A lot would have been made of that, which perhaps could have resulted in us taking our eyes off the ball a bit.

The moment we realised that promotion really could happen was when we beat Lincoln City away from home, a week prior to the game against Oldham. I was suspended for that match and spent most of it in the bar, as those were the days when you could have a drink or two if you weren't playing. We didn't have to do any running after the game like they do now. There was a lot of excitement because we were going for promotion, not that I needed much of an excuse to have a beer! Wracky got a goal about 20 minutes from the end, and then we hung on for the win. Just as importantly, our main rivals for promotion, Manchester City, surprisingly lost at home to Wycombe Wanderers. Suddenly, we were in dreamland; promotion was only one win away.

After the game finished, I rushed down to the dressing room to give everyone the good news about Manchester City losing. Unfortunately, I was that drunk I could hardly get my words out, and all the lads were laughing at me. When you come off the pitch, you often get fans telling you that so-and-so has won, while others are saying they have lost, so you never know what has really happened. That was why the lads wanted to hear the news from the horse's mouth, even if it was a pissed horse's mouth! When I finally managed to tell them the score from Maine Road, the reaction was incredible. It was a big moment for us. After weeks of ifs, buts and maybes, promotion was within our grasp. We knew we'd never get a better chance to go up, so the coach journey back home that night was something special.

Adi Viveash: That was a tough game against Lincoln. We were away from home; it was a horrible pitch and they were battling to avoid relegation. But Wracky scored a great goal and we won 1-0, which was the 13th time we'd done so that season. It was an incredible record and one that, as a defender, I'm really proud of. When we got back to the dressing room, Ray did his debrief and then Marshy came bouncing in through the door. He flung it open so hard he nearly knocked poor Ray flying! He told us that Manchester City had lost and that was when it really hit home how close promotion was. That was a very special moment, though the senior players did have to calm the others down a bit, reminding them we still had a job to do and that we had a massive week ahead of us.

We had a tremendous following from Walsall at that Lincoln game, and the noise they made after the final whistle was just incredible. The support just grew and grew that season, and I remember how proud the town was of the club. We had a real affinity with the fans and there were a lot of good people involved with the club at the time. We tried to make everyone at Walsall feel important, no matter what job they did, whether it was washing the kits, manning the turnstiles or looking after the pitch. We wanted them to feel that they were part of our success, which of course they were. It was a special time to be at the club, but we knew we had to get it right against Oldham. If we didn't beat them, we would have to defeat Fulham in the next game, or else beat Stoke City on the last day of the season. As it turned out, we didn't win either of those matches.

/// /// ///

Chris Marsh: In the days leading up to the Oldham game, Ray tried to play its importance down, but we knew how crucial it was. If you'd have said at the start of the season that Walsall could win promotion with two games to spare, they'd have put you in a straitjacket. To have our fate in our own hands, in front of our own fans, was unbelievable. But we knew that beating Oldham was our best chance to go up. Fulham were full of quality and could step up if they needed to, which perhaps spurred us on a bit. The overriding feeling amongst the players was that we needed to nail it against Oldham; to make sure of it there and then. We knew it wouldn't be easy, though. They were trying to avoid relegation and so needed the points just as much as we did. Those type of games can often be the tricky ones.

Probably now, being older, I would be anxious about the game. But I wasn't nervous at all back then. My mom and dad came to the match and one of the local radio stations were doing interviews outside the ground. They asked my parents if they were Walsall fans, and so they told them who their son was. Understandably, they were keen to find out how I was feeling about the game, so my mom told them that I'd been playing loud music that morning and was absolutely buzzing. She was right; I was ready, perhaps more ready than for any other match in the whole of my career. I know I'm saying this with the benefit of hindsight, but I couldn't see us failing to win that game. Things had gone right for us that season, and we weren't going to fall at the final hurdle.

Adi Viveash: As soon as I pulled into the car park, I could see it wasn't going to be any ordinary game. At that time on a Saturday afternoon there would normally be around 20 people milling about, but there were hordes of fans everywhere. I was mobbed as I walked into the stadium with my family and immediately felt the weight of the fans' expectations. That can become a hindrance, so when I got inside, I quickly found Tom Bradley and told him how mad it was out there, warning him that it could make the younger players a bit nervous. I do remember seeing some of them coming into the dressing room and thinking that the fans' excitement had already started to overwhelm them a bit. But then it started to settle down, with the usual sort of jokes and banter going on. We were all trying to make it a normal match, but it wasn't. I reckon that was the hardest part of the week for Ray and his staff: trying to play down the game when you can't really.

I went out for the warm-up and it was obvious the Walsall fans were there to party. Oldham were down towards the bottom of the league and still had a bit to do to avoid relegation. I remember looking at their players and they were very focused, so I knew that we had to be ready. For many of us it was the biggest game of our careers, and so we started drawing on the experience of those who had played at the highest level, such as Neil Pointon. Then we went back to the dressing room and there was a spell when it got really quiet. Ray said his last few words, telling us to believe in the process, to remember what we had done to get to this point and that he was proud of us, whatever happened that afternoon. It was a calming talk and he didn't overload us with information that we didn't need. We'd done all the hard work in the week, so there wasn't much more that needed to be said. I then recall standing in the tunnel, waiting to go out, wondering whether it would be our day.

The atmosphere when we walked out on to the pitch was phenomenal; the best I've ever experienced at Walsall. I've been there for other games when the ground has been full, such as the game against Chelsea in the League Cup in 2015, but nothing compares to the noise the fans made that day. I remember that it was bordering on being out of control on the terraces, but I knew it couldn't be like that on the pitch. It didn't help that Oldham started well, while we were a bit nervous. About ten minutes into the game, they had a long throw-in and Andy Rammell was back defending. He won the ball, but it flicked off his head and bounced off our crossbar. I think that was the wake-up call we all needed. It made us realise that we had to forget the euphoria in the ground; we had a job to do.

About 20 minutes into the game, Wracky got the opening goal. He developed a great understanding with Marshy on the right wing that season and scored a lot of times. I'm sure he would say that many of those goals were down to Marshy's movement and the fact that he had the freedom to attack, knowing that Chris could defend one-v-one if he needed to. For that goal, Neil Pointon knocked a long pass forward and Rob Steiner jumped up with the goalkeeper for the ball. The keeper got a hand to the ball but spilled it, and Wracky was on hand to slide it into the net. We started to settle down after that, got our second wind and I felt quite comfortable. The Walsall fans were going barmy and the game was finally going the way that we had felt it would go. I could also see a change in the Oldham players, as the goal had clearly deflated them a bit. Nevertheless, there was still some nervousness as we only had a narrow lead. That changed, of course, after Marshy scored. He'd been telling us all week that he was going to get a goal, but that was not unusual. He said it all the time!

I remember the timing of Marshy's movement as he burst into the penalty area with the ball and just knew he was going to score. To have the calmness to dink it over the goalkeeper, in a game like that, was just incredible. He celebrated like a loon, but you couldn't blame him. Walsall was his club; he'd been there his whole career and it was a big moment for him. I felt very confident once we'd got that two-goal lead as I just couldn't see Oldham scoring twice. But I knew I had to remain composed and think about how I could affect the people around me. We had some excitable players in our team, which can be great in the dressing room, but there are times when you need to be calm as well.

Chris Marsh: I always like to remind people that I scored the goal that sent Walsall up! It started off with Wacka throwing the ball out to me. I hit it down the channel for Wracky to chase, but their defender got there just ahead of him and cleared the ball. It only got as far as Nick Henry, who passed it up to Rob Steiner. He then held the ball up before playing it into my path as I raced forward. It wasn't the greatest of first touches from me and the ball spun a little, but then it sat up a treat and I lifted it over the goalkeeper as he came rushing out. Even though I say so myself, it was a good finish. The moment the ball went into the net a wall of noise hit me, and I can still hear it now. All the pressure that had been building up during the week came out as I celebrated the goal, sliding on my knees before being grabbed by Rams and Keatesy. As I got back to my feet, the relief I felt was almost overwhelming. To have a two-goal cushion so early in the game was just phenomenal. It was a wonderful moment that I shall never, ever forget. In fact, it makes me feel brilliant just to think about it now, 20 years later.

Adi Viveash: Ray was on the front foot at half-time, telling us that the game was far from over and that we hadn't played as well as we could. He was worried that if Oldham got one goal back, they could easily get a second, and then it would become a very different kind of match. Ray knew the opposition had nothing to lose and could afford to throw caution to the wind, so he told us to use our experience and manage the game. He was still very calm and consistent in his approach, which was reassuring. If Ray had started shouting and bawling then that wouldn't really have been him, which could have panicked us a little. Despite Ray's warnings, it was still a bit excitable in the dressing room as we all felt that Marshy's goal had put us in the driving seat.

Ray was soon proved right that the game could change, as Oldham pulled a goal back ten minutes into the second half. I remember the Walsall fans going a bit quiet after the goal and I could hear people talking in the crowd. Then suddenly a big cheer went up as they realised that we needed a lift, which we did. Neil Pointon urged us all to keep calm, while Rams was going around the team, trying to settle everyone down. Oldham, meanwhile, wanted to get on with the game, as you do when you're losing and have just got a goal back. The spine of our team was really experienced, however, and we knew how to manage games. For the next few minutes, we did what we had to do, which was going down and buying fouls. We had to take the sting out of the game because Oldham felt they had a bit of momentum. They didn't really, but just the thought that they did made them more dangerous than they actually were.

***

Chris Marsh: Any player will tell you that when you're 2-0 up and you concede a goal, you often fear the worst. But I just didn't have the feeling that was going to happen. I knew we would either score again or else see the game out, because that was the kind of season we'd had. There had been plenty of times in the past when I would have been worrying about us drawing or losing from that position, but not that afternoon. We just dusted ourselves off and went again. I was right to be confident, because with about a quarter of an hour to go Siggi got us another goal. I played the ball up to Briss on the left wing and he then cut it into Siggi, who went one way and then the other before shooting past the goalkeeper. Siggi was a good goalscorer and that was a fine goal. It was all over after that.

***

Adi Viveash: After Siggi got the third goal, I experienced nervous excitement bordering on anger as I tried to get everyone to switch on and concentrate. Then, with about five minutes left to go, there was a break in play, and I turned around to look at the Walsall fans behind the goal we were defending. They were bouncing up and down and it was wonderful to see honest, decent, working-class people getting ready to party. They were good fans who had stuck with their hometown club, and they deserved that moment. Wacka didn't have a clue what was going on and he'd gone into the mode that I'd been in, shouting at everyone to stay focused. I went over and told him to turn around, and when he did his face just lit up. I remember saying to him, 'It's done, mate. Just enjoy it.' You don't get many days like that as a footballer, and so we all savoured those couple of minutes while the game was stopped. If I hadn't told him to turn around, he would have missed that moment.

After that, it was just a case of waiting for the final whistle. The fans felt it was done and we knew it was done. We'd played a lot better that season but had still scored three goals and done enough to win the game. Saying that, it could have turned out differently if Rams's header had gone in and we'd fallen behind to an own goal. Nerves would have crept in, knowing that we had Fulham next, and then the play-offs if we didn't get the points we needed for automatic promotion. Quite often the team that finishes third doesn't manage to go up, and that could have happened to us.

It was pandemonium when the referee blew for full time. I'd never seen so many fans in the ground, so it was a bit unnerving when they all ran on to the pitch! The players didn't care about it too much because they were our fans and we knew they were just there to celebrate. You do have to be careful, though. The fans come at you at such a pace, and there's so many of them, that you can easily get injured. You can jar your neck when they grab and kiss you, which means that you're in all summer when you want to be on holiday. I was lucky because I heard the referee say that he was going to blow the whistle, and so I managed to get down the tunnel pretty quickly. But some of the other players weren't so fortunate; they were out there with no kit on!

Chris Marsh: I never liked it when fans ran on to the pitch at the end of a game as I can get a bit claustrophobic, but we're all different. Wacka would still be out there now, getting held up by the crowd. He absolutely loved it! I'd rather do what we did, which was go up into the directors' box in the stand and celebrate where all the fans can see us. Afterwards, Ray told us that he always knew we would beat Oldham, but I'm not sure he really did. There wasn't one Walsall player who stood out that day but, by the same token, no one played badly either. We just did what we had done all season, which was to follow Ray's instructions to the letter and work hard for each other. We went to the bar afterwards and got hammered, not that I can remember much about it. There was no social media in those days so you could party pretty much however you wanted to.

Adi Viveash: It was a special moment when we were up in the directors' box, with all the lads singing with the fans and pouring champagne over Ray Graydon's head. There are some amazing photos of that celebration, and I've got two of them up in my house. I remember looking out at the fans who were all over the pitch, making an amazing noise, and marvelling at how many of them were there. At times like that your thoughts go to your family and the people you love, because you want to share it with them. That half an hour was special, but it went so quickly and all you're left with afterwards are your memories of it.

Ray spoke to the players in the dressing room, saying how proud he was of us and of what we'd achieved. He reminded us that we had sacrificed a lot that season and that we should be congratulating our families that night, because he would be. Ray was quite emotional and let his guard down a bit, which was a big thing for me as he was normally a very disciplined, restrained, reserved man. I remember that at one point we were all sat down in the dressing room, taking a breath and looking around at each other saying, 'Wow! We've actually done it!' Nobody had given us a prayer at the start of the season, but to win promotion and push Manchester City into the play-offs was simply astounding. Arguably, that was as good a Walsall team as there has ever been. It just showed what can be achieved with togetherness, buying into the manager's ethic, executing his plans faithfully and sticking to your guns. Ray deserves enormous credit. He would always have been regarded as a Saddlers legend after winning that promotion, but then he managed to do it again!

The players stayed at a local hotel that night and many of us were still celebrating in the early hours of the morning. We would be going up against Fulham in a few days' time, but that wasn't really at the forefront of our minds. My overriding emotion was one of relief, plus a sense of pride in what had been achieved. Promotion was the culmination of a lot of hard work, but what really mattered was that I'd done it alongside people I liked. It's certainly up there with everything else I've been lucky enough to achieve in the game. You think those sorts of moments are going to happen a lot, but they don't, and sadly many players go through their whole careers without experiencing what we did that day.

Chris Marsh: I can fully understand why Ray Graydon is called 'Sir Ray' by the Saddlers fans. What he achieved at the club was simply phenomenal. The biggest gambler in the world wouldn't have put any money on us at the start of the season to win promotion, but we did, and Ray's hard work was at the root of it. I didn't always see eye to eye with him when I was playing, but we meet up at functions now and again and I have the utmost respect for him. He's easily one of the greatest managers Walsall has ever had.

We went away to Cyprus after the end of the season, and as club captain I was involved in sorting that out. The previous year we drew Peterborough United away in the third round of the FA Cup, but the game was postponed and so we knew we'd be playing Manchester United if we won the rearranged tie. Straight after the draw for the fourth round, the players told me to go and agree what we'd get from the club if we beat Peterborough and played at Old Trafford. They were after a bonus, of course, but what they really wanted was to go to Ayia Napa. I managed to negotiate a decent payday for us, but the players weren't much interested in that; they just wanted to go on tour to Cyprus! Anyway, a few weeks before the Oldham game, I was told to go and ask for another holiday in Ayia Napa if we won promotion. The club were fine about it and we had a whale of a time. Spending a week drinking with your mates when you're in your twenties is great, but we couldn't do it now; we're just too old!

Adi Viveash: I remember the trip to Cyprus at the end of the previous season because Jan Sorensen was sacked on the day we travelled out, which put a bit of a dampener on proceedings. Thankfully, it wasn't like that after we'd won promotion. We had a few lively days in Ayia Napa, swopping stories about games that had stuck in our memories and talking about what we would do in Division One. To play at that level was quite an achievement for a lot of the boys in the team. There were also a few other football teams out there at the same time as us, so there were a lot of people congratulating us on what we'd achieved. It was a nice moment for the lads, and it was well deserved. Having said that, it was also the last time that all of us were together as a group. Some players were getting released, which was quite tough, but that's the way football is: you just have to start again, building the togetherness and team spirit with the new players that come in.

It was disappointing to get relegated the following season, but it was still a phenomenal achievement for us to go into the last game of the season and have a chance of staying up. That away game against Ipswich Town was my last for the club, and it was the right time for me to move on. I joined Reading because it was an opportunity to get my family back home, which was important to me at that time. At the end of the match at Portman Road I had 3,000 Walsall fans shouting my name, which was emotional. It really got to me. They knew it was the end of my spell with the club and it was nice for us to be able to say thank you to each other. I was fortunate to have five great seasons at Walsall, and it was a very special time to be there.

From about the age of 25, people told me that I'd make a good youth team coach, and that has always been my ideal job. After finishing playing, I worked at Honda, WHSmith and did some courier driving while slogging away to get my coaching badges. I never imagined I would get to be a youth coach at somewhere like Chelsea, and I feel very fortunate to have had that opportunity. On arriving at the club, I didn't think I'd be there for much more than six weeks, let alone nine years! I was a coach during the era when Chelsea dominated youth football, winning six FA Youth Cups and two UEFA Youth Leagues. It was a great time to be there, helping to make those youngsters serial winners.

When you're working with the youth teams at Chelsea you have to be on the money every single day as they have some exceptional players. Most of the time there's not that much you can do to improve their natural ability, so I focused on developing their game management and tactical awareness. I enjoyed that side of the game because I could give them any game plan and they would be able to execute it. I just had to make sure that I gave them the right one! It was a stressful job, but it was rewarding to see players like Nathan Aké, Kasey Palmer and Dominic Solanke come through. Ruben Loftus-Cheek was always a phenomenal talent. I can remember him playing against 18-year-olds when he was only 15, drifting past seven or eight players with ease. Occasionally I played him at centre-half, which he hated, but I did it so he could see the game in a different way. Being at Chelsea was a great experience for me, and it remains a massive highlight of my life.

In 2017, I became assistant manager at Coventry City, which was a natural progression for me to make in football. Winning promotion in my first season there was an important achievement for me as it showed that I could be successful at different levels in the game. My drive is to be a better coach than I was a player, and I've still got work to do in that regard as I was lucky enough to play in five promotion-winning sides before I hung up my boots. Marshy and I met at Walsall and we've stayed lifelong friends. When Coventry got to the play-off final in 2018, he and his son were my guests at Wembley. They sat with my children, which was wonderful as it felt like things were coming back full circle, 20 years on.

Chris Marsh: I've done all sorts of things since I stopped playing football. I had a sandwich shop which made money, and then a restaurant which didn't. I coached abroad and now I'm working with my good friend Adi at Coventry City as a mentor to the young players. I love being around them and try to pass my advice on. Football is a short career and it's soon over, but you always have your memories. The day when Walsall beat Oldham to win promotion will live with me more than any other.

Nationwide

Tom Bennett
Midfielder, 2000–02

You could never sum up a player's career in a single game, but there are some uncanny parallels between Tom Bennett's years in football and Walsall's play-off victory over Reading at the Millennium Stadium in 2001. The proud Scot suffered two serious injuries during his two decades in the game, both of which resulted in him spending a year on the sidelines. But you can't keep a good man down. Tom Bennett recovered from the first of those setbacks by going on to win promotion with Stockport County. Then, after breaking a leg at St Andrew's, he came back to do the same with Walsall. Similarly, the Saddlers refused to lie down and die in that famous play-off final. Twice they went behind to Reading, and twice they came back before ultimately triumphing in extra time. A coincidence that Tom Bennett was at the heart of that indomitable Walsall side? I think not.

Tom Bennett came down to the West Midlands from his native Scotland in the mid-1980s, determined to carve out a career for himself in professional football. He learnt his trade with Aston Villa but was released before getting a chance to play in the first team. Next came a lengthy spell with Wolverhampton Wanderers and then a few successful years with Stockport County, the highlight of which was their 1996/97 season. As well as winning promotion to Division One, the Hatters also reached the semi-finals of the League Cup, knocking out Blackburn Rovers, West Ham United and Southampton before narrowly succumbing to Middlesbrough in the last four.

It was Ray Graydon who brought Tom Bennett to Walsall in 2000, initially on loan as the Saddlers tried in vain to stay in Division One, and then on a permanent basis as they attempted to reach that level once more. A disciplined defensive midfielder, Bennett was a vital cog in Graydon's second great Walsall side. His finest moment for the club undoubtedly came on that great day out in Cardiff when he joined the all-too-small band of players to lift a trophy in front of the long-suffering Saddlers fans.

Walsall 3 – 2 Reading

Football League Division Two Play-off Final
Sunday, 27 May 2001
Millennium Stadium, Cardiff
Attendance: 50,496

Walsall	**Reading**
Jimmy Walker	Phil Whitehead
Ian Brightwell	Graeme Murty
Zigor Aranalde	Matthew Robinson
Andy Tillson	Adi Viveash
Tony Barras	Adrian Williams (Barry Hunter)
Tom Bennett (Gabor Bukran)	James Harper
Dean Keates	Sammy Igoe (Nicky Forster)
Jorge Leitao (Darren Byfield)	Phil Parkinson
Don Goodman	Jim McIntyre (Tony Rougier)
Paul Hall (Matt Gadsby)	Martin Butler
Pedro Matias	Jamie Cureton

Managers

Ray Graydon	Alan Pardew

Scorers

Don Goodman (48)	Jamie Cureton (31)
Tony Rougier, own goal (108)	Martin Butler (91)
Darren Byfield (109)	

Referee

Eddie Wolstenholme

BEFORE THE start of the play-off final against Reading, both teams lined up to sing 'God Save the Queen'. That was fine for the English boys, but not for me. I'm a proud Scot and my national anthem is 'Flower of Scotland', so I sang that instead. It wasn't meant to be disrespectful in any way; I have lived and worked in England nearly all my life and made my home here. It's simply that hearing the Scottish national anthem stirs up deep emotions inside, and to sing it at that moment meant a lot to me. I reckon that the most patriotic Scots are the ones who don't live there, and I'm no different.

I grew up in Bo'ness, which is about 20 miles to the west of Edinburgh. An Aston Villa scout spotted me playing for a local Sunday league team when I was about 13 and invited me down to Bodymoor Heath. I spent some of my school holidays down there and then joined their youth training scheme a few years later. It hadn't been long since Villa had won the European Cup and a lot of players from that era were still around, such as Dennis Mortimer, Gary Shaw and Peter Withe. After a couple of years, Villa gave me a professional contract and I moved up to play in the reserve team.

Then Graham Taylor took over as manager. The club had recently been relegated to the Second Division and he wanted to build his own team, which meant getting rid of some of the older players. He played them in the reserves, and I was shunted across to play at right-back to accommodate them. That wasn't much good for me as I was an average right-back at best. At the end of the season, Graham Taylor called me into his office to tell me that I was being released as he didn't think I was going to reach the level he needed. I was absolutely devastated.

These days, players of that age would have parents or even agents with them in a meeting like that. I was only 18, and I was in that office with him on my own. It was an awful experience.

The next morning, I got a phone call from a guy who said his name was Ron Jukes. I'd never heard of him. He said he wanted to sign me and there was no need for a trial; I'd get a one-year deal at £100 a week and they'd see how I got on. It was brilliant that someone wanted to sign me as the last thing I wanted was to return to Scotland as a failure. The trouble was that I had no idea who this guy was, or which club he was with. 'Who are you?' I said. 'Ron Jukes,' he replied. 'Yes, but who are you?' I responded. 'Ron Jukes, head of recruitment at Wolves', came the answer. 'Who are Wolves?' I said. For the last three years my whole life had been Aston Villa. I'd heard of Birmingham City and West Bromwich Albion, but I had no idea who Wolves were. It turned out that they'd only just come out of the Fourth Division. They simply weren't on my radar.

Anyway, I joined Wolves and broke into the first team quite early on, playing at right-back to start with and then at centre-half before becoming a central midfielder. But then I snapped my cruciate ligament and was out for a year. A few seasons later I moved to Stockport County and had some good times there before breaking my leg in a game at St Andrew's in 1998. Again, I was out for an entire year. I was fortunate that both times I got injured, I had just signed a new contract and so was able to stay in the game. Football's a ruthless business and it can be very fickle at times. Many other players aren't so lucky.

I recovered from my broken leg, signed a new contract with Stockport and everything seemed to be fine. But then a new manager came in and I quickly found myself out of favour. I wanted to play and so went out on loan to Walsall, who were struggling to stay in Division One at the time. I spent all of January with the club and it went well, with the team winning three out of the four league games I played in and drawing the other. I really enjoyed that month, but Stockport's form deserted them while I was away and so they wanted me back. I played a few games for them, but it didn't sit well with me at all.

Eventually, I was able to go back on loan to Walsall and I stayed there until the end of the season. We were in a relegation scrap and it was between us and West Bromwich Albion as to who would go down. We played them in late April at the Bescot Stadium, and I scored a late winner to keep us in with a chance of staying up. We managed to take it to the last game, away at Ipswich Town, but lost and narrowly went down. It's never a nice feeling to get relegated and I think we were a little unlucky not to escape the drop.

I returned to Stockport after that, but I must have made a good impression on Ray Graydon because he wanted to sign me. Negotiations went on throughout the summer and it turned out to be a comfortable decision for me in the end. I already knew the lads and the structure of the team, plus the club were in a good position in terms of the staff members they had and the training facilities that were available at Lilleshall. I also knew that Walsall would be there or thereabouts when it came to winning promotion back to Division One, given the players they had. The stars seemed to align, and it felt right to finish what I'd started.

An important factor in agreeing to join Walsall was that Ray wanted to make me the captain. He told me that if there were any decisions he wanted to implement, he would communicate them to me first and then I'd get the messages out to the lads. He also asked me to show my experience on the pitch, take control of games if I could and give him feedback if the players felt things weren't going right. But Ray was always clear that I wouldn't be in the team just because I had an armband. I respected that because that's how it should be. I think Ray asked me to be captain because of what he'd seen when I was on loan during the previous season. I was quite a talker on the pitch and would often cajole the lads and get them going, as well as not shying away when things weren't happening for us. I also got on well with everyone, which was important as Walsall wasn't a huge club with big-time players. We were all journeymen footballers and one of our strengths was the feeling of togetherness we shared.

Looking back, there were several leaders in that team. Ian 'Sid' Brightwell, Andy Tillson and Don Goodman were all coming towards the end of their careers and any one of them could have put the armband on. They each brought different things to the group; Sid was a good lad to have in the dressing room, while 'Tills' was very well liked. He was strong in the air, had a great sense of timing and, most importantly for a centre-half, you could trust him not to duck out of headers or pull out of tackles. Tony Barras, who played alongside him, was just the same. They were both as brave as the day is long.

Don had been at some big clubs and knew what was required to win matches. He played up front with Jorge Leitao, and they were similar types of players. Both were willing to run the channels, could get you a goal out of nowhere and were incredibly fearless. Jorge was perhaps brave by naivety, whereas Don was brave by default. It was just the way he was built. Don suffered a skull fracture in a match once but recovered after surgery and carried on being exactly the same type of player that he'd always been, which is a real testament to his character. Jorge couldn't speak a word of English when he arrived, but soon made an impact and is now revered as one of the best centre-forwards the club has ever had. He's almost the Steve Bull of Walsall.

As well as getting Jorge in from Portugal, the club also found two excellent Spanish lads in Pedro Matias and Zigor Aranalde. They developed a very strong partnership, with Zigor at left-back and Pedro on the wing ahead of him. Zigor was a superb athlete who got up and down the pitch, while Pedro had a huge amount of technical ability. He was two-footed and that made him a real handful for defenders, enabling him to either cross the ball with his left or cut inside and fire it in with his right. Pedro had been at Real Madrid as a youngster but had lost his way a little in the game, as had Zigor. Along with Jorge, they really should have played at a higher level, so Walsall did well to find them and then keep them.

Ray picked me and Dean Keates in central midfield for the play-off final, though I played alongside Gabby Bukran for much of the season. Gabby came from Hungary, spoke about four or five different languages and had played all over Europe. He was used to playing in teams that had a couple of holding midfielders behind him, which enabled him to get forward all the time. To be honest, that was all he ever wanted to do. We played a strict 4-4-2, which allowed one central midfielder to attack while the other sat back and protected the back four. Gabby never wanted to sit, so I always had to. That wasn't really a problem as I was more of a pivot and was more comfortable playing from behind the ball. It just meant that I had to be very aware of where Gabby was on the pitch so I could fill in any gaps he left behind as he went forward.

Ray's approach was to bring in footballers who were round pegs for round holes, rather than trying to mould players to play in a specific position. Gabby and 'Keatesy' were both left-footed while I led with my right. That meant they were both happy playing on the left-hand side of midfield whereas I was comfortable being on the right, so it worked. When you have two players who want to do the same thing, you can end up with gaps all over the pitch and then you leave yourself open defensively. The sides that do well are those that have footballers playing to the best of their ability in their favourite position on the pitch, feeding off others who are doing the same.

I never felt I was as popular with the Saddlers fans as Gabby and Keatesy were. Gabby liked to get forward and take people on, which excited them, while Keatesy was an honest, home-grown player who worked all day long. The supporters just loved him. I was never the most flamboyant of players, or the most gregarious of characters, so there was less for a fan to latch on to with me. I remember going home after one game and listening to the local radio when a Walsall fan came on. He said he was surprised to hear that my surname was Bennett, because he thought I was called Bennett-to-Brightwell. I laughed initially but was also a bit offended. When I passed to Sid, I was keeping the ball for the team. I know

I was quite defensively minded, but that was my role in the side; the job that I did gave Gabby and Keatesy the freedom to do theirs.

I remember that pre-season training was very easy that year; there were no long runs or anything like that. I was 30 years old by then and you need to look after your body at that stage in your career, so not having a tough pre-season was right for me. Looking back, I think Ray took that approach because he had a small squad of experienced players and wanted to look after us. It clearly worked because we hit the ground running. We scored 15 goals in our first five league matches and won them all. Looking back, none of them were lucky victories; we deserved them all. We were in the top two for most of the campaign, but our hopes of automatic promotion slipped away towards the end.

One of the frustrations that season was losing too many points late on during games. Whenever we were trying to keep a lead, or hold on to a draw, Ray would take a centre-forward off, bring a midfielder on and move me back to play in front of the centre-halves, turning our usual 4-4-2 into a 4-1-4-1. Ray believed that getting more bodies behind the ball made it difficult for the opposition to score, but I think all it did was invite more pressure on to us. We were playing against Division Two sides, not Chelsea. These teams wouldn't build slowly from the back, switch play and try to create gaps they could play through; they just lumped the ball into our box and tried to make things happen from there.

Ray's game plan for defending a lead infuriated me, and though I tried to get him to change it, he just wouldn't budge. There were a lot of little things like that which the players used to fight with him about. It often seemed to us that Ray couldn't do anything wrong in the fans' eyes, but we were constantly battling with him over one thing or another. My relationship with Ray was generally sound because there was a lot of dialogue and communication between us. But we weren't mates; there was always a definite line there.

We ended up finishing in fourth place and went into the play-offs, which is always a bit of a lottery. The semi-final was against Stoke City and we drew 0-0 in the first leg at the Britannia Stadium. I always felt we were the better side and we went into the second leg at home expecting to win. It therefore came as a bit of a shock when Stoke took the lead through a great strike from Graham Kavanagh. That goal came after about half an hour, but a few minutes before half-time, we won a corner down at the Stoke end. I took all the corners for Walsall and I remember having a bit of a laugh with the away fans as I prepared to take it. Back then, the ball had to be clearly in the arc, but I placed it just outside. The Stoke fans kicked up such a fuss about where the ball was that the linesman came over to check. He made me put it back in the arc, but as soon as he went, I rolled it back out again. This just made the Stoke fans even madder, so the linesman came back over, and we ended up going through the whole routine again!

Anyway, I eventually took the corner and, to be honest, I didn't strike the ball all that well. I hit it at a decent pace, but it was too close to the near post and no one was going to get on to the end of it. I knew Stoke's goalkeeper, Gavin Ward, really well because we had been apprentices together at Aston Villa. 'Big Gav' jumped up for what should have been an easy catch, but he fluffed it, knocking the ball into the net with his hands instead. I immediately turned to the Stoke fans and had some fun with them, which just enraged them even more. That goal settled us down and gave us a good platform to build on. We went in level at half-time and then scored three goals in the first 15 minutes of the second half to put the game out of sight.

We soon learned that our opponents in the play-off final would be Reading. It's only when you look back afterwards that you realise how much was at stake in that game. We just didn't notice it at the time. From a financial perspective, many of the players' contracts were up and bonuses were hanging on the result. For the younger lads, the outcome of that match would turn out to have a big impact on their careers. There was a chance that it could go to penalties, so we spent a fair bit of time practising them beforehand. I was one of the nominated penalty takers, but it wasn't something I really wanted to do. There's a difference between those who want to take them and those who are prepared to take them. I was certainly in the latter category. Strikers often like to take spot-kicks because it's a way to get more goals, but for me it was a matter of taking responsibility. I was the captain of the team, so I saw it as part of my job. Whether it was taking the first penalty or the last, I always felt it was something I shouldn't shy away from.

It was the first year that play-off finals were held at the Millennium Stadium in Cardiff, with the old Wembley being demolished to make way for the new one. We stayed nearby at Celtic Manor and were allowed to take our families with us, which was good as it meant that we could see them before we went to the game. My wife was pregnant with our first child at the time, although she did fall asleep during the game! As the coach made its way to the ground, it had to cross a road in order to get into the stadium. I remember looking out of the window and seeing fans everywhere. They were all walking down for the game and you couldn't see the road at all, just thousands and thousands of fans.

When we got inside, a guy took us to what he described as the 'lucky dressing room'. He told us that all the winners of the matches played at the stadium so far had been in there, including Liverpool when they had won the FA Cup a couple of weeks earlier. You take it with a pinch of salt because he was probably saying the same sort of things to the Reading players. By that stage, however, you'll take anything. The dressing room was the biggest I'd seen in my entire life. In fact, it was so huge that it bordered on the ridiculous. I suppose it must have been designed for the rugby teams that would use it because no football team would ever need all that space.

We went out on to the pitch for a warm-up, and even though there were only a few thousand fans in there at that stage, the noise was incredible. The roof was still closed, and the sound just reverberated around the whole stadium. They did open it up for the game, but there was still a fantastic atmosphere. One thing that wasn't so great was the pitch. In fact, it was terrible. It was removable so that they could take it away when they held concerts there and then put it back again. It was very soft on top but rock-hard underneath, which meant that it looked like a bowling green but was awful to play on. I tried studs and moulds but neither worked.

Each time I went to strike the ball I could feel my standing leg about to give way. That made you very conscious of making a pass, whereas in a normal game you would get the ball to your feet and just play it.

As usual, Ray left us to it before the game. He was good in that way. There was no 'Braveheart' speech, or any shouting and bawling. He simply told us that we'd done all the hard work, had got to where we were, and just had to go out now and play our own game. I had played in live TV games before, but I'd never walked out of a dressing room and found the cameras in my face right from the first moment. That immediately made me very conscious of the occasion. Fireworks went off as we walked on to the pitch and they created so much smoke that it made it hard to see all the fans. I remember thinking it was the type of atmosphere that you wanted to play in every single week if you could. It was just the most brilliant feeling.

We started the game slower than we wanted to and Reading had the best of the opening quarter of an hour. They had more possession than us, looked a bit sharper than us and were a little more at it than us. That meant it was just a case of staying in the match while we gave ourselves a chance to settle down. We did manage to get into the game, but it felt like one of those matches that could go either way. It was always on a knife edge. We never felt in charge, or believed we were bound to go on and win, but then we never looked like we were out of it either. Reading never allowed us to feel comfortable throughout the match, which is a credit to them. They were a good side.

Just after the half-hour mark, Reading won a throw-in near our corner flag. The ball came into our penalty area and was flicked into the path of Jamie Cureton, who was waiting on the outside of the six-yard box. He fired in a shot, but it was at the centre of the goal and Jimmy Walker got his hands to it. Somehow, the ball then squirmed under his body and bobbled over the goal line. It was a horrible goal to concede. We were gutted for him because he was one of our most reliable players and a really good guy to have in the dressing room. When something like that happens to someone like 'Wacka', you do start to wonder whether it is going to be your day. All I said to him was, 'Shit happens. Get on with it.' There's not much else I could say. There was no point making an issue out of it or showing everybody that you're comforting him. Wacka was a strong character and we knew he'd be able to deal with it.

A few minutes later, Reading attacked again and one of their players thumped a header against the bar. We were on the ropes and we knew it. A second goal would have been massive for both teams, psychologically more than anything else. I've been in plenty of matches where you go two goals down but then get one back before half-time and the momentum swings back in your favour. But in a game of that magnitude, going two goals down would have killed us. Anyway, we got through that, created some chances of our own and went in at half-time with only one goal in it.

Ray didn't say all that much to us at the interval. He was calm and just reminded us to keep probing and getting the ball out to the wide men so that they could get crosses in towards Jorge and Don. We went out for the second half and were on the pitch on our own for a little while. We definitely didn't go out early, so I reckon Reading deliberately came out late. Perhaps they thought we would be bothered because it was raining, or maybe they hoped we would be getting cold. You can play mind games with kids, but we had too many experienced players in our team to fall for that sort of nonsense. We saw through it straight away and just kicked a ball about between ourselves until they finally joined us.

We were ready for the second half and started right. Just three minutes in, Zigor got the ball over to Pedro, who hooked a cross over towards the back post. Tills got up for it and headed the ball back across the edge of the six-yard area. Don was first to the ball, hitting it past the goalkeeper with a half-volley from close range. That goal changed the game completely. We obviously needed an equaliser, but to get it back so early in the second half really got our tails up. Sometimes on a big stage like that you can feel like you're not going to score, so we were really happy to see that one go in. The game was fairly even after that, with both sides creating chances. The biggest drama in the second half came when Tills got a head injury and had to go off for stitches. All we could do was get bodies behind the ball and try and stay in the game until he came back. We lasted out and the match eventually went into extra time.

Ray came on to the pitch to have a little word with us before it started, though he didn't say all that much; he just told us to keep doing what we were doing. Ray asked me how I was feeling, and I told him I was fine. You never say anything else unless you want to be substituted. The truth, however, was that I was dying on my feet. I had picked up an ankle injury during the week and it had been niggling me throughout the game. By the end of 90 minutes, my ankle was like a balloon and it was only adrenaline that was keeping me going. But I was never going to put my hand up and ask to come off. The only way it would happen was if Ray made the decision.

We scored our equaliser early in the second half, and then Reading did the same to us at the start of extra time. They won a throw-in and launched the ball into our penalty area. We managed to head it away, but it fell straight to one of their players who hooked it across to the edge of the six-yard area. Martin Butler got to the ball first, looping a header over two defenders and Wacka's outstretched arm. We were all good mates with 'Butts' and so were a bit gutted to see him score, though to be fair to him it wasn't a bad header.

Ray responded by making a triple substitution. He decided to take off me, Jorge and Paul Hall and replace us with Gabby, Darren Byfield and Matt Gadsby. Daz and Gabby only wanted to go forward, so bringing them on made us more of an attacking force, while Matty helped shore things up at the back as he was a more defensive player than Hally. Even though I had become drained very quickly in extra time, I was still gutted to come off, while Jorge was really disappointed. I sat next to him on the bench and remember saying that there was nothing we could do now. There was no point in jumping up and down or worrying about this or that; we just had to leave the rest of the lads to get on with it.

It's interesting now to look back at those substitutions. Alan Pardew made two changes for Reading in the second half and a third when they were 2-1 up in extra time. That was a typical series of substitutions and the conventional thing for Ray to have done was bring on fresh legs after about 75 minutes and try to win the game in normal time. However, he opted to hold his cards back until we went behind in extra time, and then made his three changes all at once. It was a relatively strange way to do things, but Ray won the game, so it's hard to argue with the decisions he made.

Walsall were still behind as the game went into the second period of extra time, and because Reading had taken the lead twice it always felt like we were playing catch-up. Yet we never thought we were out of it. We just needed a break to get back into the game, and that was what we eventually got. Gabby played a ball into the penalty area to Keatesy, who spun around Tony Rougier, catching him out with the pace of his turn. Rougier crashed into Keatesy, sending them both tumbling to the floor just as another Reading player tried to clear the ball. It cannoned into the falling Rougier and rebounded over the head of the stranded goalkeeper and into the net. That was the first moment when I thought we could win the match. Things were finally starting to go our way.

Then suddenly, within a minute, we were in front. Matty played the ball upfield to Daz, who was about 25 yards away from goal. The Reading defender got too close and Daz turned past him before firing a low shot into the bottom corner of the net. I remember watching it from the bench, looking through a thicket of legs as the ball went past the goalkeeper. It was an incredible feeling for everyone: players, management and supporters. But we never felt comfortable, even then. For the next ten minutes or so, I was a fan, just like all the other Walsall fans. The anguish and the wait were almost unbearable, and at times like that it's much easier to be out there, playing. If something happens you can possibly get back to help, but you can't do anything when you're sitting on the side of the pitch.

When the match finally ended, I couldn't quite believe we had won. We were always coming from behind in that game, so to take the lead and then hang on for the victory felt a bit surreal. We were all elated and were jumping on top of one another. Gabby got hold of a Walsall flag and started to do his 'walking the dog' celebration. We all joined in behind him as if it was a conga, grabbing each other's ankles, with the team looking like a giant caterpillar. There was no particular reason why that happened; it hadn't been planned or anything like that. It was just us losing it and doing something ridiculous in the heat of the moment.

We were given our medals and it was a great feeling to know that no one else could touch the trophy before me. The podium had been set up to face the television cameras, which was a bit weird because it meant there were empty stands in front of us, where the Reading fans had been, while we had our backs to the Walsall fans. I'd seen plenty of footballers lift trophies over the years and, finally, this was my chance to do the same. The first thing I did after raising the trophy was to run down to the Walsall fans with it. All the players were racing after me, shouting 'Where are you going with that?' There was nothing wrong with my ankle then! Once I'd done that, I let the rest of them have the trophy. I'd had my moment.

Don Goodman was given the man of the match award, which was fair enough, but there were several other players who could have won it. Both Andy Tillson and Tony Barras put in very strong performances, while Adi Viveash was outstanding at the back for Reading. I consoled him and Butts after the game, and they were fine about it, but there's not much you can say really. I felt that I did my job reasonably well, but nothing more than that. Many years later I spoke to James Harper, who was the opposition midfielder I was up against that afternoon. He'd joined Reading from Arsenal and I thought he was a terrific footballer. He gave me nothing during that game and I never felt I was dominating my position as I should. Interestingly, he told me that he never got into that game because I was always on him, stopping him from doing what he wanted to do. We both have the exact same memory of being thwarted by the other, and to hear that gave me a bit more pride in the performance I put in that day.

After the game, we met with our families upstairs in the stadium and had a meal. The players were happily celebrating the victory, but Ray was already moving on to next season. He took us to the side one by one and spent 30 seconds or so pulling us down a bit. We were all looking forward to going away on holiday for five or six weeks, but he reminded us that we needed to work hard over the close season and be fit when we came back. I think he was trying to keep us grounded but he should have respected the experience we had in that dressing room. I was 31 and there were several players older than me. We knew how to keep ourselves fit, but that was Ray; that was his character.

When you look back at your career, you can either judge it on financial success, or on the memories you've got. There will always be players who earn more than you and players who earn less, but from my point of view, memories are hugely important. That play-off final was an incredibly special occasion for me. It was the only time in my career that I got to play in a national stadium in front of over

50,000 people. The atmosphere was unbelievable and the elation I experienced at the final whistle was simply unforgettable. I had never lifted a trophy before that final, and I never got the chance to do it again. Without doubt, that day was one of my most memorable in football.

DARREN WRACK

Darren Wrack
Midfielder, 1998–2008

Arguably, the most successful period of Walsall's history was those six years between 1998 and 2004 when the Saddlers won two glorious promotions and spent four seasons in the second tier of English football. Only a small, elite group of players were there for it all, and Darren Wrack was one of them. His almost continual presence during those glory years was no coincidence, for he was a genuine match-winner on his day.

Walsall's acquisition of Darren Wrack on a free transfer in the summer of 1998 didn't generate much enthusiasm amongst some Saddlers fans. After all, how good could a player be if he couldn't get into Grimsby Town's first team? Well, how wrong the doubters were. Darren Wrack soon established himself as a coruscating right-winger who scored goals as freely as he made them. His first season with the club was probably his best, with vital goals against Bournemouth, Lincoln City and Oldham Athletic being a particular highlight as he helped drive Walsall to a well-deserved promotion.

Darren Wrack's decade with the club was a real rollercoaster ride. During that time, he won three promotions, suffered three relegations and played in all three divisions of the Football League. There was even one, all too brief, moment in late 2003 when he was part of a Walsall side that threatened to challenge for a place in the Premier League. The universal currency of football fandom is hope, and that team gave it to Saddlers fans in bucketloads. Sadly, it wasn't to be, but one suspects that Darren Wrack wouldn't have looked out of place had Walsall reached such an exalted level.

Darren Wrack suffered an horrific leg break in 2005 but fought his way back to become one of the few players to have spent ten years with the Saddlers. Over that time, he played almost 400 games for the club, scored over 50 goals and won a host of trophies. But more than that, he won a place in the fans' hearts.

Walsall 4 – 1 West Bromwich Albion

Football League Division One
Saturday, 9 August 2003
Bescot Stadium, Walsall
Attendance: 11,030

Walsall	**West Bromwich Albion**
Jimmy Walker	Russell Hoult
Danny Hay	Sean Gregan
Ian Roper (Darren Wrack)	Larus Sigurdsson (Ronnie Wallwork, Artim Sakiri)
Neil Emblen	Joost Volmer
Darren Bazeley	Bernt Haas
Simon Osborn	James O'Connor
Paul Merson (Stefan Oakes)	Andy Johnson
Vinny Samways	Jason Koumas
Zigor Aranalde	Neil Clement
Steve Corica	Danny Dichio (Scott Dobie)
Jorge Leitao (Gary Birch)	Rob Hulse

Managers

Colin Lee	Gary Megson

Scorers

Paul Merson (18, 39)	Jason Koumas (70)
Jorge Leitao (45)	
Steve Corica (57)	

Referee

Anthony Bates

THE SUMMER of 2003 was an incredibly exciting time to be at Walsall. It felt like a new era had begun as the board were investing heavily in the team, enabling experienced players such as Neil Emblen, Simon Osborn and Vinny Samways to be brought in. Compared to how things had been before, the playing budget simply went through the roof. I remember the manager, Colin Lee, walking past me in a corridor at the Bescot Stadium and saying, 'Wracky, just you wait and see who we've got coming in.' Managers say things like that from time to time, so you tend to take it with a pinch of salt. But then Paul Merson arrived. The players were just as amazed as the fans were that the club had managed to get him. 'Merse' had played for Arsenal and England and was a player of the highest calibre, albeit one who was coming towards the end of his career. It said a lot for Colin Lee that he was able to attract Merse to the club, and it also reflected well on the board who were clearly ambitious enough to go out and get a player like that.

Playing alongside Merse was a joy. He had superb vision and could do some unbelievable things with his right foot. It really was a wand. Not everyone was on the same wavelength as him all the time, but he had tremendous ability and brought something special to the team. In the ten years I spent at Walsall, Merse was one of the two best players that I shared a pitch with. The other was Vinny Samways. He was one of the finest ball-playing midfielders of his time and the range of passes he could make was simply frightening. Vinny would be a dream player for a lot of Premier League teams these days because few have the composure that he had. Even if he had five men around him, he wouldn't panic. Vinny always seemed to have time on the ball and would be able to pick a pass out, no matter how many players were bearing down on him.

Merse and Vinny may have been the stars of the team, but they had a lot of good footballers around them. In midfield there was Simon 'Ossie' Osborn, who was another strong passer of the ball, as well as Steve Corica, who would pop up in holes and make things happen. Then, up front, we had Jorge Leitao, a strong, industrious striker who never stopped running around. Jorge was always up for a battle and scored bags of goals for the club. Just as importantly, he was one of the lads.

Colin Lee liked to set the team up with three central defenders and two wing-backs. Darren Bazeley usually played on the right flank while Zigor Aranalde would be on the left. 'Baze' was an experienced defender who joined us from Wolves, while Zigor was brought over from Spain by Paul Taylor. They were both excellent at their jobs. The three defenders stationed between them at the start of the season were Danny Hay, Neil Emblen and Ian Roper. Danny was a New Zealander who was only at the club for a couple of years. There's always a bit of banter in the changing room and anyone new gets it thrown at them right away. Danny was a bit strait-laced when he first joined us, but eventually let his guard down and got the gist of it. 'Embo' was a midfielder for most of his career but played as a centre-back for Walsall. Like Danny, he was solid, experienced and knew what he had to do. 'Ropes' used to get a lot of stick from Ray Graydon about his weight and looking after himself, but he was so much better than his appearance suggested. He was a no-nonsense defender who always looked to clear the ball away from danger as soon as he could, and not much got past him. Ropes should have played at a higher level than he did during his career. He really was that good.

Another player in that team who should have had more time in the limelight was Jimmy Walker. 'Wacka' was an incredible shot-stopper and he deserved to have done more at Tottenham Hotspur and West Ham United than sit on the bench, which was pretty much all he did, to be honest. I think his height probably counted against him, but it shouldn't have done. Being a good goalkeeper is all about having agility and pulling off saves. For me, Wacka was up there with the best keepers in the land.

Looking back at the team that started against West Bromwich Albion, one thing that strikes me now is how mature it was. Eight of the team were in their thirties while the youngest player was Ropes, who was hardly a novice at the age of 26. Colin Lee had clearly decided that the best way to try to maintain Walsall's Division One status was to have a very experienced squad.

Colin Lee came in as manager after Ray Graydon had been sacked. Prior to his appointment, I only really knew of him from his time in charge at Wolverhampton Wanderers, and when he'd been a player at Chelsea and Spurs. What changed most under the new manager was the style of coaching. Ray was a bit more 'old school' in his methods while Colin was more forward-thinking and hands-on. There was a lot of variation in Colin's training sessions and they were inventive and enjoyable. If I had to sum up the difference between them, I would say that Ray was more of a manager than a coach, particularly in the type of coaching sessions he put on, while Colin was more of a coach than a manager.

Colin brought Dave Merrington with him when he took over at Walsall and the two of them were very good for me. Dave was a bubbly, excitable character who liked a laugh and a joke with the lads. He only stayed at the club for a few months, which was a shame as he was a great character to have around. I found Colin to be a very easy manager to talk to and he was a likeable person. He was good at getting messages across quickly and helping us to understand how he wanted the team to play and what our individual jobs were.

After Colin had been at the club for a few weeks, we came up with a nickname for him. For some reason he reminded us a bit of a vampire, so we christened him the 'Dark Lord'. There was nothing malicious about it at all. It was just part of the fun and games that go on in the changing room, though we never called it him to his face! Overall, I'd say that Colin was my favourite out of all the managers I played for at Walsall. He was excellent at helping players to develop and he took my game on to a different level. That's not taking anything away from the other managers as I enjoyed working with all of them, but I think Colin brought the best out of me.

Colin wanted the team to be creative and inventive in its play and you can see that by the type of footballers he brought in. He recruited some great flair players in Steve Corica, Merse and Vinny and that helped to change the mentality at the club. For a long, long time it had been 'little old Walsall' but, somehow, he managed to talk the board into upping the budget so that he could bring those calibre of players in. Signing those footballers was a real declaration of intent about where he wanted to take the club.

Persuading Merse to join Walsall was no mean coup for the club, and the fans packed out the ground to see him make his debut against West Bromwich Albion. It was a tough opening fixture as they had just come down from the Premier League and still had a lot of top players in their side. There was a lot of expectation amongst the Albion fans and I think their team may have underestimated us a little, though they shouldn't have as Walsall had a lot of good footballers at the time.

One thing I remember was how glorious the weather was that day. It was boiling hot and the game was played in bright sunshine. I started on the bench but came on after only ten minutes or so. Ropes jumped for a header, fell awkwardly, injured his back and couldn't carry on. It must have been quite serious as it took a lot to get Ropes off the pitch; he would run through brick walls for the team. Colin kept the same formation by moving Baze across to centre-half, while I replaced him at right-back. It was a bit of a different position for me, but that wasn't a problem as I was used to playing all over the pitch for the club. Over the years I played at right-back, left-back, on the wings, in central midfield, as a striker and as a number ten. In fact, I think I played everywhere for Walsall except central defence and in goal.

West Bromwich Albion started the stronger and had a couple of half-chances, but it didn't take us too long to get into our stride. I'd only been on the pitch for a few minutes when we got our first goal of the afternoon, and what a brilliant one it was. I won a throw-in and took it quickly. The ball went to Steve Corica on the right wing and he passed it at knee-height to Merse, who was unmarked on the edge of the penalty area. Rather than trying to bring the ball down, he unleashed an incredible volley that looped over the goalkeeper and crashed into the back of the net.

Inevitably, Albion came back at us, missing a good chance to score before Wacka pulled off a fine save to keep us in front. It looked like we'd be taking a 1-0 lead into half-time, but then we got two goals in quick succession that effectively finished them off. The first was another superb strike by Merse. We won a free kick in our half of the pitch and Vinny took it, sending an inch-perfect pass out to Zigor on the left-hand side of their penalty area. His cross went into the box, but an Albion defender got there first, knocking it out to the edge of the 'D' where Merse was waiting. He hit it first time, sending a screamer into the top right-hand corner of the net. The goalkeeper had absolutely no chance.

Our third goal wasn't too bad either. There was some delightful one-touch football involving me, Merse, Vinny, Ossie and Jorge. Albion just couldn't get the ball off us. The final pass in the sequence went to Ossie, who raced through the heart of the opposition defence with the ball seemingly glued to his feet. He went past the last defender and shot at goal from the edge of the penalty area. His strike beat the goalkeeper but not the post, though thankfully Jorge was first to the rebound, knocking it into an empty net. The goal itself may have been a bit of a scrambled effort, but the build-up play was something special.

Everyone was buzzing in the changing room at half-time, and you were almost pinching yourself about what had just happened. At times like that you don't need to say too much and so the team talk was almost non-existent. I really can't remember Colin saying anything to us. We were on a real high, but we didn't make the mistake of relaxing too much. There were just too many experienced players in the team to allow that to happen. We knew we still had a job to do if we were to put the game to bed, and the way we came out in the second half showed that we didn't take anything for granted.

We continued to pass the ball around well, switched it from side to side and waited for openings to arise. Embo went close with a header from a perfectly delivered Merse corner. Then, about ten minutes after the interval, we scored a fourth goal which completely killed the Albion off. The move began and ended with Steve Corica. He won a free kick just inside their half of the pitch, which Vinny took. He passed the ball out to me on the left wing and I took it forward before laying it off to Ossie. He then passed it to Steve who played a one-two with Merse. The ball was played back a bit behind him, so he had to flick it up in the air to get it away from the Albion defenders who were closing in on him. The ball then bounced just outside the penalty area, sitting up perfectly and inviting itself to be struck. Steve got right underneath it, hitting a swooping volley that flew over the goalkeeper's head before nestling in the back of the net. It was such a well-timed strike that the Albion keeper barely moved his feet from the floor; there was just no way he could get to it.

West Brom managed to get a goal back about a quarter of an hour later, but it was a bit of a lucky one. Jason Koumas went on a run through the centre of the pitch and hit a shot from outside the penalty area. It probably wouldn't have troubled Wacka, but it took a deflection off Baze and ended up in the bottom corner of the net. Given the way we were playing that afternoon, however, it was only ever going to be a consolation goal. We kept the ball well throughout the match, and the longer it went on the more possession we had. We were also able to slow the game down, which was important as it was blisteringly hot. My recollection is that we were a lot fitter than the Albion players, but we may just have run the energy out of them, popping the ball around between us and making them do all the chasing. Heat can take its toll on players, especially when you're getting battered. At times like that you start to wonder how you're going to get back into the game and then the cohesiveness of the team begins to disintegrate, with players getting at each other whenever a pass goes astray.

You could sense that the West Brom players were getting frustrated, but I don't remember any of them losing their composure and lunging into tackles or doing anything sinister. The challenges they made were no different to those that you would normally get in a game. When they finally realised that the game was dead and buried, they stepped off the gas a bit and we just knocked the ball around between us. In the last few minutes of the game they even stopped chasing the ball; they knew they'd been beaten fair and square and were just going to have to take it. When you lose like that, you just want it to be over and done with so you can get off the pitch as quickly as possible.

Looking back, the difference between the two teams that day was the quality of our finishing. All the goals we scored were special, with three of them being goal of the season contenders. Everyone who was there will have their own favourite, but mine are Merse's two strikes. They set the tone for the game and got us going. The fact that we raced into a lead and put a lot of daylight between them and us, particularly by half-time, also had a big impact on the eventual outcome. I think there was a fair amount of disbelief amongst the Albion fans for much of that match. They clearly thought we wouldn't be able to keep playing to such a high standard and that they would get back into the game at some point. But they never did.

That game against the Albion was the finest performance by a Walsall team that I was ever involved in. It just had all the ingredients of a classic. At a personal level, I'd started off in the team during pre-season, was dropped, but then came on as an early substitute and so had a chance to stake my claim once more. In addition, there was a lot of optimism around the club because of the calibre of players that had been brought in. Even the fixture itself was special as it was a big local derby against a team that had just come down from the Premier League. If all that wasn't enough, it was also the opening game of the season, plus it was a beautiful, hot summer afternoon. You couldn't have asked for a more perfect result and a more perfect day. I was very lucky to have been part of it, very lucky.

One inevitable consequence of that victory was that it sent expectations rocketing. Merse's two goals, and the way that the team played against the Albion, painted a picture of what the season could hold for the club. It was a dramatic statement of intent: 'Come and look at us and see what we can do.' As professionals, we knew we had to maintain realism and keep our feet on the floor. We knew that league success is all about consistency rather than one-off results. However, the fans started to dream a little, and to be honest I think the players did a bit as well. I know I certainly did. We had some incredibly talented players at the club, perhaps some of the best that Walsall has ever had. At that precise moment in time, anything seemed to be possible.

We carried on playing good football throughout the autumn and got some decent results. I remember we beat Wigan Athletic 2-0 and I got criticised in the press afterwards, even though I had scored both goals! For the first one I picked the ball up on the halfway line and then surged forwards, playing a one-two with Merse as I bore down on the penalty area. The reporter complained that I held on to the ball for too long before passing it to Merse. The reason I did that was so I could draw the players on to me, creating space behind them that I could run into when Merse played the ball back to me. Football reporters: what do they know? The move worked out just as I had hoped, and I was able to lift the ball over the goalkeeper as he tried to narrow the angle by spreading himself. For the second goal, Vinny played another inch-perfect pass from the centre circle out to Chris Baird on the right wing. He beat his man, fired the ball across the face of the goal and then I slid in to meet it at the far post.

Not too long after that we beat Nottingham Forest by four goals to one, which was another impressive result against one of the more fancied teams. I was marked in that game by Wes Morgan, who went on to make a big name for himself at Leicester City. He was still a teenager back then, but he was well thought of and a lot was expected of him. Wes scythed me down a couple of times that night, though I do remember nutmegging him for one of the two goals that I scored, which seemed to be appropriate retribution!

We then got another fine result on Boxing Day, beating Cardiff City by a goal to nil away from home. The scoreline suggests a narrow victory, but we played really well and some of our passing was out of this world. We weren't far outside the play-offs at that point in time and I remember thinking that we were still there, still winning and still playing good football. There was always a sense of realism, but as the

New Year dawned there didn't seem to be any reason why we couldn't continue doing well for the remainder of the season. We started to dream a little bit more, and there was nothing wrong with that. I think that players should be ambitious, not just at an individual level but also for their team. If you're not, then you have to question what you are in the game for. You should want to be regarded as being a good player. You should want to be part of a successful team. You should want to be remembered.

Sadly, 2004 did not bring us what we had hoped it would. One of the first signs that things were beginning to go wrong came in a home game against Coventry City in mid-January. They got an early goal and then Stefan Oakes was sent off, though I did manage to grab an equaliser just before half-time. Coventry went back in front a few minutes after the interval and so we started to chase the game, which wasn't easy with only ten men on the pitch. They soon began to pull us apart, got a third goal, and then a fourth and it became very easy for them. We lost all discipline and ended up losing the match by six goals to one. Hindsight is a wonderful thing, but if we had just kept it tight and lost by the odd goal then it wouldn't have been the end of the world. Losing by that margin at home was not a great result, though I don't remember anyone hitting the panic button at that time. We just viewed it as a bit of a freak result.

Frustratingly, the team continued to struggle, and it didn't help that we lost Merse for a while either. He was trying to deal with a gambling addiction and went to Arizona for treatment. We played six league games while he was away and didn't win any of them. Losing a player of his ability was always going to affect the team, though it was down to the rest of us to adapt to his absence and make the right decisions on the pitch to compensate for him not being there. Merse was back by mid-March, but by then Vinny had left. Vinny's home was in Spain and he was allowed to fly back there after matches. Doing that amount of travelling is never easy and eventually Vinny decided to knock it on the head. Losing someone of his quality was a big blow, and it inevitably had an impact on the team.

Walsall slipped further and further down the table, and with four matches to go we found ourselves only two points above the relegation zone. It was at that point that Colin Lee was sacked, following a dispute over him talking to Plymouth Argyle about becoming their manager. His dismissal came as quite a shock to the players. I really enjoyed my time under Colin, and I know a lot of my team-mates did as well. He was an exceptional coach and he had a lot of time for us. It was a shame that the board didn't persevere with him as he had the right ideas about how to take the club forward.

Merse took over as player-manager until the end of the season, though he was under no illusions about how hard a task it would be, particularly given his lack of experience. His first game was away at Norwich City, which ended in a 5-0 thrashing. That was followed by successive 1-0 defeats to Sheffield United and Crystal Palace, though we had chances to win both of those games. We did beat Rotherham United in our final fixture, but still went down on goal difference. We'd amassed 51 points, which would normally be enough to avoid relegation, but not that season. In fact, scoring only two more goals would have saved us. Football is a game of fine margins, and we found ourselves on just the wrong side of the dividing line.

I had three promotions and three relegations in the ten years I spent at Walsall, so there was never a dull moment. The highest high I experienced was winning promotion from Division Two in my first season at the club. We had a team that was patched together rather than put together, and all the pundits predicted that we would go down. We went on to defy all expectations, finishing second ahead of clubs such as Manchester City and Stoke City. It was our team spirit that won us that promotion. Whenever we went on a night out, everyone went, without exception. I know it's disapproved of these days, but we didn't just go out once a month; we went out every week. Don't get me wrong, we had some good players, but the fact that everyone had each other's backs made it very hard for other teams to break us down. Many of the friendships I made back then I still have to this day, which pretty much tells its own story.

In the early years of my career it was an open secret that players went out and most managers turned a blind eye to it. Then more attention got paid to sport science, nights out became much more frowned upon and the drinking culture slowly ebbed away. There's a lot to be said for that, but I think something has been lost along the way. These days squads can become quite fragmented, with different cliques forming and players disappearing straight after training. A lot of modern footballers want to do their own thing these days, rather than spend time bonding with their team-mates. That doesn't appear to be a healthy development to me. Players also appear to be less resilient than my generation was. I think they complain a bit too readily about the number of games they are asked to play and can be a little too quick to rule themselves out when they get a slight knock. We would play 50-odd games a season without grumbling and would always try to soldier on if we had a minor injury. For better or worse, I reckon footballers had a lot more character in my day.

If winning promotion in my first season at Walsall was my highest high, the lowest low was not being involved when we reached the play-off final at the Millennium Stadium. It didn't come as a complete surprise as I could see by the shape of the team in training that I probably wouldn't start. I still hoped to get a place on the bench, but it wasn't to be. If that wasn't disappointing enough, after the team left the changing room Ray told me that he was going to put me on the transfer list. Talk about a double whammy! The three relegations I suffered were bad enough, but you can handle going down as there's always next season. From a purely personal perspective, however, what happened on that day in Cardiff was really tough to take. What it did do, though, was give me a bit of extra drive. I remember thinking, 'I'll show you', and I believe I did.

Ray had signed me from my hometown club, Grimsby Town. Alan Buckley was their manager at the time, and I remember him pulling me out of training one day and saying that Walsall wanted to have a look at me. He told me it was a good club and let me go down to play for them in a pre-season friendly. Walsall were impressed and so I signed for them straight away. I don't think I was really given a chance at Grimsby and always felt that my history with the club counted against me a little bit. They had wanted to sign me as a schoolboy, but I turned them down in favour of Derby County. I signed for Grimsby a few years later when Brian Laws was in charge, but he soon left and Alan took over, which didn't turn out to be so great for my prospects in the end.

It was when I joined Walsall that my career really took off. Playing week in, week out enabled me to show what I could do, which I had only done sporadically at Derby and Grimsby. There was a lot of hype about me in my first season, and after we'd beaten Oldham to win promotion Ray Graydon told me that he'd already turned down a few bids for me. At the start of the following season, Fulham came in with an offer and I came very close to joining them. I remember getting a phone call from my agent to confirm that my package had been sorted and the move was just waiting on an agreement from Walsall. It was an exciting moment as Fulham were on their way to the Premier League and I had to pinch myself that it was really happening. I even called the Fulham ClubCall line to check! Frustratingly, the two clubs couldn't agree on a transfer fee and so I stayed at Walsall.

Lots of players have hard-luck stories about big moves that never quite came off, and I'm no different. Joe Royle showed an interest when he was in charge of Manchester City, but he decided to sign Terry Cooke instead. Neil Warnock also wanted me to join him once. The package he offered was terrible, but he was one of those managers who took players with him from club to club if you did what he wanted on the pitch. Who knows where I might have ended up if I'd taken that opportunity? I only found out about the biggest 'what if' of my career when I was living with Merse. He told me that John Barnes had considered signing me when he was manager of Celtic. Sadly, he had one of the shortest-ever managerial tenures at the club, so nothing came of that either!

I was comfortable at Walsall, but looking back, maybe that was the problem. I settled in very quickly and soon felt a part of everything that was going on. I got used to the club environment, and they became accustomed to me. I had so many good times at Walsall, but I never really got out of my comfort zone and sometimes you need to do that in life. I have always believed that I should have played at a higher level more consistently during my career and putting myself on the edge may well have helped me to achieve that. It's often only when you get older and wiser that you see the moves you maybe should have made.

In saying that, I have a lot of fond memories of Walsall. My first impressions on arriving was that it was a well-run club, and I have never changed my view of that. Everyone there knew each other and there were never any barriers, which can develop at bigger clubs. If you had time for people, they would have time for you. I'm always made to feel very welcome at Walsall and I think that speaks volumes for the club.

DEAN KEATES

Dean Keates
Midfielder, 1996–2002, 2006–07

Perhaps understandably, Walsall fans tend to have fairly low expectations. We don't demand that our players be world beaters, but we do expect them to try. And boy did Dean Keates try. He was our very own *Rocky:* a scrapper who just never knew when he was beaten. Any opposition midfielder would soon know they were in for a tough afternoon as 'Deano' would just never, ever give up. In fact, playing against him must have been as much fun as being pursued by a wasp for an hour and a half.

A native of Walsall, Dean Keates stood on the terraces at Fellows Park as a youngster and fulfilled his dreams by going on to play for his hometown club. His first spell with the Saddlers was marked by two promotions, the second of which was secured with a play-off final victory over Reading that owed a lot to his tireless running.

Bringing 'Deano' back to the club in 2006 was a masterstroke as it helped to reconnect a club in freefall with its rather disillusioned fans. He became the driving force behind Walsall's promotion push, and for him to score the goal that helped secure the League Two title was real *Roy of the Rovers* stuff. That moment really did seem to be written in the stars.

When he finally hung up his boots, a career in management beckoned. Wrexham was his first appointment, and then in 2018 he made an emotional return to Walsall. He took over a team that appeared to be heading for relegation and kept them up with a couple of points to spare. If his life was a Hollywood movie, this would be the moment when the credits rolled. Sadly, there wasn't to be a happy ending to this story. A blistering start to the following season soon had fans dreaming of promotion, but results began to deteriorate, the club slipped inexorably down the table and his services were dispensed with after a 3-1 defeat at home to Oxford United that left the club on the brink of relegation. His spell in charge didn't end the way that anyone would have wanted it to, but one thing remains undeniably true: Dean Keates has always been, and shall always be, *one of us*.

Swindon Town 1 – 1 Walsall

Football League Two
Saturday, 5 May 2007
County Ground, Swindon
Attendance: 14,731

Swindon Town	Walsall
Phil Smith	Clayton Ince
Jack Smith (Ashley Westwood)	Craig Pead
Jamie Vincent	Danny Fox
Barry Corr (Lukas Jutkiewicz)	Anthony Gerrard
Jerel Ifil	Chris Westwood
Andrew Nicholas	Michael Dobson
Michael Pook	Kevin Harper
Blair Sturrock	Dean Keates
Chris Roberts	Martin Butler
Lee Peacock	Trevor Benjamin (Darren Wrack)
Sofiane Zaaboub	Ishmel Demontagnac (Hector Sam)

Managers

Paul Sturrock	Richard Money

Scorers

Jerel Ifil (52)	Dean Keates (90)

Referee

Mike Jones

THE TITLE-WINNING game against Swindon Town was the most memorable moment of my Walsall career, but it might never have happened. When I first left the Saddlers in 2002, there were a few weeks during that summer when I had to seriously contemplate a life outside football. A year earlier, Walsall had won promotion to Division One through the play-off final at the Millennium Stadium and everything looked rosy. But things can change quickly in football. We struggled the following season and Ray Graydon was sacked, with Colin Lee replacing him as manager. One of the first things that Colin did was to bring Martin O'Connor back to the club, telling me that he needed some experience in midfield to help us get out of the relegation zone. He told me I still had a bright future at the club and that there would be a new contract for me in the summer.

Unfortunately, ITV Digital collapsed at the end of that season and a lot of money disappeared out of lower league football as a result. A lot of negative repercussions were felt throughout the game, and what it meant for me was an offer of just a six-month contract plus a 50 per cent cut in pay. I decided to take a gamble and turned it down in favour of seeing what other options might become available. I went a couple of months without a club and then went on trial at Port Vale. After a few weeks there I went to see the manager, Brian Horton, as I was due to be the best man at my friend's wedding. It clashed with one of their pre-season games and I needed to know whether there was going to be anything for me at the club. If there was, I would play the game as my mate would understand that I had to. If not, then I didn't want to let him down for no good reason. Brian told me that he would love to sign me but had thought I was only holding out for more money from Walsall and so had just signed someone else instead. So, that was the end of that.

I was 24 and in danger of dropping out of the game completely. I spent three weeks training on my own and began to consider what I could do with my life instead. When I was growing up, I was always outside, running around with a ball under my arm or climbing trees. I couldn't imagine working in an office, so I thought about going into the police force, or maybe becoming a fireman. I was in the wilderness, but then Jan Mølby rang me up out of the blue. He'd recently taken over as manager of Hull City and had been impressed when he'd seen me play for Walsall. I went up there on a pay-as-you-play contract, but I wanted a longer deal than that. The club was going through a massive transition at the time and the chairman, Adam Pearson, told me that they were in the process of moving a lot of players out. He gave me his word that as soon as that was done, I would be the first player they'd offer a new contract to. I've been given a lot of words in football, and you don't always get what you've been promised, but Adam was as good as his word. A few weeks later, I was offered a year-and-a-half contract.

Moving to Hull was one of the best things that ever happened to me. I had been in my comfort zone at Walsall, surrounded by friends and family and playing at my hometown club. Leaving all that behind made me grow up. It also helped that things went well on the pitch. Hull moved from Boothferry Park to the new KC Stadium during my first season at the club and I had the honour of scoring the opening goal there in front of a full house. A year later, Hull finished second in the table and won promotion to League One. After that, I teamed up with Jan Mølby again, this time at Kidderminster Harriers, before having a spell at Lincoln City. Then, in 2006, I got a call from Walsall.

Paul Merson was the manager at the time, but he wasn't the one who brought me back. When I arrived at the Bescot Stadium, Jeff Bonser pulled me to one side and told me that Merse hadn't signed me; he had. He said he was fed up of paying players who didn't give him anything back, but I had always earned my money, which was nice to hear. Walsall were really struggling in the league at the time and my first game was away at Brentford. It ended in a 5-0 thrashing. The following Monday was one of those days that you never forget. I was driving down the M6 for training when I got a call that my kids' mom had gone into labour. Danny Fox was travelling with me, but I had no choice other than to kick him out at Junction 15, swing the car around and shoot back home. That afternoon I was sat at the hospital when I heard the breaking news that Paul Merson had been sacked. I'd played for him for less than a week.

The following Saturday, I was made captain for the home game against Scunthorpe United. It was almost four years to the day since I'd last played at the Bescot Stadium, and it was great to be back. I scored in the first half but as the match drew to a close, we found ourselves a goal behind, as well as being down to ten men. Thankfully, we managed to get a late equaliser to cap off what had been one of the wildest weeks of my life. The club had changed massively since I'd been away and was no longer the place it had once been. Everything we'd achieved when I was there had been built on the back of a great changing room, but that was all gone. The squad was full of loan players who had little care for the team, or for the club. Mick Halsall had a few games in charge and then Kevan Broadhurst was brought in to try and keep us up. Sadly, it didn't work out, we were relegated to League Two and a lot of players left the club soon afterwards.

During my first spell at Walsall, Chris Nicholl, Jan Sorensen, Ray Graydon and Colin Lee didn't give me any responsibility at all. I was just a young kid who came in every day and got told what to do. It was a different Dean Keates who returned to the club. I was 28 by that time and one of the senior players. When Richard Money took over as manager, he pulled me, Martin Butler, Michael Dobson, Chris Westwood and Darren Wrack to one side. He told us that we were his five senior players and that he needed us to be his eyes and ears in the changing room. He wanted us to handle any issues that arose but was clear that if anyone stepped too far out of line and we couldn't deal with it, then we could go to him and he would sort it out. But, to be honest, the changing room was so good that season that I don't recall Richard having to get involved in anything. That was something that I picked up from him and used when I went into management.

We didn't go anywhere during pre-season. Richard just took us up to Lilleshall for a few days and spoke about what he wanted us to achieve. The aim was promotion, so he worked out how many points we'd need based on the average number collected by teams that had gone up previously. He then broke the season down into blocks of five games and calculated that we needed to get ten points from each block. If we got more than ten, then we'd have something in the back pocket in case we had a dip in form later in the campaign. Richard reckoned that if we could set that sort of pace, we would go into the last game of the season with a chance of winning the title. Talk about Mystic Meg!

I really enjoyed my time under Richard, and we had a good relationship. He came in with some different ideas and I bought into the way he coached straight away. Richard had spent the previous year in Australia, coaching the Newcastle Jets in the A-League. That became an ongoing joke in the changing room as he'd come back with a bit of an Aussie accent! Richard had a real attention to detail, leaving none of us in any doubt as to what our role on the pitch was and what he expected of us. That meant there was nowhere to hide and no one else to blame if you didn't do your job.

Richard wanted us to play a traditional 4-4-2 and drilled the style of play into us so effectively during pre-season that it didn't need to be refreshed for the rest of the campaign. We knew what we were about. There wasn't much video analysis of games back then and all we got was a pamphlet with a couple of set plays in it. We always defended corners the same way, with a change only being made if I wasn't in the team. I was always stationed on the back post as I was never going to win a header, but if someone taller came in then they'd be given an opponent to mark. Richard was keen on having a strong spine to the team and embarked on a big rebuild to get what he wanted.

Clayton Ince was brought in from Coventry City during the summer to be our first-choice goalkeeper. He was a big man in every sense of the word. He was well over 6ft tall and must have been touching 19 stone. He took a lot of pressure off our defence whenever balls came into the box because he would come and claim absolutely everything.

If Clayton shouted and put his name on the ball, no other player on the pitch was going to be crazy enough to go anywhere near him. He was also a big personality in the changing room. Clayton came from the Caribbean and had a very laid-back, chilled-out approach to life.

The two central defenders in front of Clayton that season were usually Anthony Gerrard and Chris Westwood. 'Gez' joined us when he got released from Everton and he was a typical Scouser: very chirpy and loud and in your face in the changing room. But he could back it up on the pitch, which was why he went on to play at a higher level with clubs such as Cardiff City and Huddersfield Town. Even though he was only a youngster at the time, he was still quite vocal on the pitch and helped to organise the way the team played.

'Westy' is a Black Country lad like me and we're a similar age. I played against him a lot of times at youth-team level, but it wasn't until we were both at Walsall that I got to know him. After that, we played together at Peterborough United, Wycombe Wanderers and Wrexham and he became one of my closest friends in football. He wasn't all that big for a centre-half, but he read the game well, anticipated things before they happened and put himself in the right place to deal with it. Westy was also a great talker on the pitch, which is a dying breed in the game now. Not many modern players can talk their way through a game like he could.

The central midfield pairing was me and Michael Dobson, who captained the side that season. The way we played required one of us to stay back while the other broke forwards. 'Dobbo' often sat in front of the back four and that gave me the opportunity to get up the pitch. I usually got four or five goals a season, but that year I scored 13, which was easily the highest tally of my career. I couldn't have done that without Dobbo being so unselfish. He was the unsung hero of that team.

In front of us was the team's target man, Martin Butler. Like me, he had risen through the ranks at Walsall, moved away and then come back again. 'Butts' was only a few years older than me and he became a first-team player while I was still in the youth side. It didn't really work out for him in his first spell at Walsall as he struggled to get picked ahead of Kevin Wilson and Kyle Lightbourne in attack. When he did get in the team he was often played out on the left wing, which was not his preferred position. When you're a youngster coming through you need to get a break, which can happen if someone gets injured or suspended, but he just never got it. He was eventually sold to Cambridge United and went on to score loads of goals for them before getting a big money move to Reading. It was a great decision by Richard Money to bring him back home as he did a lot for the team. Butts never gave the opposition back four a moment's rest. He was always in their faces, which allowed the midfield to move up and support him, keeping us high up the pitch.

The spine of the team was strong, but we also had some great players on the flanks. The right-back, Craig Pead, was one of the funniest kids I ever played with. He had the perfect personality to be a football player. 'Peady' gave absolutely everything in training and always had a smile on his face, though he suffered a lot with injuries, which did for him in the end. For most of the season, Mark Wright played in front of Peady. His job was to bomb down the wing and get one-v-one with defenders. The pitch at the Bescot Stadium was even widened to give him more space to run into. Towards the end of the season Kevin Harper was brought in on loan to give him some competition. He was another direct, head-down winger who would get balls into the box. Like several of us, he had been at Walsall before and he came back with a wealth of experience which helped us to get over the line and win promotion.

On the other side of the pitch, we had Danny Fox at left-back. I first met him when I was on holiday and we got chatting around the pool. I was at Lincoln City at the time, while Danny had just left Everton and signed for Walsall. I told him all about the club he was about to join and found out that he only lived ten minutes away from me in Cheshire. We car-shared when I came back to Walsall, and he was forever complaining about having to play on the left wing when he wanted to be a left-back. In the end I told him to stop moaning and go and tell Richard how he felt. It was the right move for Danny because what you want from a left-winger is electric pace and the ability to carry the ball up the pitch, which weren't his attributes. Anyway, he went to see Richard, started playing at left-back on a regular basis and soon got a move to Coventry City on the back of his performances in defence. A year later he was at Celtic, so I reckon he owes me one!

Ishmel Demontagnac played in front of Danny in that game against Swindon Town. His nickname in the changing room was 'Asbo' as he could be a bit of a loose cannon at times, though he was a lovely lad. 'Ishy' was at his best when coming off the bench towards the end of a game, particularly when the opposition were sat in and we were struggling to break them down. We would get the ball to him about 20 yards out and he would take three or four players on, pulling them out of position and creating space we could exploit. I remember standing in the middle of the pitch during one game as Ishy sent three defenders one way before going the other, watching as all the fans behind the goal fell for the same trick! Everyone else in that team was a consistent '7-out-of-10' type player, but Ishy was different. On his day he was a born match-winner.

One of the substitutes that came on against Swindon was Darren Wrack. He made his comeback that season from a horrific injury, having suffered two compound fractures and damage to his ankle ligaments in a tackle. 'Wracky' showed great resilience in returning, though he never got back to the level he'd been at previously. He had to change his game as a result and ended up playing quite a few games in central midfield. At his peak, Wracky was an incredible player. I remember playing away at Bournemouth when we were going for promotion during Ray Graydon's first season in charge and getting absolutely spanked. We had our tin hats on until Wracky got the ball on the halfway line, took it up the pitch and smashed it into the net from 25 yards. That goal won us the game. If I was to pick my all-time top Walsall 11, Wracky would be in it. We've been best mates for over 20 years, and I know he'll be a friend until the day I die. I just can't speak highly enough of him.

From mid-September onwards, we were never out of the top two in the table. In fact, our form was so strong that the opportunity to win promotion came with four games to spare. We travelled to Notts County and had a massive following, with over 3,000 Saddlers fans filling the stand behind one of the goals. We needed a win to go up and got it with only a few minutes of the match remaining when Trevor Benjamin scored to put us 2-1 in front. 'Benji' was brought in on loan towards the end of the season to give

Hector Sam some competition in the supporting striker role. Hector could do some great things when he had the ball at his feet and his back to goal, but Benji offered us something a bit different. Benji was a gentle giant, despite easily being one of the strongest guys I've ever met. He had phenomenal brute strength.

Benji fitted into the changing room straight away. At the time we had this rule that you never shut the toilet door when you went in. If you did, then there would be consequences. I remember on his first day at the club, Benji went into the toilet only ten to 15 minutes after arriving. He made the mistake of shutting the door so Gez and Peady threw a huge bucket of ice water over the top of the cubicle. Benji came out, absolutely drenched from head to foot. The lads were creased up laughing, but all Benji said was, 'So, is that how it is, then?' He was a great lad.

I was fortunate to be in some great changing rooms at Walsall when I was younger, but that was the best one I ever had the privilege to be in. There wasn't one player who didn't have the right attitude, or who didn't buy into what we were trying to achieve. The changing room really matters in football because it's a sanctuary. Sadly, the way players relate to one another has changed for the worse over my 20 or so years in the game. Footballers are much more self-obsessed these days and their priority is to look after themselves. If you walk into a changing room now, you'll often see players sitting there, looking at their phones and not talking to one another. If you walk into the canteen, you'll see them eating with a fork in one hand and their phone in the other, ignoring the person sat in front of them. The first thing I did when I became a manager was to ban phones. I wanted footballers who would communicate with each other, because if they are silent in the changing room, they'll take that on to the training ground and then out on to the pitch.

We had a great journey back from Notts County after winning promotion and celebrated that night because we'd achieved our objective for the season. But we didn't take our foot off the gas. We met up on the following Tuesday and talked about what we wanted from the rest of the season. Every player wants to be able to look back on their career and say that they won something, and we were no different. We wanted to be the first Walsall team to win a league title in almost 50 years. We wanted to write our own little bit of history. Richard had given responsibility to the five senior players at the start of the season, and it came down to us five again. We took the lead, telling everyone that we had to keep going and get to that final game against Swindon with a chance of still winning the title. We wanted to be champions.

By the time the Swindon game came around, we were where we needed to be. Walsall were top of the table, equal on points with Hartlepool United but with a superior goal difference. It was in our own hands and we didn't need to rely on anyone else. Richard didn't need to say too much to us before the game. He knew he had a good bunch of professionals and trusted us to do what was needed. His only message was not to let the opportunity slip. Saddlers fans came in huge numbers to the game and there was a real party atmosphere, but we had to switch ourselves off from that. We could enjoy it during the warm-up and after five o'clock, but once we walked down the tunnel, we were professional sportsmen there to do a job. We had to play the game, not the occasion.

There was a lot riding on that match for both teams as Swindon needed a point to confirm promotion alongside us. Sometimes promoted teams can play with a more carefree attitude, but that wasn't our outlook at all. We weren't on the beach; we wanted to win the title. That made for quite an edgy, scrappy game and it wasn't the greatest of spectacles, to be honest. Perhaps unsurprisingly, it was 0-0 at half-time. We found out at the interval that Hartlepool were winning, which meant that we had to get all three points if we were to become champions. I remember thinking that I really didn't want to be sitting there on the coach home, thinking about having just missed out on a title we were so close to winning.

A few minutes into the second half, Swindon got a goal and it looked like things were slipping out of our hands. Then, not long afterwards, there was a buzz from the Walsall fans, and we all wondered what was going on. We got told on the pitch that Hartlepool had been pegged back, so all we needed now was a point. The dream was on again. The tension was incredible, and then Richard got sent off for over-protesting at one of the official's decisions. Despite being quite a reserved guy, he did have a fiery side to him and that came out when he saw someone get a decision wrong right in front of him. Like us, Richard wasn't content with promotion. He really wanted to win the title; not so much for himself, but for the club. When you want something that badly you can easily lose your cool, and that was all that happened. The players on the pitch weren't bothered by it at all. He'd drilled our roles and responsibilities into us, and we knew what we needed to do, whether he was stood there on the side of the pitch or not.

We carried on chasing the point we needed but were running out of time. The game had gone into injury time when we won a throw-in, about 15 yards from their corner flag. We all knew what our jobs were at set plays and mine was to stay at the edge of the box as I was never going to win a header. The ball was thrown deep into their penalty area and one of the Swindon players managed to nod it away from goal. As he did this, I moved a little further back, creating space between me and the opposition defence. The ball came straight in my direction, dropped and then sat up a treat. I hit it on the half-volley, and from the moment I made contact I knew it was going in. I followed the ball the whole way, watching as it nestled in the stanchion.

I still get goosepimples talking about that goal, even over a decade later. To fully explain what it meant to me, you need to understand who I am and where I came from. I grew up on a council estate in Bentley and lived there until I was 15. We then moved to Beechdale, where my dad was from. I learned to play football at the bottom of the hill in front of Emmanuel Church, which was right next to where we lived. I was out playing there every hour I could. My dad took me to watch the Saddlers play at Fellows Park, though it was mainly on Tuesday nights as I played Walsall district games at the weekend. We had to walk for about three miles down the canal towpath to get there because my dad didn't drive.

My favourite players back then were David Kelly, Chris Marsh and Mark Rees, though the one that made the greatest impact on me was David 'Mini' Preece. Like me, he wasn't the biggest, but he could control a game. I had no idea at the time that I would go on to play in central midfield for Walsall, just like him. I went to King

Charles Primary School in Bentley and then Willenhall Comprehensive School. My teachers often told me that if I applied myself to my schoolwork as I did to my PE lessons, I could be a 'Grade A' student, but I didn't take it in. When it came time to leave school, they told me all I could expect was a place on a Youth Training Scheme.

Thankfully, I had other options. Lots of clubs from all over the country were interested in me, including most of the local ones. I went to Wolves a few times, but I didn't like it there, so it came down to a choice between the Albion and Walsall. The Saddlers had been after me for years and I decided to go with them as I thought that would provide me with a shorter path to becoming a first-team player, which is how things turned out. Kenny Hibbitt was the manager when I joined the club, but he was soon replaced by Chris Nicholl. I have the utmost respect for Chris because he made me resilient. As a kid, I was often told that I might not make the grade because of my height, but Chris never mentioned it once. The only thing he ever commented on was the length of my hair!

When I was growing up, I modelled myself on Jesper Olsen, a left-winger who played for Manchester United and Denmark. I played all my youth-team and reserve games on the left wing, but Chris gave me my debut at left-back. I then had a few games at left-back or on the left wing before Jan Sorensen converted me into a central midfielder. Mark Blake got injured during an away game at Bristol Rovers, and at half-time Jan asked me whether I wanted to replace him in the middle of the park. I would have played anywhere to get on to a football pitch, so I immediately said yes. I'd never played as a central midfielder in my life, but it went well, and Jan kept me there for the rest of the season. I had started out as a tricky little left-winger and then, almost overnight, my game changed completely. But that was fine with me; I just wanted to play.

I was fortunate to have two promotions with Walsall under Ray Graydon, left the club, came back and then had to suffer a relegation. That goal against Swindon mattered so much to me because Walsall was my club and I just loved playing there. Everything had come full circle for me. I had stood in the stands as a fan, and here I was scoring the goal to give the club its first title for almost half a century. It was the most surreal experience of my career. The emotions I felt in that moment were almost overwhelming. It had been a tough season off the pitch as I'd lost my mom, and I had lots of my friends and family in the stand that day. Who knows, perhaps it was fate?

After the goal went in, there was virtually nothing of the game left. We went back into our own half and then the referee blew the whistle. A point was enough for us to win the league and for Swindon to get promoted, so both sets of fans were ecstatic. A lot of home fans ran on to the pitch, but there was no trouble. It was just a joyful afternoon for everyone involved. Pitch invasions can be hard for me, given how small I am. If lots of people run on, I can just disappear underneath them. When I was at Kidderminster Harriers we played away at Northampton Town on the last day of the season, and they won to claim a spot in the play-offs. As I was running off at the end of the game a fan punched me in the back of the head and I ended up scuffling with him, which is not what you want to happen on a football pitch.

Back in the dressing room, Richard spoke to us, but not for long. At times like that anything a manager says just goes into one ear and out of the other. Emotions were running high and all the players were like a bottle of pop waiting to go off. Anyway, he congratulated us, thanked us for our hard work and told us that we should be proud of what we'd achieved. And then it all kicked off. Champagne corks were flying around everywhere, while the players were bouncing up and down and throwing everything they could get their hands on to into the air. On the journey home, we got stuck in traffic and decided to pull into a pub and have a beer with the Walsall fans. There was no social media back then, so you had to do things like that to reach out to supporters.

A couple of days later we had a civic reception at the Council House to celebrate our title win. We reported to the Bescot Stadium, got on the open-top bus and then drove through streets lined with Saddlers fans. It was great to be able to show the trophy to the fans and to share that moment with them. At a personal level, it was without doubt the best season of my career. I finished as the club's top goalscorer, won the Walsall Player of the Year award and got voted into the PFA League Two Team of the Year. However, I couldn't have achieved any of those things without the players I had around me. They were just a great bunch of lads.

That goal I scored against Swindon turned out to be the last ball I ever kicked for Walsall Football Club. Right from the start of 2007, I wanted to sit down with the club and sort out a new contract, but they had no interest in talking to me until the season was over. That left me open to offers and, given the year I'd had, plenty came in. I never envisaged leaving Walsall, having put so much into getting the club promoted, but then I went down to Peterborough United and met their manager, Darren Ferguson. He sold the club to me and made it clear how important I was to his plans. It was a big thing for me to leave my hometown club for one that was still in League Two, but it was a new opportunity.

Daz guaranteed that I'd be a League One player within 12 months, and I was. He also promised that Peterborough would be in the Championship the season afterwards, and the club were. Daz has always been there for me. When I got the manager's job at Wrexham, he was the first person to get in touch. When I took over at Walsall, he was straight on to me. Then when I got the sack, he was the first person to text me. It was a tough decision to leave Walsall for Peterborough, but it was made easier by how I felt I'd been treated by the club. I left without any regrets and went on to win two promotions with Peterborough, which I don't think would have happened if I'd stayed at Walsall.

Looking back, I wouldn't change a thing in my career, even if I could. I made over 700 appearances as a professional, won six promotions and played at Wembley a few times. If you'd have offered that to me when I was a 15-year-old running around on a council estate, I'd have taken it. My career got as good as it ever could have. I had a relationship with the fans at every club I played for, and I think that's because they saw me as an honest player who went out on to the pitch and gave everything I'd got. I gave 110 per cent for every team I played for, but it was probably 120 per cent for Walsall. The club will always be special to me.

ADAM CHAMBERS

Adam Chambers
Midfielder, 2011–19

When Adam Chambers arrived at Walsall in 2011, few could have expected that the 30-year-old would spend the best part of a decade at the club. It looked as if the club had signed an ageing central midfielder, but as the years passed fans could be forgiven for thinking Peter Pan had been recruited instead.

The revitalisation of Adam Chambers's career was no fortuitous accident. Under the wise tutelage of Dean Smith, he stopped being a box-to-box player, reinventing himself instead as a defensive midfielder. He repaid the favour by becoming Smith's faithful lieutenant on the pitch; an experienced, calming presence amongst a team brimming with exciting young talent.

A year after Adam Chambers signed for Walsall, he was joined at the club by his twin brother, James. It was a move that saw their careers finally come full circle. They had started out playing in the same school and Sunday league teams before becoming apprentices together at West Bromwich Albion. They made their professional debuts for the Baggies within a few months of each other and went on to become the first twins to play for the same team in the Premier League.

It may have appeared that their fates were to be forever entwined, but their paths soon diverged. Adam went on loan to Sheffield Wednesday before spending five years at Leyton Orient. James, meanwhile, went his own way before being reunited with his brother at Walsall in 2012. It was a fitting finale for the two Black Country boys; their playing careers bookended by spells at the Albion and the Saddlers.

The highpoints of Adam Chambers's time at Walsall came in 2015 and 2016 when he captained the first Saddlers side to reach Wembley, before almost winning promotion to the Championship a year later. He continued to be a mainstay of the team but succumbed to a foot injury at the start of the 2018/19 season which saw the Saddlers relegated. It was a demotion that many felt would never have happened if he'd still been there to protect an increasingly frail back four. As with many of the best things in life, Adam Chambers proved hard to replace.

Walsall 0 – 0 Preston North End

English Football League Trophy,
Northern Area Final Second Leg
Tuesday, 27 January 2015
Banks's Stadium, Walsall
Attendance: 10,038

Walsall	**Preston North End**
Richard O'Donnell	Thorsten Stuckmann
James O'Connor	Calum Woods
Paul Downing	Tom Clarke
James Chambers (Ben Purkiss)	Paul Huntington
Andy Taylor	David Buchanan
Michael Cain	John Welsh (Alan Browne)
Adam Chambers	Neil Kilkenny
Anthony Forde	Chris Humphrey (Jack King)
Romaine Sawyers	Paul Gallagher
Jordan Cook (James Baxendale)	Kyel Reid
Tom Bradshaw	Kevin Davies (Sylvan Ebanks-Blake)

Managers

Dean Smith	Simon Grayson

Referee

Nigel Miller

I ALMOST picked my debut for Walsall as my most memorable match. It was a special moment, not just because it was my first game for the club, but also because of who it was against and the circumstances surrounding it. By the summer of 2011, I had been at Leyton Orient for five years. I had another 12 months left on my contract and was happy there. I'd had a few calf injuries during the previous season and so had been in and out of the team. Then the manager got in touch to say that Walsall were keen to take me on and so he was going to help me get back to the West Midlands. The trouble was that I was in no rush to go home; I enjoyed living in London.

I'd have been much happier about the situation if they had just been straight and told me that I was no longer part of their plans. Instead, there was all this nonsense about helping me to get back home. I'd been at the club for quite a long time and it left a bitter taste in the mouth. I did a week or two of pre-season training, but it was uncomfortable as I was having awkward conversations with the manager after each session ended. Eventually, I spoke to the club chairman, Barry Hearn, as I'd always had a good relationship with him. He sorted out how I could leave the club and I'll always be grateful to him for stepping in. The last thing I wanted was to be at a club where I had a sour relationship with the manager.

Anyway, I joined Walsall and, as luck would have it, the first game of the season was at home to Leyton Orient. I would be playing against a team that I had been contracted to until they told me I wasn't wanted any more. In the lead-up to the game, I remember telling friends and family how badly I wanted to win it. Not only did I score the only goal of the game, but it was an absolute cracker: a 30-yard strike that went right into the top corner. I was overjoyed and recall making my way over to the opposition bench to let them know just how I felt. My next thought was that the game was only 20 minutes old, and there was still a long way to go before I'd know whether it was the winner! I hadn't pushed to leave Leyton Orient, but looking back now, it turned out to be a great move for me.

Initially, I wondered what I was letting myself in for at Walsall. They had finished onc point above the relegation zone in League One at the end of the previous season, while Leyton Orient had only missed out on the play-offs by a point. The two clubs were at opposite ends of the table, but I was pleasantly surprised by what I found when I arrived. Walsall had a much better training ground than Leyton Orient and there were some excellent people behind the scenes. One of those was Jon Whitney, who was the physiotherapist and fitness coach at the time. I'd had a lot of injury problems over the years, but Jon helped me to get through them and I was finally able to play consistently. The longer I spent at the club, the more and more I came to love it.

One of the factors that attracted me to Walsall was that Dean Smith was the manager. I've known him since I was a kid. My best friend's dad used to throw parties and I regularly saw Dean at those as he was my pal's cousin. The next time I came across Dean was when I went on loan to Sheffield Wednesday for the last few months of the 2003/04 season. He was the captain there and he and his wife took me under their wing as it was the first time I'd lived away from the West Midlands. He always reminds me about that whenever I see him. We've spent a lot of time together away from football over the years and his family have become like a family to me.

The next time our paths crossed was when I was at Leyton Orient and Dean was assistant manager to Martin Ling. I could tell straight away he was making good progress as a coach and that he enjoyed being a leader. Dean has a lot of qualities as a manager, but the one that stood out for me was the way he handled individuals. I was always of the belief that everyone in a team should be treated the same, but Dean got the best out of people by knowing whether they needed a kick, a nudge or an arm around the shoulder. I saw first-hand at Walsall how well he dealt with players who'd had issues at other clubs and had been given a second chance with the Saddlers. He knew exactly what needed to be done to help them develop and flourish.

The times I spent at Walsall under Dean's stewardship were amongst the most enjoyable of my career. That was partly down to being back home, but it was also because of the style of football we played. Under some other managers I often ended up feeling like a robot, kicking the ball forward and not taking any chances. Dean trusted his players to make good decisions, which made football much more of a pleasure. It's fair to say, though, that Dean was not an overnight success. There were some lean times during his first couple of years at the club and I could see that the fans were getting restless. The team could play some good football outside the box, but we didn't make enough chances, or score enough goals. We were also inconsistent. When we clicked, we looked amazing, but too often we appeared a bit toothless.

There were a few occasions when the board could have gone in a different direction, but thankfully they kept faith with Dean and their patience was rewarded in the end. With a few tweaks and additions to the playing squad, Dean got the balance right and put together a team that could have good possession of the ball, as well as being an attacking threat. The players always believed in what Dean was trying to do; it just took us time to build up an understanding of what was needed and to be confident playing that style of football. When it went well, I remember coming off the pitch and having opposition managers, coaches and even chairmen telling us how well we'd played. Players from other teams often asked us what we did in training to be able to play so fluidly and how we all seemed to know what our team-mates were doing.

Walsall were able to play such attractive football because of the type of players that Dean recruited. He brought in footballers that not only had good technical ability but were also hungry to learn and develop. He constantly challenged us to be better and created an environment at the stadium and the training ground which made it a joy to be there. At some clubs you just clock in and clock out but everyone liked being at Walsall, and I always wanted to stay longer. There was a good bond between the players, and we had a good laugh together, though everyone put a shift in when it was time to work. There are many ways to play the game, but Dean's style of football was the most enjoyable I came across during my career. The only problem is that you get spoiled when you've had something that good.

As the team developed, I stopped being a box-to-box player and became more of a defensive midfielder. My job was to act as a screen for the back four, winning possession of the ball and getting it forward to our attacking players. I've never been a prolific goalscorer, but one consequence of my deeper role was that I very rarely got into positions where I could have a shot at goal. When I got that debut goal against Leyton Orient the fans probably thought the club had acquired a goalscoring midfielder, but it didn't turn out that way. In fact, I only scored once more in 300-odd games for the Saddlers! Dean used to have some fun at my expense about that, but it was all done in a good spirit. The relationship I had with him was easily the closest I've had with any manager during my career.

We didn't have a good start to the 2014/15 season and were joint bottom of League One in mid-October. We had some young footballers in that team, and they tend to be more inconsistent than the more senior players. That's because they are still learning their trade, figuring out what their strengths and weaknesses are and getting used to first-team football. But our league form picked up after that and we also made headway in the Football League Trophy. We knocked out Rochdale, Sheffield United and then played Tranmere Rovers away in the Northern Area semi-final. We were 2-0 down at half-time, but it never felt like we were out of it; we knew we had players who could create chances and players who could take them. Anthony Forde got a goal back midway through the second half and then Michael Cain equalised with a good strike from outside the penalty area with just ten minutes to go. Michael came on loan to us from Leicester City and was a good addition to the squad. Clubs in the higher divisions were often keen to lend us their young players because of the style of football we played, as well as the quality of coaching they knew they would get at Walsall. The game eventually went to penalties and we were confident about winning as we had some technically gifted players, and it helps when you can trust your technique in that situation. We also knew that Richard O'Donnell could make a save, and that was how it turned out. 'OD' palmed one of the Tranmere penalties past the post and then Paul Downing tucked his spot-kick away to give us the win.

Our opponents in the Northern Area Final were Preston North End, with the first leg being played up at Deepdale. They were pushing for promotion and several of their team had played in the Premier League, including Jermaine Beckford, Kevin Davies and Paul Gallagher. They were favourites to get to Wembley, but even though we were inconsistent, we knew that on our day we were a match for any team in the league. They got off to a flyer and created chance after chance to score, but we somehow managed to keep them out. When you've been in the game for a long time you learn that teams like that do start quickly and are going to have spells when they're on top. As OD pulled off save after save, I was left thinking, 'Bloody hell, we could be two or three down here!' OD was an excellent shot-stopper and he made some incredible point-blank saves from Beckford to keep us in the game in that first half.

Ten minutes before half-time, we almost scored a goal ourselves. We won a free kick in a good position and Andy Taylor stepped up to take it. He was a steady left-back who had played in the Championship for Sheffield United and was one of the more experienced players in the squad. He struck a great free kick which beat the goalkeeper but hit the foot of the post. If his shot had been an inch or two to the right, I'm not sure it would have been saved. It was probably a good job that Andy took that free kick as it meant that Anthony Forde took the next one that we got late in the second half, but I'll come back to that later …

Dean Smith and his assistant Richard O'Kelly were very positive at half-time. They always believed in us and were good at making those little tweaks that can make a big difference out on the pitch. We hadn't had as much possession of the ball as we would have liked so they urged us to get back to the basics of our game. Many of Preston's chances had come from crosses into our box, so we also talked about how we could get tighter on their wingers and stop those crosses at source. We were much stronger in the second half as a result and the game was there for the taking.

With only a few minutes left to go, their goalkeeper made a poor pass forward and it went straight to Romaine Sawyers. He got the ball about 40 yards from goal and took it straight up the pitch before getting bundled over just outside the penalty area, which won us a free kick. It was typical of Romaine to get us into such a good position. He was always our 'go-to-guy', a number 10 who operated in pockets of space and made things happen. His awareness and vision were excellent. He got a lot of joy out of setting up chances for other strikers and scored some very good goals himself. It didn't matter whether Romaine was marked when you gave him the ball as he was strong enough to look after it before finding a way to get us going forward. He could be exceptional at times. In fact, I remember thinking during games that I was glad that I didn't have to play against him. I would probably have had to kick him!

The fans seemed to be split in their views of Romaine, though I'm not sure why because he was a class act. His laid-back style perhaps didn't endear him to some, but I reckon that helped him in the way he played. Romaine joined us from West Bromwich Albion, and I think he had a point to prove because it hadn't worked out for him there. He was certainly good enough to play at a higher level and showed that when we played Chelsea in the League Cup early during the following season. There were some top internationals in their side, but Romaine held his own against them. He didn't look out of place at all.

Andy Taylor and Anthony Forde stood over the free kick, but I didn't know which one of them was going to take it. 'Tayls' had hit the post in the first half, but 'Fordy' was a good striker of a dead ball as well. Getting the ball up over the wall and then down again is a difficult technique to get right. Not many players can do it, so we were fortunate to have two players who had mastered the art. Goalkeepers watch loads of videos and so will know where the ball is likely to go if you've only got one free-kick specialist in your team. If you've got two, that makes it much more difficult for them as they're not sure what's coming. I don't know how Tayls and Fordy decided who was going to take that free kick. Maybe they had an arrangement where they took turns, or maybe it depended on who was feeling the most confident. I never got involved as captain as I didn't want to get into the middle of that. They were a good couple of lads so I knew they would be able to sort it out between themselves.

I stood at the end of the Preston wall for the free kick, trying to get in their goalkeeper's eyeline. Fordy gave their goalkeeper the eyes and then shaped himself to hit it into one corner before whipping it the other way at the very last moment. It was such a good free kick that the goalkeeper barely moved before the ball hit the back of the net. Free kicks are hit at such pace these days that goalkeepers have to look at the player's body shape to try to gauge where the ball is going to go. If you can disguise what you are going to do then it can really catch goalkeepers out, and that was exactly what Fordy did. I was pleased for him as he was a chirpy, funny guy who was great to have around in the dressing room.

It was a nice feeling to go in front as I knew what was at stake. Living close to the area, I saw a lot of Walsall fans leading up to the game and they told me that we had to get to Wembley as the club was one of the few never to have played there. It was never going to be easy to beat Preston over two legs, so it felt good to get our noses in front. We were one of those teams that were emboldened when we took a lead as we knew that the opposition would have to come at us and that would give us more space to attack into and create chances in. And so it proved.

A few minutes later, Preston made another mistake when one of their defenders played a back pass to the goalkeeper without realising that Tom Bradshaw was lurking. 'Bradders' latched on to the ball and kicked it through the goalkeeper's legs from a tight angle. It was typical of him to score a goal like that as he was always ready to pounce when the slightest of chances arose. Sometimes his goals were spectacular and sometimes they were scruffy, but all that mattered to him was finding a way to get the ball in the net. Bradders provided an attacking threat that we'd lacked before he joined and was an absolute goal machine for us. He went on to play at a higher level and was capped by Wales, which was well deserved. Bradders was a positive, enthusiastic lad who was always prepared to put in the hard work needed on the training ground in order to improve.

We saw the game out and were thrilled to have a two-goal buffer to take back to the Banks's Stadium. OD was given the man of the match award, which was well earned given the string of saves he made in the first half. He didn't just keep us in the game; he kept us in the tie. There was a lot of cautious excitement in the dressing room afterwards. Your emotions are running high because you've won a game at a difficult place to go, but you have to supress them because it's still only half-time really. Some of the younger lads did start to get a bit carried away so the senior players had to dampen their enthusiasm a little. If you're not careful your mind can wander, and it can feel like you're already at Wembley.

The Banks's Stadium was packed for the second leg, which only happened a handful of times during my Walsall career. What made it unique was that the great majority of spectators were Saddlers fans. I've played in games when the ground has been full but we've given two sides of it to away fans, either because we were playing a big Midlands club in a pre-season friendly or a team that had dropped down to League One from a much higher level. But that night the Banks's was full of Walsall fans who wanted us to finish the job and get to Wembley. The expectation amongst the fans had been building throughout the day and you could sense their growing excitement. They'd been to work, chatted about the match all day and were clearly up for it. The fact that it was a night game also gave it a special feel. It's an absolute joy to play in that sort of atmosphere and you can feel yourself feeding off everybody else's energy. You want every game to be like that.

It's not always easy to go into a second leg with a lead as you don't know exactly how to play it. You can sit back and defend, but that just invites pressure. Dean's approach was to pick the same team as he had for the first leg and tell us to 'go out and do it again'. That made it easier for us as it meant playing as we normally would, rather than trying to do something novel. The early part of the game was quite tense, with the two-goal lead playing on our minds a bit. We knew that getting to Wembley for the first time was such a big thing for the club and the fans, so we really didn't want to let that lead slip. Momentum can be really important in football and we knew that conceding a goal would give them the impetus to push on. We therefore tried to keep the score at 0-0 for as long as possible and it was still goalless at half-time, which was fine with us.

We didn't change our plans for the second half. Our overriding desire was not to do anything silly that would give them a leg-up and allow them back into the tie, though it would be great if we could get a goal. Preston had some very good forwards and were flying high in the league, so you knew that if they got one goal, they could get two or three quite quickly. We kicked towards our fans in the second half and were much more of a threat, with Bradders, Fordy, Romaine and Tayls all going close with shots and headers on goal. It would have relieved a lot of pressure if we could have scored, but we just couldn't get the ball over the line.

Preston weren't giving up on the tie and they brought Sylvan Ebanks-Blake on for the last half an hour of the game. There aren't many League One teams that can take a player like Kevin Davies off and replace him with someone who, on his day, could be even better. Preston had that strength in depth and Ebanks-Blake soon made his presence felt, forcing a good save out of OD from a point-blank header and then rattling the crossbar with a blistering shot from just outside the penalty area. OD had been the hero in the first leg, and he came to our rescue several times in the second half. He made a good stop from a free kick, but his finest moment came as Preston peppered our goal from a corner. OD parried the ball twice in quick succession before Paul Downing kicked the ball off the line from their third effort.

It was difficult to keep them at bay and there were times when we had no choice other than to barricade the goal and put bodies on the line. Preston were kicking towards their own fans, which added to the anxiety of it all as you could hear their fans willing them to score from behind the goal. It seemed like every 30 seconds a player was asking the referee how much of the game was left. The first time he was asked he said '20 minutes', and someone in our team replied, 'Seriously?' Personally, I'd rather not know how much time is left to play as it can just be a distraction.

Keeping Preston out for two whole games was no mean feat, given the strikers they had, and our back four deserved a lot of credit for that. They weren't the biggest, but they were very composed on the ball. That really suited our style of play and was what Dean wanted from us. My brother, James, was the senior player at the back and he marshalled the other guys. He would often alternate positions with James O'Connor, with them switching between central defence and right-back, depending on who we were up against. They were similar types of players as they were comfortable on the ball but could still be aggressive when they needed to be.

My brother got on very well with Paul Downing, who was the other regular centre-half. 'PD' had been through West Bromwich Albion's academy, but hadn't been able to break into the first team and so came to Walsall. The two of them were always talking about football and it was a good relationship, with the senior pro constantly giving good advice to the younger one coming through. PD had a good passing range and that made him an important player for us. We often found that teams would try to counter our style of play by sitting back and making it difficult for us to pass through them. When that happened, PD would get us moving forwards by playing diagonal balls out to our wingers and getting them one-v-one with defenders.

As the match wore on you could sense that the energy levels were dropping amongst the Preston players. They'd given everything, bombarded our goal but just couldn't score. It wasn't working out for them and you could tell that they felt it wasn't going to be their day. But that didn't mean that we could relax. Football is one of those games where things can change very quickly. They could get a scrappy goal from a deflection and suddenly their tails would be up again, putting us on to the back foot. We kept going and fittingly the match ended with another good save from OD. He got down low to a shot from the edge of the penalty area, and as soon as he got back up to his feet the referee finally blew the whistle. We'd done it!

I started to celebrate with my team-mates but suddenly the Walsall fans were all over the pitch. There are only a handful of clubs that have never played at Wembley, and Walsall had finally stopped being one of them. It was wonderful to see the relief on the faces of the fans and how much it meant to them. As a footballer you play for yourself and you want to progress in your career, but when you have a relationship with the fans you want to do it for them as well. Seeing what it meant to them that night was a reward just in itself, and that is why it is my most memorable match. Inevitably, people tried to pull off my shirt as I walked off. In fact, they tried to take off everything I was wearing, including my shorts! Thankfully, I managed to keep everything on, and I've still got the shirt at home somewhere.

One of my favourite memories was James Baxendale getting hoisted off the pitch on top of a fan's shoulders. He certainly took a lot of flak from the rest of the players for that one! To be fair, Bax was a good lad who was always at the centre of the banter going on in the dressing room, so it had to be him really. There were some great celebrations in the dressing room that night, but for me it was never a case of being proud of a personal achievement. There were a lot of good people at the club, from the management to the board and the staff and it was special because *we* had all got to Wembley. Lots of people had worked hard for that moment, not just the players. We were the first-ever Walsall team to reach Wembley, so we'd made a little bit of history and that was a prize *everyone* deserved. It's a memory that will live with me forever.

Playing at Wembley isn't an everyday occurrence, so lots of things went on before the final that didn't normally happen. There were a lot of interviews to be done, as well as getting a new suit. I've still got it somewhere, though I don't know if it still fits! It was a great time and I enjoyed it with good people, which made it an even better experience. We weren't sure how many Walsall fans would make the trip down to Wembley, so to sell almost 30,000 tickets was simply incredible. It just seemed that anyone who'd ever had any association with the football club wanted to be there, no matter how slight that link was.

It was the third time that my brother and I had played together at Wembley, though the previous two games had both been played at the old stadium. The first was in a kids' tournament that took place before a play-off final when we were about 11 or 12 years old. The second time we played there was for the West Bromwich Albion youth team, though there weren't any fans in the ground for that match. This time was different because it was the new Wembley, it was a big occasion and there were over 70,000 fans in the stadium, making it the most well-attended game in the whole country that weekend.

It was a proud moment for me to lead Walsall out on to the pitch at Wembley, especially as lots of my family and friends were there. My only regret is that I wish the performance and the result could have been better. We came up against a very good Bristol City side that went on to win the League One title that season. Added to that, we just didn't hit the heights on the day that we were capable of. We were inconsistent all throughout that season and it turned out to be one of those days when we didn't perform as well as we could. You can analyse why that was so, and some may ask whether we over-celebrated getting to Wembley, but I don't think that was the case.

We were hampered a little because a few of our players were carrying injuries and were 50-50 for the game. I remember Sam Mantom coming back into the team after a long time out, which was tough for Michael Cain as he'd played in the previous rounds. Bradders was also struggling with his hamstring, and he was a big player for us. You could tell during the game that he was half a yard off the pace, which had a real impact as that can be the difference between scoring a goal or not. You could argue that he shouldn't have played, but it's not always that simple. There were plenty of times when Bradders had played with a hamstring injury and had gone on to get a goal for us. We were hoping that it was going to turn out that way again, but it wasn't to be. You can make perfect decisions in hindsight, but it's not always so easy in the heat of the moment. I've never watched that game back, though I might be able to one day!

That run to Wembley gave us a lot of self-belief and we took that momentum into the following season. We were very confident before it started as it felt like everything that Dean Smith had been building was finally coming together. The younger players were a year older and developing quickly, while there were some great additions to the first-team squad, including Jason Demetriou, Neil Etheridge, Rico Henry and Milan Lalkovič. The style of play was embedded, plus we had a good understanding of what Dean wanted from us, which enabled us to find the consistency that had so eluded us in previous seasons.

It turned out to be one of the most enjoyable seasons of my career, not just because we won a lot of games but also because of how we won them. We played fluid, attacking football and had some great results, such as beating Nottingham Forest 4-3 and Blackpool 4-0, both away from home. We were in contention for automatic promotion for much of the season and went into the final game of the season still in with a chance of it. We concentrated on doing our job, beating Port Vale 5-0 away from home, and hoped and prayed that Doncaster Rovers could do us a favour against Burton Albion. Sadly, they didn't.

We tried to refocus for the play-offs, but subconsciously we found it difficult to deal with just missing out on promotion. You do get a bit of a drop when it doesn't work out for you, and that's what happened to us. Despite losing to Barnsley in the play-offs, that Walsall team is still the best that I have ever played in. I was lucky enough to win the club's player of the year award, but it could have gone to several other of my team-mates that season. Personally, I would have given it to Romaine Sawyers as he was a real class act in League One that year.

I spent over 20 years in football, having started out as a trainee at West Bromwich Albion when Alan Buckley was the manager. Richard O'Kelly was my youth coach and he was exceptional at his job. I learned so much from him about all aspects of the game and his tactical knowledge was excellent. There was a greater focus on work ethic when I was coming through the ranks, but that has changed a bit over the years and now more attention gets paid to developing a young player's technical and tactical abilities. I could see that in the players that Walsall recruited from Albion's academy; the understanding that Paul Downing, Sam Mantom and Romaine Sawyers had of the game when they arrived at the club was so much better than I had when I was their age. I think some of that is down to the technology footballers have access to these days. Players can now clip their own parts of a game, analyse their performances and develop their knowledge of the game. When I was young, we only had grainy videos and you could hardly tell who on the pitch was who, let alone learn anything from them. But that's how the game is. It never stands still. The one thing that stays the same about football is that it is always changing.

About the author

Simon Turner's first book, *If Only: An Alternative History of the Beautiful Game*, told the stories of teams that were denied glory by the fickle finger of fate, something fellow long-suffering Walsall fans will easily identify with. He lives in Lichfield with his wife Val, daughter Ellie and son Edward, whose baffling infatuation with Aston Villa sadly shows no sign of abating.